# THE UK PC
# starter kit

## 2000 edition

# THE UK PC
# starter kit

## 2000 edition

# ROB YOUNG

Prentice
Hall

An imprint of Pearson Education

London ■ New York ■ Toronto ■ Sydney ■ Tokyo ■ Singapore
Madrid ■ Mexico City ■ Munich ■ Paris

PEARSON EDUCATION LIMITED

Head Office:
Edinburgh Gate
Harlow CM20 2JE
Tel: +44 (0)1279 623623
Fax: +44 (0)1279 431059

London Office:
128 Long Acre
London WC2E 9AN
Tel: +44 (0)20 7447 2000
Fax: +44 (0)20 7240 5771

First published in Great Britain in 2000

© Pearson Education Limited 2000

ISBN 0-130-26999-9

*British Library Cataloguing-in-Publication Data*
A catalogue record for this book is available from the British Library.

Many of the designations used by manufacturers and sellers to distinguish
their products are claimed as trademarks. Pearson Education Limited has
made every attempt to supply trademark information about manufacturers
and their products mentioned in this book. A list of trademark designations
and their owners appears on page x.

10 9 8 7 6 5 4 3 2 1

Typeset by Pantek, Maidstone, Kent.
Printed and bound by Biddles of Guildford and King's Lynn.

*The publishers' policy is to use paper manufactured from sustainable forests.*

# CONTENTS

Contents ▶

# Trademark notice

# Acknowledgements

Pearson Education has made every effort to seek permission to reproduce the screenshots used in this book. The Publishers wish to thank the following organisations for permission to reproduce material: Maps.com, Microsoft Encarta Encyclopedia, Microsoft Internet Explorer – UK Plus, Time Out.

# INTRODUCTION

**M**any people are having to deal with PCs from a standing start. Perhaps you've suddenly found yourself grappling with a PC at work, or your children are using PCs at school and blinding you with technical gibberish. Maybe you want to work faster, organise your business, or connect to the Internet.

In *The UK PC Starter Kit* you'll find clear explanations and advice to help you decide what you need, buy with confidence, and start obtaining results from your PC. Instead of just leaving you to muddle through alone, *The UK PC Starter Kit* will help you graduate from 'nervous novice' status by acting as a comprehensive reference whenever you want to buy new hardware or software, solve a problem, or become more expert at using Windows.

## How is this book organised?

This book is split into six major parts to help you find the answers you need quickly and easily.

**Part 1, Getting to know your PC** looks at the PC itself: its internal bits and pieces such as memory and disks, external devices like mouse and keyboard, and optional add-on gadgets such as a printer or a digital camera. What are all these things? What do they do to each other when they get together? What should you have in *your* PC?

**Part 2, Getting to grips with Windows** gives you all the details you'll need to work with *Windows 98 Second Edition*. Learn how to open, save, edit and print files, switch between programs, customise Windows to suit your way of working, and keep your system running smoothly.

**Part 3, Choosing and using software** examines the types of program you can use on your PC to accomplish different tasks, and the most popular titles in each category. With plenty of tips and clear advice on what to buy, you'll learn how to install and uninstall software and begin getting results from the programs you choose.

**Part 4, Surfing the Internet** shows you how to get connected to the Internet and what to do once you're online. Find out what you need and where to get it, learn how to send and receive email messages, and start surfing the World Wide Web.

The *Appendices* section includes useful information to help you choose and buy a PC, and a 'JargonBuster Super Reference' to help you decipher what everyone's talking about!

The *Directory* gives you an indispensable collection of contact details for companies and stores that sell computer software and hardware, provide access to the Internet, or offer other computer-related services. If you decide to connect to the Internet, you'll also find a useful list of companies' Web sites from where you can download software or find answers to problems.

## How should I use it?

This book is organised in such a way that you can read it from cover to cover if you want to, but you certainly don't have to. I like books that you can dip into and learn something new from reading just a couple of paragraphs, so don't feel guilty if you like to do that too! You can use the Contents pages or the Index to locate what you need, or just flick through until you see something you'd like to know more about. You'll find plenty of cross-references to tempt you towards other parts of the book. However, I do have a few suggestions:

▶ If you are new to computing, I recommend that you read the first two parts of the book, which will help you discover what your expensive new gadget can do and set you on the road to mastering your PC and Windows.

▶ If you have upgraded to *Windows 98 Second Edition* from an earlier version of Windows, skip straight to Part 2 to learn about the new features and software built into this new edition.

▶ If you have had a PC for some time, find out what you can get from your PC by adding extra hardware (in Part 1), or installing new software (in Part 3). You may still find some useful Windows tips in Part Two (particularly if you've been using an earlier version than *Windows 98 Second Edition*, the version I've covered in this book).

▶ Looking for a quick and easy way on to the Internet? If you already know a little bit about your PC and Windows, grab the CD from the inside back cover of this book, turn to Part Four, and you'll be online in minutes.

## Icons and conventions

Throughout the book I've used a few special features and conventions that make it easier to find your way around. In particular you'll see that chapters are split up into bite-sized chunks with subheadings. If something looks a bit complicated or dull, just skip to the next heading.

You'll also find some icons and text in boxes containing extra information that you may find useful:

A question-and-answer format highlighting questions or problems that may present themselves while you're reading about something or trying it out for yourself.

A selection of handy hints, tips and incidental notes that may save you some time, point you in a new direction, or help you avoid pitfalls.

Explains any technical terms that couldn't be avoided, or any related jargon you may encounter when dealing with a particular subject.

I've also used different type styles to make certain meanings clear:

**Bold type** indicates a new term being encountered, or text that you will type into a program yourself.

*Bold italic type* means that you will type this text yourself, but I don't know exactly what it will be. For example, if you have to type the name of a file you want to open, you might see something like **open** *filename*.

Finally, although I've referred to the 'Enter' key throughout, on your keyboard this may be labelled 'Return'. In fact it may not have a label at all, but it's the large irregular-shaped key to the right of the letter keys.

# WHAT'S ON THE CD?

## Licensing Agreement

This book comes with a CD software package. By opening this package you are agreeing to be bound by the following.

The software contained on this CD is, in many cases, copyrighted, and all rights are reserved by the individual licensing agreements associated with each piece of software contained on the CD. THIS SOFTWARE IS PROVIDED FREE OF CHARGE, AS IS, AND WITHOUT WARRANTY OF ANY KIND, EITHER EXPRESSED OR IMPLIED, INCLUDING, BUT NOT LIMITED TO, THE IMPLIED WARRANTIES OF MERCHANTABILITY AND FITNESS FOR A PARTICULAR PURPOSE. Neither the book publisher nor its dealers and its distributors assumes any liability for any alleged or actual damage arising from the use of this software.

## How to use the CD-ROM

In Windows 95 and 98, just insert the CD-ROM into your CD drive and close the drive tray. Within a few seconds a window should appear containing clickable options that include **Software Directory** and **Web Directory**. Move the mouse over any of these options to read a brief description, or click the option to install the program or view the Directory sections in your web browser.

If the window doesn't appear automatically when you insert the disk, double-click My Computer followed by your CD-ROM drive's icon, and then double-click the icon labelled **Autorun** (it has an icon that looks like a CD).

To view the contents of the Software and Web Directory sections, you'll need a web browser. If your PC doesn't have a web browser installed, you can install Microsoft Internet Explorer 5.01 from the CD-ROM either by choosing **Install Internet Explorer 5.01** from the CD's Autorun program, or by following the instructions in the paragraph above, then opening the **MSIE501** folder and double-clicking the file called **ie5setup.exe**.

# CD-ROM Contents

## Virgin Net

The CD-ROM contains everything you need to connect to the Internet without charge using Virgin Net's outstanding service. Within minutes you'll be surfing the World Wide Web and exchanging email messages with family and friends. Turn to the pages at the back of this book for more details about connecting to Virgin Net, or choose **Install Virgin Net Software** from the CD's Autorun program.

## Software Directory

The Software Directory section will open in your web browser, letting you read descriptions of the software programs included on the CD and install any of them on your PC with a couple of mouse-clicks. Click a category from the left side of the browser and a list of software titles will appear below it. Click the software title you want to find out more about. In this section you'll find indispensable utilities such as WinZip, Mighty Fax and Acrobat Reader; popular graphics software including Paint Shop Pro and GIF Animator Light; multimedia titles like Illuminatus and Media Center Plus; and Internet programs to help you get the most from your Net connection.

## Web Directory

Once you've set up an Internet connection, use the Web Directory to browse through over 1100 of the hottest World Wide Web sites sorted into 24 categories. Pick a category from the left of the browser window and then click a link from the list that appears on the right to visit some of these great sites.

# 1

# GETTING TO
# KNOW YOUR PC

# WHAT IS A PC?

# What is a computer?

In its most basic terms, the computer is a device that accepts some form of input (you punch in a number, for example), processes it in some way (adds it to the number you'd punched in previously), and produces an output or result (gives you the answer to its piece of addition).

Obviously we're talking calculators here. The pocket calculator is a non-technical, non-frightening example, but it has all the basic attributes of the modern computer: it has a small keyboard for input, a processor to do the calculations, a small amount of memory to let it remember one number whilst dealing with another, and a screen to display its output. The major difference is that the calculator knows only one trick, and it isn't likely to learn any new ones. In fact, the very first home computers, way back in the mid-1970s, were little more than glorified adding machines, but they had one extra vital ingredient: ambition!

# So what is a PC?

PC is simply an abbreviation of personal computer. This general term could be applied to any moderately small computer containing everything it needs to 'compute' by itself. The idea behind a computer being 'personal' is that it should be cheap enough that each user should be able to have his or her own machine rather than sharing it with the entire office, and small enough that it fits on a desktop or sits on your lap (or, recently, even in the palm of your hand).

This general definition could encompass a vast range of computers and manufacturers including Apple Macintosh, Atari, Amiga and Acorn. In recent years, however, the term has taken on a new *generic* meaning and now refers specifically to a computer that is **IBM Personal Computer-**compatible, the type of computer made by Dell, Gateway, Packard-Bell, and thousands of other large and small companies. A computer that is IBM PC-compatible is able to run the well-known **Microsoft Windows** operating systems, and it's this that sets the PC apart from an Apple Mac or an Amiga more than anything else.

# What can you use it for?

If you're wondering whether to take the plunge and buy your first PC, you've probably got a few ideas about what you'd use it for. Here's a tiny sample of the possible uses to help push you in the right direction:

▶ Take pictures using a digital camera (no need for film or expensive processing), edit and store them on your PC, or create an electronic photo album on CD.

▶ Use the Internet and email to keep in touch with friends and family, do your shopping at online stores, read electronic editions of magazines and newspapers, and find Web pages about your favourite hobby, football team or rock band.

▶ Simplify your business – store information in databases for instant retrieval, manage accounts using spreadsheets, print letters, invoices and envelopes using a word processor.

▶ Listen to audio CDs (or create your own!), watch DVD video disks, or enjoy TV and radio while you work.

▶ Send faxes straight from your PC without a separate fax machine, and receive incoming faxes to print or read on-screen and store for future reference.

▶ Record your own high-quality digital sounds and music, create animations, and edit video footage.

▶ Retire your game console and play the latest 3D action games on your PC.

▶ Design and print full-colour brochures, newsletters, cards and stationery.

## Software

JARGON BUSTER

The general term used to describe a computer program, or a set of computer programs. A program is a set of instructions that a computer uses to determine what you see on the screen, and what happens when you type a key on the keyboard or click a button on the mouse. Most programs help the computer work with one particular type of information: a graphics program will let you create pictures and retouch photographs, for example, but it won't help you manage your household accounts. For each type of software program you need, you'll usually have a wide choice of titles, prices and features.

The list of possible uses could go on forever, and it's getting longer every day, but it's important to realise that your PC may not be able to do all these things right from the moment you unpack it. What you can use it for depends upon what software is installed and (in some cases) what extra hardware you have. Most computer packages come with a useful range of software to get you started, along with the most common hardware 'extras', and you can add new software and hardware to your PC at any time to expand its capabilities.

## Hardware

**JARGON BUSTER**

Hardware is a blanket term that describes all the electronic components of a computer: a piece of hardware could be anything from a mains plug to a monitor. Think of it this way: would it break if you dropped it from the top of a building? If it would, it's hardware.

▶ *If you don't yet have a computer, skip ahead to Appendix C for advice on choosing and buying your first PC.*

## What's in the box?

The odd thing about PCs is that they tend to be bought a piece at a time. You'll almost certainly want to add extra capabilities to your machine somewhere along the line, and you might want to replace some of its internal organs for bigger, better or faster versions. All those separate pieces of computer hardware are available straight off the shelf, and we'll take a closer look at them in the next few chapters.

New computers are bought in just the same way. You decide what you need, wander into the computer store or pick up the phone, and say: *'It's got to have one of these, and one of those, and I want a built-in thingummy and a couple of wossnames'*. The retailer will put all this together for you, check it works, and present you with a couple of large cardboard boxes. But apart from a year's supply of polystyrene, what will those boxes contain?

Well, you may have some add-on goodies such as a printer or scanner, but besides those there are five basic elements to a computer. We'll look at each element in more detail later on, but here is a thumbnail view.

## System unit

This is the largest component, a case which houses the computer itself. In here, if you were to look, you'd find the **motherboard**, a large circuit board containing the processor, memory chips and expansion slots. In the drive bays towards the front of the unit you'd spot a **hard-disk drive**, a **floppy-disk drive** and a **CD-ROM** or **DVD-ROM drive**. Looking at the outside of the unit, the floppy-disk and CD-ROM drives are a little more obvious, having slots to insert disks, buttons and lights to indicate when a drive is busy. You should also find a power switch, a reset switch and varying numbers of coloured lights (some manufacturers seem to be frustrated disc jockeys!).

**JARGON BUSTER**

## Drive bays

A drive bay is a slot in the front of the system unit where more disk drives can be installed. Drive bays are two different sizes, $5\frac{1}{4}$-inch and $3\frac{1}{2}$-inch, to accept different-sized drives. CD-ROM drives are $5\frac{1}{4}$ inches wide, floppy-disk and tape drives are usually $3\frac{1}{2}$ inches. Most new PCs will offer at least three bays, two or more of which will already have drives fitted.

## Monitor

The large item that looks a lot like a TV screen. In the computer's input/process/output sequence, the monitor is the main output device, letting you see the results of your input and the computer's processing. The monitor connects to a socket on the back of the system unit, which in turn connects to a circuit board called the **display adapter**. The display adapter tells the monitor what to display.

## Keyboard

The keyboard is one of the two ubiquitous input devices, passing what you type into the system unit for processing by means of a single cable. This cable also provides a tiny power supply to the keyboard.

## Mouse

Not the small furry thing that chews through your cables, but the second of the two input devices. Movement of the mouse around a small area of your desk controls the movement of an arrow-shaped pointer on the monitor screen. By itself this doesn't accomplish much, but the mouse also has two or three buttons: clicking these buttons will make the computer do different things depending upon what you're 'pointing' at when you 'click'.

## Software

Okay, this is a bit of a sly one. You might find a small amount of software in the box (most deals on new computers include a few games or product samplers on disks which you can install or ignore as you wish) but the most important software should be already installed and ready to use as soon as you unpack and switch on your PC.

Fundamentally this software will include an **operating system**, a collection of programs that handles the vital task of interpreting your input and telling the rest of the system what to do to make you happy. Unless you've been living down a hole for the last few years, you've probably heard of **Windows**, the most popular operating system for PCs. Depending on the deal offered by the computer store, or what software you specifically asked for, you might have other software packages included too. The store will almost always install the software itself and make sure it all runs correctly: if they didn't, they'd risk the expense of sending someone out to help you if you got into difficulties!

### Disks and manuals

Although most of the software will be installed on your computer when you receive it, you should still have been given the original disks and manuals. For example, you should have a clearly-labelled CD-ROM and user guide for Windows 98, usually shrink-wrapped in a single package.

# Setting up your PC

Where you site your desktop PC takes some careful thought. You'll need to be within easy reach of power sockets (and a phone socket if you have a modem), and to have enough desk space for external devices such as keyboard, mouse and printer to be accessible. Remember that monitors take up a lot of space – if necessary, pull your desk out from the wall a little way so that you can move the monitor further back. Also, make sure the monitor is situated and angled in such a way that it can't reflect sunlight or a lightbulb into your eyes.

The system unit is the other bulky device that needs to be found a home. You'll need to leave at least six inches of fresh air behind it, partly because of the cables that have to be plugged in, but primarily to ensure that its internal components don't overheat. Desktop cases are intended to be placed behind your keyboard with the monitor placed on top of them, though you may prefer to place it elsewhere. Small tower-cases are usually placed on the desk beside your monitor; larger tower-cases are intended to be placed on the floor. Remember that you'll need to reach the floppy-disk and CD-ROM drives from time to time, and avoid putting the case anywhere it can be jolted or kicked.

**BY THE WAY**

## Storm protection

When you're not using your PC, unplug the whole system from the mains after turning everything off. To guard against electrical spikes and storms, you might also choose to add a surge protector, available from most computing or electrical stores.

Make sure none of the connected cables are stretched taut between devices, and keep all the 'spaghetti' at the back as tangle-free as you can. Take special care to secure all this cabling in some way so that no-one can drag it off the desk by getting their feet caught up in it! Lastly, choose somewhere comfortable: your monitor should be in front of you, and at eye-level without the need to stretch or slump; you'll need room to rest your hands in front of the keyboard; you'll need space on your desk for a mouse-mat, and some elbow-room to move the mouse.

The various ports and sockets on a PC are detailed in Chapter 3, and are probably labelled, so plugging everything in should be a simple job. However, never *ever* plug or unplug devices on the system unit while the computer is switched on! If you bought additional devices to install yourself (particularly internal devices such as expansion cards), don't install them until you're sure the rest of the system is working perfectly.

## Turning on, turning off

The most important rule to remember in turning your PC on and off is: *try not to do it!* In general, try to turn your computer off only when you won't be using it again for a day or two. The surge of power into the unit each time you start up, and the change in temperature of the internal components, can shorten their life-span if it happens unnecessarily often. Turning the PC off and immediately back on again should only ever be done in desperate circumstances and you should pause for a few seconds in between. Whenever a restart is necessary, use the Reset switch on the system unit to do it.

**GOOD QUESTION!**

## Can I really leave my PC on for days at a time?

Yes, and it's a good idea to do that. Modern PCs and monitors have power-saving features that automatically switch them to 'stand-by' mode after a period of inactivity, rather like modern TVs. You'll find out more about these features in Chapter 11.

## What next?

With everything connected up and plugged in, you're ready to switch on and start using your PC. To take this next step, skip ahead to Part 2 where you'll learn the correct routines for starting and switching off your PC, and begin finding your way around Windows 98.

In this chapter we've looked at the five main pieces of a PC, but you have probably got some other pieces too – maybe a printer, a scanner, or a digital camera. Then there are the pieces you won't be quite as aware of (they're tucked away inside the system unit): you've certainly got a hard-disk, a floppy-disk drive, and a CD-ROM or DVD-ROM drive. You've probably got a modem and a soundcard too. In the remaining chapters of Part 1, we'll take a look at what these gadgets are for, how to use them, and what else you can add to your PC setup if you choose to.

# 2

# INS AND OUTS OF THE PC

If you've never used a computer before, there's no escaping the fact that you are about to expand your vocabulary with words like **processor**, **megabyte**, **files** and **hard-disk**. You might not be able to throw them casually into everyday conversation, but they'll crop up whenever you want to buy computer hardware or software. So let's start by taking the mystery out of some of these words.

# What's going on in there?

The basic principles of how the computer operates are pretty straightforward – the PC works very much like you do:

▶ Your brain receives input from your ears, eyes and so on; the computer receives input from the keyboard and the mouse (and, perhaps, one or two other optional devices you've connected).

▶ You probably have a filing cabinet or a drawer where you keep your important files and documents; the computer contains a **disk** for the same purpose.

▶ You have a brain for working things out; the computer has a **processor**.

▶ You have various methods of outputting the results of your brainwork, such as writing or speaking; the computer might output its results to be displayed on the monitor, printed on paper, or stored on a disk.

▶ As you try to think out a tricky problem, you keep as many of the details in your mind as you can; the computer has its own forms of **memory** to do a similar job.

▶ If a job comes in that suddenly requires your full attention, you make notes about the first job on a piece of paper so that you can come back to it later; the modern PC is able to empty its memory enough to handle a different task and then 'read' this same information back in when it wants to use it again.

# The brains behind the operation

In the internal workings of the human being, nothing at all can happen without the active participation of the brain. The same is true of the computer, but the 'brain' in question is a small microchip called a CPU (central processing unit) or **processor**.

Because the processor plays a vital part in everything the computer does, it's constantly working behind the scenes and juggling a large number of tasks in blindingly quick succession. Exactly *how* fast it can handle each task is one of the main yardsticks we use in determining that subjective factor, the *power* of the computer. To a large extent, the faster your processor, the more powerful your PC.

**JARGON BUSTER**

## Data

A sort of synonym for 'information'. While the computer is storing it or working with it, it's data – a meaningless stream of numbers to you and me; when some sense has been made of it all and it's presented on screen or paper, it's information.

# Ins and outs

To continue the 'brain' analogy just a little longer, the processor sends data to most parts of the PC's 'body', and receives data back from most of them. But notice the use of the word *most* – not every part of the system will receive data, and not every part will send it. The computer is made up of three types of hardware component: input devices, output devices, and combined input/output devices.

▶ An **input** device *sends* data to the processor but doesn't need to receive anything in return: the mouse is a good example of an input-only device.

▶ An **output** device *receives* data from the processor and presents it to us in some way, examples of this being the monitor and the printer.

15

▶ An **input/output** device *exchanges* data back and forth with the processor. The archetypal input/output device is the hard-disk: sometimes the processor will send data to the disk to be stored; at other times it will retrieve data from the disk to be used.

# Bits and PCs

As you can tell from the brief outline above, there's a lot going on, and data is endlessly being passed around the system. But what is this data? What form does it take?

Computers work only with **binary numbers**. The binary system is a method of counting in base two which involves using combinations of the numbers 0 and 1, equating to 'off' and 'on'. On the surface this may seem limiting, but if the processor only has to distinguish between these two possible states it can therefore handle immense streams of these digits (generically known as *data*) in a very short space of time. Each of these 0s and 1s is called a **bit**, short for BInary digiT.

Because a single bit by itself can't convey much information, bits are grouped into sets of eight called **bytes**. A byte is far more meaningful, offering 256 different combinations of 0s and 1s, so a single byte can communicate numbers from zero to 255. As a point of interest, one byte is equivalent to a single typed character.

## Kilobytes, megabytes and gigabytes

Bits and bytes are terms used to count quantities of data, but they're pretty small measures and computers have to deal with much larger chunks of data. For example, a small word-processor program with fairly limited features could be around 200 000 bytes in size. Because we're dealing with numbers of this order most of the time, two additional terms are used: the **kilobyte** (abbreviated to **kB**) which equals 1024 bytes, and the **megabyte** (abbreviated to **MB**) which equals 1024 kilobytes or 1 048 576 bytes. Another term being encountered more and more frequently as technology progresses is the **gigabyte** (abbreviated to **GB**), equal to 1024 megabytes.

These terms are used most frequently when discussing the capacities of two particular types of computer hardware: memory and hard-disk.

## Hard-disks are never 'too big'!

Programs and operating systems are getting bigger all the time (for example, Windows 98 will typically take around 200 MB of space on your hard-disk), so the greater the capacity of the hard-disk, the better.

# Memory and storage

The computer, as we know, deals with huge amounts of data. However, at any one time only a comparatively tiny amount is actually being processed, and a small amount is travelling between the various components. So where is all the rest of it?

By far the largest amount of data is *stored* ready for use whenever it's needed (which might be in a couple of minutes' time, or might be next year!) and the main storage medium is the **hard-disk**. This is a magnetic disk inside the computer on which all your programs are kept, together with the documents you create when using those programs, and all the other software required to control the computer itself.

**Memory** is a type of short-term storage, and the modern PC has several types of memory at its disposal. The most important of these is called **RAM** (random access memory) which comes in the form of small modules on cards that slot into the computer's motherboard. Every program and document you use at any one time (including the operating system) is read from the hard-disk and loaded into the computer's RAM. When the RAM is full, the computer has to find alternative places to put some of this data temporarily. These alternatives do exist, but they can't send back the data as quickly as RAM when it's next needed, which results in the whole computer slowing down. The bottom line here is: there's no such thing as too much RAM!

## Motherboard

**JARGON BUSTER**

A large circuit board inside the system unit on which most of the computer's major components are situated. The design of the board ensures that everything attached to it (including any devices you add later) will be able to communicate with everything else.

# Files, programs and documents

Returning once again to the 'human body' analogy, data is the *blood* of the computer, being passed around its major organs all the time and keeping the whole thing working. Although all this data moves around as a stream of bits, it needs to be grouped and stored in a more organised way to let you find what you need quickly and easily. These groups of related data are called **files**, and a file will be either of two types: a **program** or a **document**.

A **program** is a file that contains a specific set of instructions or commands to the computer itself. Some of these programs will be run automatically when your computer starts (or, indeed, while you're using it) to make the computer work as it should. These are part of the operating system. Other programs you will run yourself when you need to use them – a word-processing application when you want to write a letter, or a graphics application when you want to draw a picture.

## Application

**JARGON BUSTER**

An application is a type of program that is used to create something – a drawing, a table, a database, and so on – as distinct from a program that provides entertainment (such as a game) or lets you change system settings or dial a phone number. These words tend to be used interchangeably – people talk about **graphics software**, a **graphics program** and a **graphics application**, all meaning the same thing.

A **document** file is something you create yourself. When you run your word-processing application and write a letter, this letter is being stored in short-term memory (RAM) while you're working on it. When it's finished and sitting on the screen in front of you, you can choose what to do with it. You can, if you want to, print it out on paper ready to send to someone, close down the application and forget it – if you do this, the RAM will forget it too. Or you can *save* the letter as a file that you can look at and edit in the future; in effect, this means you're moving your letter from the short-term memory to the permanent store (the hard-disk). Files that you create yourself in this way, containing meaningful information, are called 'documents'.

**3**

# UNDER THE HOOD: THE IMPORTANT STUFF

Of all the hundreds of possible bits and pieces that could make up your PC system, some are vital, some are desirable, and many more are optional add-ons that one user would regard as essential and another would consider to be frivolous luxuries. In the next few chapters we'll look at what's available and how to choose the devices you need, whether you're buying a complete new system or upgrading your current machine. Where better to start than inside the system unit itself, home of the indispensable parts that make your computer 'compute'!

# Brain and brawn: the processor

The processor is the *brain* of the computer, the chip that makes all the calculations and produces the results, so it's one of the most important parts of the machine despite its diminutive size (roughly 4 cm square). You'll sometimes see it referred to as a **microprocessor** or a **CPU** (central processing unit), but these names all refer to the same thing. Because of its essential nature, the type of processor included is used to describe the computer and distinguish it from other PCs: if someone says they have a powerful computer, what they really mean is that they have a computer with a powerful processor.

## What does it do?

Just like the human brain, the processor does a vast number of things. It obeys instructions one at a time, obeying them so fast that they all appear to be happening at the same time. In any given fraction of a second, the processor will take a look at the keyboard socket to see if you typed anything, and at the mouse socket to see if you moved or clicked the mouse; it might send more data to be displayed on the monitor, and read data from the computer's memory store or hard-disk. If you have other devices attached to your computer such as a printer or a modem, it will be watching these for incoming data and/or sending data to them.

So however calm and unflustered it all seems on the surface, the processor is actually going like crazy underneath. It follows that whatever you do and whenever you do it, you're going to interrupt its well-organised routine. Just as the human brain is adept at swapping back and forth between different tasks, the processor uses the computer's memory-chips (the RAM) to keep track of what it was doing before you interrupted it.

## What do you need?

If you've looked at advertisements for PCs, you've probably noticed that they prominently feature a line that looks something like this:

**Pentium III 700 MHz**

This line is one of the most important to check in any computer ad. The first part of the line (**Pentium III**) refers to the *type* of processor-chip, the second refers to the chip's *speed*. The speed is given in *megahertz* (pronounced 'megga-hurts') and measures how fast the processor works. In general, the higher the speed, the less time you'll have to wait for the computer to do what you're asking.

**GOOD-QUESTION!**

## Do I really need a fast processor?

Not necessarily. The things that really tax a processor are graphics and video (the latest action games, 3D modelling, graphic design), digital sound recording, and very large spreadsheets and databases. For ordinary home or small-office use, the main benefit of a faster processor is that it helps to 'future-proof' your PC by making it better able to handle the demands of tomorrow's software.

The two big names in processors are Intel (whose much-hyped Pentium processor you've probably heard of) and AMD. From Intel, you have the choice of the Pentium III and the Celeron (and, perhaps, the older Pentium II). From AMD there's the Athlon and the K6-2. The Celeron sits at the budget end of things, suitable for someone using their PC as a tool for the home or small office rather than as a multimedia or entertainment machine. The Pentium III and Athlon are preferred for more intensive use, and for games and multimedia. The K6-2 is positioned somewhere in the middle, but it's more of a challenger to the Pentium III than the Celeron.

When it comes to a choice between an Intel processor or the equivalent from AMD, it's more a question of price than anything else – there's little to choose between them in terms of quality. AMD's pricing tends to be a little below that of Intel, putting some cash back in your pocket, or perhaps a faster processor for the same price.

# Memory – the more the merrier

Memory is a short-term holding place for data that is currently in use, is about to be used, or has just been used. In fact, there are *several* holding places of different types that the PC uses in different situations, and they vary in speed and effectiveness. The most important of these is called **RAM** (random access memory): as long as your computer has enough RAM, all the files currently in use are held there and your PC should respond quickly when you try to do something. However, when the RAM becomes full, the computer starts using the much slower hard-disk to supplement it. The more the hard-disk has to be used, the slower your machine will run.

The answer, of course, is to have enough RAM that the computer rarely (or never) needs to use the hard-disk as temporary memory. So how much is *enough*? Don't go for anything with less than 64 MB (megabytes), and regard 128 MB as being the optimum amount for most uses. Some new PCs are still being sold with only 32 MB of RAM, but any retailer will be happy to slot in another 32 and relieve you of a small amount of extra money.

## Need more memory?

RAM comes on small circuit boards called **DIMMs** (dual inline memory modules). Most PCs have three internal slots for DIMMs, with the installed memory occupying one (or perhaps two) of these slots, so it should be possible to add more memory by installing another DIMM in a vacant slot.

A second type of memory is called the *cache* (pronounced 'cash'), a lightning-fast store that holds recently-used data in case it's needed again. You'll sometimes see this referred to as 'external cache' or 'level 2 cache'. Pentium III systems come with 512 kB of cache memory, as do AMD's Athlon and K6-2. Intel Celeron systems have only 128 kB.

# Hard-disk – the bigger the better

Think of your files (operating system, applications and documents) as a car: when you want to *use* your car you take it out on to the road, and drive around Processorville, RAM City and other nearby places. When you don't want to use it you *park* it somewhere. Once you've parked it, you can leave it there as long as you like. That might be just a minute or two, or it might be months or even years.

The disk is a car-park for your files, and there are two common types: the **hard-disk**, and the **floppy-disk** (sometimes referred to as a **diskette**). Of these two, the hard-disk is by far the more important because it can hold much more data. Since the most significant consideration about any storage device is *how much* data you can store, hard-disks are noted by their capacities in gigabytes (GB).

To put hard-disk size into some sort of perspective, when you take delivery of your new PC your hard-disk will already have Windows 98 installed, perhaps a suite of office applications (see Chapter 21), and a few other 'freebie' programs. At a rough estimate, 350 MB of your hard-disk is already in use, and that's before you start adding other programs you want to use and storing the files you create yourself.

## Don't try to fill your hard-disk!

The intention with a hard-disk isn't to fill it. If the disk has plenty of empty space, your PC will always be able to find somewhere on it to store data quickly and easily, and remain that much more responsive as a result.

If there's any budget stretching to be done, a large hard-disk is the reason to do it. It isn't easy to replace the disk you've outgrown with a larger one and transfer all your data to it, and adding a *second* disk is a lot more expensive than buying a large one at the outset. Regard a 4 GB disk as the absolute minimum; something over 6.4 GB is a safer bet. Many systems include hard disks ranging from 13 GB to over 30 GB: while this is overkill for most of us, you might want to consider something of this size if you plan to put your computer to a number of different uses involving a large number of different programs, or you expect to work extensively with large files such as graphics, sounds, videos or desktop publishing.

# A floppy-disk drive for sharing files

Now is a good time to clarify that word 'drive'. A disk is literally a circular magnetic piece of metal on which data is stored. The **drive** is the surrounding box that contains the disk and the various components that read data from it and write more data on to it.

The hard-disk and its drive are bought as a single unit and hidden away inside your PC's system unit. The drive for floppy-disks is a $3\frac{1}{2}$-inch wide unit installed at the front of your system unit with a slot for inserting disks and a button for ejecting them.

All new computers come with a single $3\frac{1}{2}$-inch floppy-disk drive, and one is usually enough. A floppy-disk holds only 1.44 MB of data which isn't really sufficient for day-to-day work with files, and computers read floppy-disks *much* more slowly than they read from your hard-disk. The main use for a floppy-disk is to copy files on to it to give to someone else, or to keep safety copies of small files. The disks themselves are cheap (around 20p each).

An alternative to the ordinary floppy-disk drive is the SuperDisk drive, although it hasn't really caught on as well as expected. SuperDisk drives use their own type of disk and store a much more useful 120 MB, but still have the ability to work with standard floppy-disks.

▶ *The options for removable storage are increasing all the time, offering better alternatives to the humble floppy. Turn to Chapter 6 to find out about some of these.*

# A BIOS to get things started

Like the floppy drive, you don't need to specifically ask for a computer with a BIOS – it's definitely got one. BIOS is an acronym for Basic Input/Output System. As the name suggests, the BIOS plays an important part in transferring your *input* (from the keyboard, for example) to the processor, and transferring the processor's *output* to the monitor and other devices. As far as this goes, it is comforting to know that *something* is doing that, but it's not terribly interesting and we won't dwell on it. However, before the BIOS embarks on this full-time job, it has a sort of paper-round to take care of first: it has to get your system working.

The BIOS is a set of small programs stored on a special chip whose basic role is to tell your computer about itself. When you turn on your computer's power-switch, the BIOS's programs spring into action and start a sequence known as the **POST** (power-on self test). Until the PC knows it has a hard-drive, a floppy-drive, memory, a keyboard, and so on, and that they're all properly connected and working, it can't start to use them. You will see the BIOS details displayed briefly every time you turn on your PC, in white on a black background.

# And holding it all together...

Everything we've mentioned in this chapter, and every other piece of hardware you want to add to your system, ultimately connects to the **motherboard**, a large circuit board inside the system unit that lets everything 'talk' to everything else. Generally speaking, the larger the motherboard, the more room there is for future expansion – easily adding more devices to increase the power or capability of your PC. The size of the motherboard is determined by the style of case it has to fit into, so let's start by looking at what is available.

## Choose your case

The case of the system unit comes in three flavours, although each will vary in size and layout according to the manufacturer:

**Desktop** – the original case design, roughly 4 inches high and 15 inches wide, designed to sit behind the keyboard with the monitor on top.

**Mini tower** – looking like an upended desktop case, this stands on your desk beside the monitor.

**Full tower** – a larger version of the mini tower that sits on the floor.

Very often, the computer you've got your eye on will be available with a choice of case styles, so it doesn't hurt to ask if you don't see any mention of the style you want.

## Counting the drive bays

Drive bays are slots in the front of the system unit into which additional drives can be installed. When you take delivery of your new PC, you'll probably find that two of these are in use already, holding the floppy-disk drive and a CD-ROM drive. The remaining bays have plastic covers to protect them from your lunch until they're needed.

Drive bays come in two sizes and most modern PCs have at least two bays of each size. The $3\frac{1}{2}$-inch bay holds a standard floppy-disk drive and some types of backup drive (see Chapter 6). The larger $5\frac{1}{4}$-inch bay is for CD-ROM or DVD-ROM drives, backup drives, and an older type of floppy disk-drive now rarely used.

Like most things in the computer world, the more drive bays you have available, the better. This is going to depend to some degree on your choice of case: a full tower case might have a total of six or seven bays, whereas the desktop or mini tower might have only three or four. If you expect to use or copy floppy-disks in any great quantity, a spare $3\frac{1}{2}$-inch slot will let you add a second floppy drive. Otherwise $5\frac{1}{4}$-inch drives are the more plentiful, so a PC with a CD-ROM/DVD-ROM drive already installed and one or more free bays of this size is ideal.

## Memory and expansion slots

Hidden away in the dim recesses of the motherboard is a rack of **expansion slots** into which you can plug **expansion cards** that add new capabilities to your PC. These cards are 4–8 inches long and about 3 inches wide. If you were to look inside the system unit you'd see at least two of these cards: one is the device that keeps the picture on your monitor updated (more on that in Chapter 4), and the other handles the task of moving data around between all the different pieces of your system. Other types of card might contain a modem to let you send faxes or connect to the Internet (see Chapter 6), or add sound capabilities (Chapter 5).

To complicate the issue a little, there are two types of slots and cards used in modern PCs:

**ISA** (industry standard architecture) – an old technology that the computer industry still cannot seem to shake off.

**PCI** (peripheral component interconnect) – a recent format that lets cards handle data faster and with less involvement from the processor.

A new PC should have at least three of each type of slot, and you would ideally want two of each to be empty unless your PC already has a soundcard and modem installed. Some types of expansion card will be ISA and others will be PCI. A few devices can be bought in either format, but the PCI version will be more expensive. You don't need to know how these work, but there is one important point to remember: try to keep track of how many free slots of each type you have. It's heartbreaking to come home with a new PCI card and find that all your PCI slots are full!

Most recent systems also include a single **AGP** slot, which stands for accelerated graphics port. This lets you use one of the latest and fastest AGP graphics cards (see Chapter 4) to give the best possible display of games, video and 3D graphics. If your PC has an AGP slot, the odds are that you've already got an AGP graphics cards installed in it.

A smaller set of slots in the motherboard holds the chips containing the RAM. These chips are called DIMMs (dual inline memory modules), and a single chip might contain 16, 32, 64 or 128 MB of memory. You'll usually have three of these slots, but ideally no more than two should be in use when you take delivery of your computer: if your PC has 64 MB of RAM, you should have one 64-MB DIMM chip. At any time in the future, you can buy another DIMM to install in the free slots to increase your PC's total RAM.

## Don't fry your hardware!

Never, ever connect or disconnect your mouse, keyboard or any other device while your computer is switched on: it is one of the surest ways to turn electronic technology into frazzled desktop ornaments. The one exception is devices connected to USB ports (see below), which can be plugged and unplugged at will – your PC should recognise the arrival of a new USB device as soon as you connect it.

## Ports and sockets

The back of the system unit is where everything gets connected together,
and you'll find a dazzling array of sockets (some of which, inexplicably, are
known as **ports**). On most systems each socket will be labelled, but here is a
quick rundown of what you may expect to find:

**Main power** – a three-pin male socket that powers the whole system and
looks like an electric kettle connection.

**Monitor power** – a three-pin female socket that powers the monitor (unless
the monitor has its own power cable and mains plug).

**Monitor display** – a 15-pin female socket that sends the display signal to
the monitor.

**Keyboard** – a five-pin DIN (circular) socket to connect and power the
keyboard, now rarely used.

**Serial ports** – two 25-pin male sockets called COM1 and COM2 (short for
'communications') to which the mouse, external modem and other devices
can be connected. Some PCs and devices use a nine-pin socket or cable, but
you can buy a cheap adapter to connect the two types.

**Parallel port** – a 25-pin female socket that might be labelled LPT1 or Printer
Port, to which printers, scanners and a few other devices can be connected.

**PS2 ports** – one or more six-pin female sockets, used for mouse and
keyboard.

**USB ports** – a new type of port included in recent PCs, and you've probably
got at least two of these. Up to 127 separate devices can theoretically be
connected to a single USB port, by linking them together in a chain. USB
ports let you install a new device by simply adding it to the end of the
chain. The only catch is that the devices you buy must be built specifically
for connecting to a USB port, but the range of compatible devices has
increased hugely over the last year or so.

## If I can plug 127 devices into a single USB port, why do I need two of them?

You'll probably never have 128 extra devices to plug in, but you may come across a device that won't work when attached to a chain of other devices (or won't allow other devices to be plugged into it), so extra USB ports certainly do have a value.

Many of the expansion cards you install on your system will add extra sockets. These are fitted to one edge of the card, and this edge is visible at the back of the system unit when the card is installed. If you add a soundcard, for example, you'll have a speaker-output socket, a headphone socket, and a game port for plugging in a joystick.

**4**

# THREE ESSENTIALS – MONITOR, MOUSE AND KEYBOARD

Although the system unit contains all the technical wizardry that *is* the computer, by itself it's not much use. To actually work with the computer you need a monitor to see what's going on, and a keyboard and mouse to communicate with the system. In this chapter, we'll tell you what to look for and what to avoid, whether you're buying an entire system or just looking for a more comfortable keyboard.

# Picture this – your ideal monitor

The most important thing to consider in a monitor is its size, and you'll see 14-inch, 15-inch and 17-inch monitors bundled with new computers (although larger sizes are available separately). The first piece of advice here is simple: don't buy a 14-inch monitor. Although the difference between 14-inch and 15-inch seems small, that larger size represents an extra 15 per cent of viewing area. If a 14-inch monitor is quoted in the price of a computer, ask what it costs to upgrade to a 15-inch – most companies will happily quote for this, and the small additional cost is money well spent.

The price jump to a 17-inch monitor is greater, but this is the recommended size, particularly if you will be using your computer for more than a few hours a day. For particular uses, 17-inch or larger monitors are worth their weight in gold (which, admittedly, is what they seem to cost at the moment): if you'll be working with large spreadsheets, desktop publishing or artwork and graphics, you'll want to see as much information on screen at once as you possibly can. Remember that it's better to pay £150 extra for a large monitor now than to pay £400 upwards to replace your current monitor next year.

**JARGON BUSTER**

## OSD

Monitor adverts love to talk about their OSD without telling you what that is. It's short for 'on-screen display', and means that you can adjust the monitor picture from options displayed on the screen rather than trying to understand what a dozen little buttons on the monitor's case are supposed to do.

Size is important, but it isn't everything. You'll be spending many hours gazing at this thing, so here are two extra features to check before buying:

▶ It must be **non-interlaced**. Interlaced monitors use a method of updating the screen that creates a constant flicker, making them very unpleasant to work with.

▶ It should have a **dot pitch** of 0.28 mm or less. The dot pitch is the spacing between the tiny dots that make up the display: as a rule of thumb, the smaller the dot pitch, the greater the clarity.

## You need a graphics card

The graphics card is the expansion card that controls what your monitor displays, and it is referred to by a number of different names including **display adapter** or **graphics adapter**. For your monitor to display anything at all a graphics card is required, but a monitor can only be as good as the graphics card that drives it, so it pays to buy carefully. Your graphics card will probably be of the AGP type (see page 29) and plugged into your system unit's single AGP slot.

Graphics cards come with their own built-in memory (RAM) modules, and the quantity of RAM on the card determines the maximum **resolution** and **colour depth** your monitor can display. The resolution refers to the number of dots per inch (**dpi**) that your monitor can display. You don't want to work at anything less than $800 \times 600$ dpi, and the next largest resolution, $1024 \times 768$ dpi, allows much more information to be displayed at any one time. The colour depth refers to the number of colours used to draw what you see on the screen. You can choose from colour palettes containing a rather washed-out 16 colours up to a true-to-life 16.7 million colours.

Both of these settings need particular quantities of RAM on the card: if your card has insufficient RAM, you might find that to use the True Colour palette (16.7 million colours), for example, you'll have to drop to a much lower screen resolution.

## Refresh rate

**JARGON BUSTER**

The image on the monitor is updated a number of times every second, and the time interval between each update is called the refresh rate. If the rate is fast enough you won't be aware it's happening, but if it's too slow, the screen will appear to have a constant flicker.

For general use, go for a graphics card with at least 8 MB RAM, and make sure that it can provide a refresh rate of 72 MHz or higher at a resolution of 1024 × 768 dpi. These combined features will give a crisp, clear image and allow you to use the vibrant True Colour palette at 1024 × 768 dpi. If you're a fan of arcade-quality games or plan to work extensively with graphics or video, you'll want a card with at least 16 MB RAM and perhaps a graphics accelerator. Many cards allow you to add more memory whenever you want to, but you should make sure of this and find out what the maximum is before you buy.

## Double your viewing space

**BY THE WAY**

Windows 98 will let you use two or more monitors, doubling your viewing space and making it easy to refer to one document while working on another. Install a second graphics card and plug a monitor into it, and Windows will handle the rest automatically next time you switch on. Remember that your PC only has one AGP slot, which is probably occupied by your current graphics card: when you buy the second one, it will have to be a PCI card (see page 29).

▶ *For the best game play and movie playback on a PC, the typical graphics card doesn't really cut the mustard. Turn to page 46 to find out about the add-ons and alternatives.*

# Meet the mouse (and friends)

The original type of input device for a PC was the keyboard, and that was fine for the purpose because most of the original operating systems and programs were text-based. The arrival of Windows, with its friendly buttons and icons, required a more intuitive method of working and the mouse became a ubiquitous feature of PCs. Most mice plug into one of your PC's USB or PS/2 sockets, although a few still use one of the computer's serial ports (COM1 is recommended for a serial mouse).

The mouse is a small plastic box sculpted to fit under your palm, with two or three buttons at the front and a cable (or tail!) leading to the PC's system unit. A ball in the base of the mouse enables it to roll around your desk, and sensors inside measure the direction and speed of travel. The movement of the mouse controls the movement of a small pointer on the monitor screen in a thoroughly intuitive way – move the mouse to the left and the pointer moves to the left, and so on.

## Basic rodent care

Never swing the mouse around by its tail, tempting though it is. And if it stops working, don't flush it down the toilet!

The movement of the mouse enables you to position the pointer wherever you want it, but that doesn't actually *achieve* anything useful by itself. However, once the pointer is placed over an icon or button, pressing (or *clicking*) one of the mouse's buttons will perform some kind of action. Exactly *what* happens will depend upon the operating system, the object you're clicking on and a variety of other things, but a mouse-click might run a program, display more details about the object in question, or present you with a list of options (known as a **menu**) to choose from, as shown in the following screenshot.

▶ Clicking a mouse-button on this icon produces a menu of options. Moving the pointer on to one of these options and clicking again will select that option.

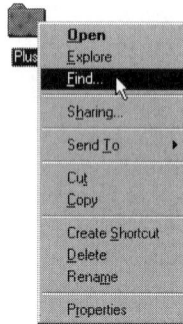

| |
|---|
| **Open** |
| Explore |
| Find... |
| Sharing... |
| Send To ▶ |
| Cut |
| Copy |
| Create Shortcut |
| Delete |
| Rename |
| Properties |

The best-selling mouse is made by Microsoft and revels in the exotic name of Microsoft Mouse. New versions of this mouse add a small wheel to the usual two-button setup which greatly increases the mouse's talents, and the most recent versions replace the ball with an optical tracking system: this system casts an eerie red glow under the mouse, and removes the age-old problem of the ball gathering dust from your desk and then refusing to roll.

## The trackball

The trackball is like an upside-down mouse, with the ball on top. The design of trackballs can vary from the mundane to the eccentric, and the buttons can end up just about anywhere. However trackballs all have one thing in common: they're stationary. Instead of moving the whole device around your desk, your hand rests on it and moves the ball in its socket; one benefit of this approach is that no arm-movement is required.

## The graphics tablet

The tablet features a touch-sensitive square pad that sits on your desk, and the movement of the on-screen pointer is controlled by the movement of your finger or an attached stylus over the pad's surface. Clicking is done by tapping the pad or using buttons on the tablet's case, or a combination of the two. The larger-sized tablets give about the best possible input method for graphic-design and artwork applications.

# Meet the keyboard

The computer keyboard is remarkably similar to its typewriter counterpart, despite the much wider range of actions called for by a PC. For example, the same QWERTY layout is used, the Tab, Shift, and Caps Lock keys survive, and there's even the equivalent of a carriage-return lever called the Enter (or, sometimes, Return) key.

## QWERTY keyboard

**JARGON BUSTER**

The standard UK keyboard layout, named after the first five keys found on the top row. The QWERTY system was originally designed as a counterintuitive layout to slow down typists who were reaching such great speeds that the typewriter keys kept getting stuck in a bunch. Obviously this can't happen on a computer keyboard, but by now we're all too used to it to change.

As this *is* a computer keyboard a few extra keys have been added, so let's take a look at them.

▶ The standard 102-key computer keyboard.

**Function keys**. A row of keys usually located at the top of the keyboard numbered F1, F2 and so on. Different operating systems and programs assign different commands to some of these keys, usually serving as alternatives to clicking an option with the mouse.

**CTRL and ALT keys**. These work rather like the Shift key, in that they are used in combination with other keys to produce a result. These key combinations are used mostly to select options from menus, once again as an alternative to using the mouse.

**Arrow-keys**. These are four keys for up/down/left/right which are chiefly used either for moving the cursor around a block of text or for navigating through lists or groups of icons.

**Page Up/Page Down keys**. Because modern operating systems display each document in its own 'window' (a box on the screen), it may not be possible to view the whole of a long document at once. The Page keys provide one method of moving up and down the document a screenful at a time, rather like rolling a piece of paper backwards and forwards through a typewriter.

**Home/End keys**. These provide a quick method of moving the cursor to the beginning or end of a line, or to the top or bottom of a long document or window.

**Del**. Short for 'Delete', and not surprisingly used to erase the files or section of text you select in advance. In a word-processor, it deletes the character immediately to the right of the current cursor position.

**Backspace**. In a word-processor, this deletes the character immediately to the left of the current cursor position, moving the cursor back one step in the process.

**Esc**. Short for 'Escape', this key is commonly used to back out of something you've started and would rather not finish – a sort of Cancel button.

**Enter**. This is sometimes labelled 'Return'. In word-processing and similar software, it functions like the carriage-return lever on a typewriter, beginning a new line. In general Windows use, you can press Enter to confirm that you want to go ahead with something when several options are presented and you've chosen the option you want.

**Numeric keypad**. A group of keys on the right of the keyboard. This group contains copies of the numerical and arithmetical keys on a calculator (together with a second **Enter** key). These keys actually have dual functionality: with the key marked **Num Lock** turned on they function as calculator keys; with **Num Lock** turned off they double as an extra set of **Home/End/Page/Arrow** keys.

**Windows keys**. Three extra keys specifically for use with Windows. There are two identical 'Win' keys with a small flag motif and one 'Menu' key with a drop-down menu and a little mouse-pointer.

## Why are there two Ctrl, Shift, Alt and Win keys?

**GOOD QUESTION!**

The duplicate **Ctrl**, **Shift** and **Win** keys can be used interchangeably. For touch-typists, one key may be more easily accessible than the other. The **Alt Gr** key to the right of the Space bar is slightly different from the **Alt** key to the left – it does the same as pressing **Ctrl** and **Alt** together.

The main factors to consider when buying a keyboard are key spacing and responsiveness – a good keyboard will have a slight spring in its action that cushions your fingers. The *sound* of a keyboard can make a difference too – most users like to hear a slight click as they press a key, but some keyboards give a very plastic, rattly noise which can grate on your nerves after a short time.

# GETTING EQUIPPED
# FOR MULTIMEDIA

A couple of years ago, you could buy a PC or you could buy a **multimedia** PC. The multimedia PC was the desirable, all-singing, all-dancing machine that supposedly elevated the dull office computer to the status of a complete entertainment centre by adding a soundcard, speakers, and a CD-ROM drive.

Today the 'multimedia' tag has been all but dropped: you'd be hard put to find a PC that *doesn't* have these extras nowadays, and a whole host of other goodies may be bought to extend your computer's entertainment capabilities. In this chapter we'll explore some of the multimedia add-ons available.

**JARGON BUSTER**

## Multimedia

A method of presenting information using a combination of sound, video, animation, graphics and text, but the term is getting wider all the time as new media such as television and radio are being added to the PC's capabilities.

# CD-ROM: music, games and more

The CD-ROM drive has become as fundamental to a PC as its hard-disk, and far more useful than a floppy-disk drive. The main reason for this is the size of modern software applications. A few years ago, it was common to buy a major software title, like Windows or Microsoft Office, and be presented with 30 floppy-disks, making the whole process of installing the software painfully slow. Today, the latest version of the same program could easily fill 60 or more floppies. But a single compact-disk (CD) can hold 650 MB of data, and your PC can read that data from a CD *much* faster than it can read data from a floppy-disk, so the CD has become the preferred medium for selling most types of software.

It doesn't sound much like multimedia so far, though. Following is a quickfire list of rather more entertaining reasons to own a CD-ROM drive.

▶ With a soundcard and speakers (explained below), you can play ordinary audio CDs just as you do with your home hi-fi.

▶ The best arcade-style games come on CD-ROM disks – for blazing action, sound, and fast-moving graphics, only a CD-ROM can hold this much data and play it quickly enough.

▶ Multimedia software titles such as interactive encyclopaedias and books can be bought only on CD-ROM.

The only difference between CD-ROM drives is their speed. You'll see some marked as 28-speed, others as 40-speed and so on. The faster the quoted speed of the drive, the faster it can read data from the disk, making software installations speedier and video playback smoother. The speed of the drive doesn't affect the playback of audio CDs though – your Diana Ross CDs won't suddenly sound like Pinky and Perky on a faster drive!

## CD and CD-ROM

The two names refer to exactly the same type of disk, but the term 'CD' usually refers to an audio-disk that you can play on your home stereo system, and 'CD-ROM' means a disk that contains computer data (definitely not for playing on your stereo). The 'ROM' part stands for read-only memory – data on the disk is stored permanently and cannot be erased.

New technologies have brought drives called the CD-R (recordable CD-ROM) and the CD-RW (rewriteable CD-ROM). Neither type of drive can read a disk as quickly as a plain CD-ROM drive, but they have other powerful features that we'll look at in Chapter 6.

# DVD-ROM, the new CD

DVD stands for digital versatile disk, and it builds on some of the best capabilities of the compact-disk. The DVD-ROM drive looks no different from a CD-ROM drive, and it can work with audio CDs and data CD-ROMs, so most new PCs now include a DVD-ROM drive instead of CD-ROM.

The biggest improvement is in the capacity of these disks. At the moment a DVD can store over 4.7 GB of data, and this will soon increase to an amazing 17 GB (roughly double the capacity of the average hard-disk). This means that a single disk can hold a full-length cinema movie and soundtrack, and there's a wide choice of DVD movie titles available that may be watched on your home computer.

There are a couple of catches with the DVD system to be wary of when it comes to playing DVD movies. First, many DVD-disks and drives are coded with one of six 'distribution zones' such as USA and Canada (region 1) or Europe, Japan and South Africa (region 2). A disk encoded for one zone can only be played on a drive coded for the same zone. Second, you may need some extra hardware to get watchable results from a DVD movie-disk (see below).

## 3D graphics, games and movies

In Chapter 4 we looked at graphics cards, the device that tells your monitor what to display. A good graphics card with plenty of built-in memory can give you a clear, flick-free picture with vibrant colours, perfect for ordinary PC use. These days, though, many users want to watch DVD movies, play the latest 3D action games, or work with video or 3D modelling, and the standard graphics card isn't designed to handle this sort of workload.

You may not have a *standard* graphics card, of course. There are plenty of cards around that have a built-in **3D graphics accelerator** and include support for DVD movie playback, such as the ATI Rage Fury series or Matrox Millennium G400. If yours hasn't, one option is to replace it with a card that has. The other option is to buy a separate 3D accelerator card which you'll plug into a spare PCI slot in your system unit.

## Hear sounds and music with a soundcard

Your PC has a small internal speaker that enables it to beep indignantly at you if you do something it doesn't like. Without an expansion card called a **soundcard**, that's the only sound your computer will ever make. These days, just about everything comes with its own soundtrack: computer games rely heavily on sound effects for realism, applications provide confirmatory audio feedback when you click a button or select an option, and a lot of new software now comes with a CD-ROM-based tutorial that literally talks you through the manual.

On a more musical level, connect your CD-ROM drive to your soundcard and you will be able to play your audio CDs while you work. If you have a creative leaning, you can use special software to record your own musical masterpieces.

The bog-standard soundcard is a 16-bit stereo card. Some types of music format will sound pretty atrocious, but this type of card is fine for playing back sound effects, speech, and audio CDs. For better quality sound, go for a 64-bit card from manufacturers like Creative, Yamaha or Ensoniq, particularly if you play computer games, videos or DVD movies, or you want to create your own music. A few cards offer snazzy extra features such as 3D surround sound.

## SoundBlaster compatibility

Whatever type or brand of soundcard you buy, check that it has SoundBlaster (SB) compatibility. Although the SoundBlaster is a brand of card, it quickly became extremely popular to the extent that most games expect to be using a compatible card.

## You'll need speakers too!

Well of course you will. Among a little bundle of sockets to appear at the back of your system unit after the soundcard is installed, you'll find one labelled Speaker Out or something similar. If your PC comes with a soundcard, you'll get speakers too, but some of these are hideously under-powered and tinny for music playback. If the sound quality matters to you, there are several options available:

▶ Upgrade to a three-piece system that adds a subwoofer for better bass performance.

▶ Connect the Speaker Out to the CD or Tape input on your home stereo system instead.

▶ Connect the Speaker Out to a cheap amplifier and stereo hi-fi speakers (Tandy is a good place to look for these).

### Get interactive with a microphone

Your soundcard will also provide you with a socket into which you can plug a microphone, and this is one of the cheapest peripheral devices you can buy, at roughly £10. Until recently, a microphone simply allowed you to record speech and other 'live' sounds into your PC, which has limited usefulness. Now the microphone has come into its own in two important respects.

The first of these is the ability to control your computer by voice commands: instead of clicking buttons with the mouse, or typing streams of text, you can select options by saying their names and dictate text into your word-processor. The software needs a little training before it can understand you well, but with continued use it will 'learn' your speech patterns and its accuracy will improve.

### Full and half duplex

Make sure you get a **full duplex** soundcard to make best use of a microphone. A **half-duplex** card can record sound or play it back, but it can't do both at the same time, so using your microphone for phone calls is something like a walkie-talkie conversation: you need to turn it off to hear the other person talk (no good for arguments). A full duplex card can record and play simultaneously, exactly mimicking the way you use a telephone.

The second great advantage of the microphone is that it works hand-in-hand with your modem (see Chapter 6). Not only can the microphone/modem partnership replace your telephone, but if you have a connection to the Internet you'll be able to make international phone calls for much the same price as a local call, or talk to other Internet users in online chat rooms rather than typing your side of the conversation.

## Gameplay with a joystick

The joystick is a device known and loved by computer-game fans and ignored by everybody else, but it has essentially the same features as a mouse: a handgrip for controlling the movements of objects on the screen, and a variety of buttons and triggers for wiping out all alien life-forms. If your PC has a soundcard, you'll probably find a game port on the card for plugging in the joystick. If your card doesn't have a game port, you'll either need to buy a dedicated game card or replace your soundcard with one that does. (If you don't have a soundcard, buy one! Most games use sound, so you'll kill two birds with one stone.)

Gameplay isn't a subject we're going to dwell on too much, so while we're here it's worth pointing out a few basic pros and cons. On the positive side, there is a huge number of games available for the PC, and the better ones (when you're lucky or informed enough to find them) can be every bit as good as their arcade and game-console counterparts. On the negative side, games, more than anything, test your PC to the limits with their need for a speedy processor, a good supply of RAM on the graphics card and 3D acceleration, and a high-quality soundcard.

# Digital photography and video

The digital camera is a comparatively new gadget that wants to replace your ordinary film camera. Instead of using film, digital cameras come with a slot-in memory card that stores photographs digitally (as a computer file). When the card is full, just connect the camera to your PC, copy the pictures to your hard-disk for storing, viewing, editing or printing, and start snapping again.

Digital cameras are not the easiest of devices to shop for, unfortunately. Although many share similar features (the same features you'll find on a film camera, plus a few more), prices can vary by hundreds of pounds, picture quality is hugely variable, and there are important considerations such as the size, cost and type of memory to weigh up. Try to test-drive a promising camera to ensure that its quality lives up to its specifications, and check the following:

▶ Cameras are battery-driven of course. Some use disposable AA batteries while others use rechargables. Check the battery life and recharge time.

▶ Some cameras will connect to one of your PC's USB ports, others to a serial port. The USB connection provides a much faster way to get the pictures from your camera to your PC.

▶ When set to the highest picture quality, the pictures will fill up the camera's memory quickly. For serious use, you'll want at least 16 MB of memory on the slot-in card, and you may want to purchase extra cards if you expect to do a lot of snapping before you're back at your PC.

Some digital cameras can also take a short burst of video (no more than a few seconds). This is better treated as a gimmick than a feature, but digital camcorders are starting to appear for the home-movie fan with deep pockets.

## TV and radio while you work

One of the few things the modern PC can't do is to lift you up gently and put you in front of the TV when you've finished for the day. While they work on that one, they have delivered the next best thing: as long as your PC is equipped with a soundcard, speakers, and a reasonable graphics card, you can slot in a TV tuner card to watch television (either full-screen or in a small window) or listen to the radio while you work.

### The aerial challenge

BY THE WAY

To receive a TV picture, remember that you shall need to connect the card to your main TV aerial – an indoor aerial won't give good results.

Although this is a relatively new technology, it is improving all the time and combined radio and TV cards are available, saving a valuable expansion slot. One of the best combined cards, which has the bonus of instant Teletext and requires a PCI slot, is the Hauppage WinTV series. For simpler installation in modern PCs, you can buy an external version that plugs into your USB port.

Once you have all these bits and pieces in place, you can use a Windows 98 feature called WebTV to set up your TV tuner card and retrieve program listings and other information from the Internet.

# OPTIONAL EXTRAS – LUXURY OR NECESSITY?

There are more peripheral devices available for your PC than you can shake a stick at, and new ones are arriving all the time. In this chapter, we take a look at some of the most popular add-ons, along with the choices you'll have to make and the pros and cons of each option.

# Printers – the good, the bad and the ugly

The printer has been a mainstay in the peripherals market since the birth of the personal computer, so there is a vast amount of choice to be had in this area; prices range from about £75 to £8000. So let's narrow it down a bit: you probably don't want a dot-matrix printer. This is a 'cheap and cheerless' printer that's fine if you just want to print something roughly for reference, but has very poor presentation. Its one redeeming feature is that it can be used to print NCR stationery such as invoices. (If you do buy a dot-matrix printer, choose a 24-pin rather than a nine-pin model for better definition.)

That leaves a choice of either an inkjet or a laser printer, and brings us to the basic decision that has to be made: do you need to print in colour, or will a black and white printer do the job?

For colour printing, even a cheap laser printer will put a £2000-sized hole in your pocket. Colour inkjet printers print more slowly, but they are much more affordable at £75 upwards, and the results can be superb. Most colour inkjet printers use a system of two swappable cartridges. One contains black ink only, for use in non-colour work such as letters. The other contains either three- or four-colours which are mixed to create full colour output. A superior system uses four separate colour cartridges, but always look at a sample output before buying to make sure you are getting the quality you need. Inkjet printers worth a look are Hewlett-Packard's DeskJet series, the Canon BJC and the Epson Stylus series.

## Paper choice

Choose your paper carefully. For colour printing especially, special coated paper should be used to prevent colours bleeding or soaking through the page. This paper can be expensive if you use it all the time, but there's no reason not to use ordinary copy paper when printing drafts and reference copies.

For black and white printing, the inkjet printer has been all but vanquished by the arrival of budget-priced laser printers, starting at around £300. The laser printer produces output that can at least match the quality of the best inkjet, but it does so at a much speedier 8 to 12 pages per minute (compared with one to three pages per minute for an inkjet). Models to look for include the Brother HL series and OKI's OkiPage series.

Finally, a few points worth checking on the subject of printers:

▶ When inkjet printers claim a 'pages per minute' speed, these are optimistic approximations based on how much print an average page contains. Laser printer speeds can be trusted.

▶ Check the output quality, measured in dpi (**dots per inch**). The higher this figure, the better the quality. 600 dpi is a good score for a budget laser printer; a colour inkjet should be able to manage 600–720 dpi, and some can offer over 1000 dpi.

▶ Make sure your printer comes with an automatic sheet-feeder. If it doesn't, you'll have to insert pages to be printed manually.

▶ Remember that printers have additional costs in their 'consumables' – special paper, replacement cartridges or refills for inkjets, toner and drum for laser printers. For heavy-duty printing, the price difference in consumables for one printer model and another might add up to a tidy sum over a long period.

# Fax and Internet with a modem

The surge in popularity of the Internet and the sudden rush to buy modems is more than coincidental; we'll look more closely at the Internet in Part 4, but if surfing the Net sounds like your thing, you'll need to join the queue at the modem counter.

Other uses include the capability to send and receive faxes from your computer instead of having a separate fax machine (the software you need for this will usually be included), and to dial the phone from your computer to save the exertion of all that button-pushing. Modems with voicemail ability will let you use your computer as an answer-phone, storing incoming messages to hard-disk (provided you leave your computer running when you're away from your desk or out of the office). To record and play back voicemail messages you'll need to have a soundcard installed (see Chapter 5), but some voicemail-compatible modems include a basic soundcard in the package.

## Lighting and siting

BY THE WAY

Keep your modem at least a few feet away from any fluorescent lights – they can cause interference, lost data and even dropped connections if they are too close.

Unarguably the main use of a modem is for Internet connectivity and this is where your choice of device becomes important. The job of a modem is to convert computer data into sound so that it can be sent down a telephone line, and to convert it back to data at the other end: the faster it can do this, the more you'll enjoy the multimedia-rich Internet experience. Modem speeds are measured in bps (**bits per second**), and the standard buy is a 56 000-bps device. Most new PCs come with one of these already installed.

The big decision when buying a modem is whether to go for an **internal** modem (which plugs into an expansion slot) or an **external** modem. The external modem is slightly more expensive and needs to be plugged into a power socket like any stand-alone electrical device, but it is simple to install and has the benefit of a panel of flashing lights that tell you what's going on. As internal devices, modems can be more complicated to install than some other expansion cards. If you prefer to have your modem tucked away inside the system unit, look for an internal modem with Plug and Play compatibility to automate as much of the setting-up as possible.

### Home Highway: faster Internet access

Although modems claim a speed of 56 000 bps, you will actually never get much beyond 50 000 bps from them. Other factors, such as the quality of your phone line, can also conspire against you to give a much lower speed. An alternative is to upgrade to British Telecom's Home Highway service, which gives you a digital line with a fixed speed of 64 000 bps. It has a couple of other benefits too:

▶ You will effectively have two telephone lines, allowing you to make and receive phone calls while surfing the Net, or make a phone call and send a fax at the same time.

▶ Where a normal modem warbles and screeches for 30 seconds or more when you try to connect to something, this system makes a connection silently in about five seconds.

To upgrade to Home Highway, you will first have to arrange for BT to convert your telephone line and put a new box on your wall. Second, you will have to replace your modem with a **terminal adapter** or an **ISDN card**. (Both devices do the same job, but the first is an external unit and the second is an expansion card.) The standing charge for a Home Highway line is higher than that for an ordinary telephone line, but the increased speed and reliability should make up the difference.

# Scanning for a paperless office

Okay, the truly paperless office will probably never happen, but the scanner is the device that makes it theoretically possible. A scanner works rather like a photocopier, but instead of producing a duplicate on paper, it copies the original into your PC. When scanning pictures, graphics and photographs, this allows you to load the image into photo-editing software, remove scratches and colour defects, apply filters and so on, and save or print the finished result. Text-based documents can be stored as image files for reference, and special OCR software (which will usually be included with your scanner) can convert these documents into text that can be loaded into your word-processor, edited, and saved as a much smaller text file.

**JARGON BUSTER**

## OCR

This stands for optical character recognition, a clever software trick that can recognise printed text and convert it into text that you can edit and save with your word-processor, as if you had typed it yourself.

55

Like most peripheral devices there are choices to be made, and scanners come in two types: the flatbed and the document scanner. The flatbed looks like a four-inch high photocopier, slightly larger than an A4 sheet of paper, with a hinged lid. This is the more flexible of the two, allowing easy scanning of photographs and documents along with open books and magazines. Some flatbed scanners include auto sheet-feeders for scanning multiple pages without any intervention. Budget flatbeds such as the Umax Astra and Agfa SnapScan start at under £100.

The document scanner is a physically smaller machine, ideal if you are short of desk space, which will accept only single sheets, fed between two rollers. These are as easy to use as the flatbed, but lack its flexibility. The undoubted king of document scanners is the Visioneer Strobe, which is as popular for the software it includes as for its scanning quality, and can also be found for under £200. The excellent software, Visioneer Paperport, can be bought separately and used with any scanner to organise, store and retrieve scanned documents.

A variant on the document scanner is the handheld device, which looks like a large mouse and has to be rolled slowly over the document to be scanned. The potential 'curse of the wobbly hand' means that handheld scanners are best avoided for OCR work but the results are pretty consistent in other areas, and clever software can stitch together large images that you scan in multiple strips.

Here are a few points to consider when shopping for a scanner:

▶ Like printers, scanning quality is measured in dpi (**dots per inch**). For OCR work this measurement makes little difference, but 600 dpi upwards is desirable when scanning photographs and graphics. Bear in mind that a scan 600-dpi can still only be printed at 300 dpi if you have a 300-dpi printer.

▶ Not all scanners are colour models, so check what you're buying. Colour is unnecessary for OCR work, but you're likely to want to scan photographs in colour.

▶ A scanner that has TWAIN compatibility is useful; it allows you to scan straight into many different applications and start working with the results immediately.

▶ Many scanners are SCSI devices (see later in this chapter). If you don't have an SCSI expansion card, you will need to buy and install one, or look for a scanner that plugs into a USB, parallel or serial port instead.

# Backup drives for safety and convenience

When you buy your PC it's a major purchase and a valuable asset. As time goes on, you'll begin to realise that you're collecting a disk full of equally valuable (and in some cases irreplaceable) files. If your PC is damaged or stolen, or your hard-disk stops working, what would you do? The odds are that your lost data would suddenly seem a lot more important than your lost computer.

For this reason, it's usual to keep **backups** (copies) of vital files on separate disks. One option is to regularly copy the files that matter to floppy-disks, but for any serious quantity of data, this could take a mountain of floppies and a full day's work. A better solution is to buy a dedicated backup drive, which uses removable tapes or disks capable of storing hundreds or even thousands of megabytes of data.

For true backup use (as opposed to archiving, which we'll look at in a moment), speed and capacity are what matter most. For this, a **tape streamer** is ideal. These are drives that use low-priced magnetic tape cartridges, and each reusable cartridge can hold up to 750 MB of data. Popular manufacturers are Hewlett-Packard, with their Colorado series, and Connor.

## Check the backup copy

Because magnetic tape is recognised as being a less than perfect medium, the software bundled with tape drives includes a **Verify** procedure that checks the data it has just stored against the original. It might double the start-to-finish time of the procedure, but it's a good idea to select this option, particularly if you reuse the same tape over and over (as you would normally expect to).

Archiving is a similar process, but it's done for a different reason and so requires different hardware. Over time, your hard-disk is likely to gather large files such as images or videos that you rarely need to use, but need to keep handy. Rather than have them wasting valuable hard-disk space, wouldn't it be useful if you could move them to a separate disk where they are still quickly accessible but not in the way? That's archiving.

Tape streamers don't make good archive drives due to the way they store data. Rather like listening to a music cassette, if you want something that's near the end of the tape, you have to wait while the tape is wound forward. For archiving purposes you want high capacity with easy retrieval, and the ideal devices for this are drives that use disks that look like the humble floppy (although they're more expensive, needless to say). The most popular of these is Iomega's Zip drive, which takes 100-MB or 250-MB disks (depending upon which model you buy), closely followed by its big brother, the Jaz drive, which can handle 2 GB.

## Create your own CDs with CD-R

For your own archiving use, the Zip and Jaz drives mentioned above may be ideal, but they're not the best choice if you want to share files with other computer users – not everyone has one of these drives, so they wouldn't be able to use the disk you sent them. Everyone has a CD-ROM or DVD-ROM drive, though, and blank CD-ROM disks are cheap, so a recordable CD-ROM drive (or **CD-R**) will let you create high-capacity disks readable on almost any computer. A blank CD will hold up to 650 MB of computer data, or 75 minutes of stereo sound.

The basic CD-R drive will let you record data to a disk in up to 99 separate recording sessions (or until the disk is full, whichever happens first). These disks cannot be erased, so they don't make ideal backup devices but they do offer a cheap way to permanently store files you don't need on your hard-disk.

## One thing at a time

Recording to CD requires a constant stream of data to be sent from the PC to the CD drive. In the case of CD-R, if the data flow is interrupted, the disk will usually be ruined. It is best to shut down any other programs and override your screen saver before starting to record on a CD-R, leaving the PC to concentrate on the job.

An alternative to CD-R is **CD-RW**, or rewriteable CD. These drives let you record on to the cheap CD-R disks (with the same 'no erase' restriction), or the more expensive CD-RW disks. CD-RW disks can be used just like your hard-disk or a floppy-disk: an old file can be replaced with a newer copy, or the whole disk can be erased to let you start again.

One final option to watch for is recordable DVD. The DVD disks have enough capacity to store the entire contents of a medium-sized hard-disk, and recordable drives are slowly starting to appear. At this early stage, they're still expensive and manufacturers haven't agreed on a standard, so they're best avoided for a while, but they will at least have the effect of pushing down the prices of CD-RW drives.

# SCSI: speed and expandability

SCSI (pronounced 'skuzzy', short for small computer systems interface) provides a slightly different system for installing add-on hardware devices to your PC, but a very fast one. A SCSI expansion card is fitted to one of your expansion slots, and then up to eight SCSI-compatible devices can be connected together in a chain linking back to the card. These are usually storage devices like hard-disks and CD-ROM drives which benefit from SCSI's lightning-fast speeds, but SCSI can control all sorts of devices. And if you want to add even more devices (or you have compatibility problems with some of the devices), you can add a second SCSI controller.

# Easy networking with a NIC

If you have two or more PCs in your office or home, it makes sense to connect them together so that you can access data stored on one while working at the other. This is known as **networking**, and your group of connected computers is known as a LAN, or local area network.

Connecting two or more Windows' PCs is a reasonably hassle-free experience. First, each PC needs a **network interface card**, or NIC, which plugs into an expansion slot, with a cable joining the two computers. A Novell NE2000-compatible Ethernet card should cost no more than £35, and a Plug & Play compatible card will automate the setting-up that makes the two computers 'talk' to each other.

**GOOD QUESTION!**

## Is there any other way to connect two PCs?

A less convenient way is to connect a cable between the computers' parallel or serial ports and use a Windows feature called direct cable connection. Start the DCC program on both computers and set one as the Host and the other as the Guest, and you'll be able to copy files between the two.

A detailed explanation of networking is beyond the scope of this book, but the basic principles are straightforward enough: to be able to use data on another computer (or a device connected to it, such as a printer) it needs to be *shared*. In Windows, you can opt to share a device or the contents of a folder by clicking it with the right mouse-button and selecting the **Sharing…** option on the menu. Assign a memorable name to the item, choose whether it should be protected with a password, and Bob's your uncle. To access this item from elsewhere on the network is a simple case of referring to it by name.

# Gadgets and gizmos

The PC has been around long enough that an endless array of gadgets and small, expensive plastic things has found its way into the stores. Here are a few of the presents you might want to buy for your computer.

**Mouse mat.** A rubber pad with a plastic or cloth covering that makes a better surface for smooth mouse control than a desktop. These come in all sorts of shapes, designs and colours – some have a built-in wrist-support (another little extra you can also buy separately), or a tray for holding pens and other office bits and bobs.

**Mouse house.** A rodent residence designed to keep the little guy dust-free while you're not using him. There are several million cheaper ways of doing this, but none is quite as cute.

**Keyboard cover.** A fitted cover for your keyboard that keeps the crumbs and coffee out, but still lets you tap away.

**Computer covers.** Separate plastic dust-covers are available for monitor, system-unit and keyboard to keep them clean and dust-free while you are not using the PC. The monitor-cover is an especially sensible buy.

**Copy holder.** A plastic arm that attaches to the side of your monitor with a clip to hold papers you need to refer to while working. A cheap and very useful accessory.

**Anti-glare filter.** A thin mesh that fits over the front of your monitor and cuts reflections from nearby lights and windows to help prevent eye-strain. These filters can also increase your privacy by making the screen-contents difficult to see from an angle.

# 2

# GETTING TO GRIPS WITH WINDOWS

**7**

# STARTING AND EXPLORING YOUR PC

So you're the proud owner of a shiny new PC. You've diligently attached everything that needed to be attached, and you're sitting comfortably and waiting expectantly. Over the next few chapters you'll learn how to find your way around Windows, work with programs and documents, and customise things so that they look and work the way you want them to.

As you read on, remember this one simple fact about computers: they exist to help you do what you do quickly and easily. Essentially that means creating, opening, saving and printing files. They can do other things too, such as playing audio CDs, but you didn't buy a PC because you wanted a really expensive CD player!

# Getting started

Task number one needs little introduction: to use the PC for anything remotely useful you'll need to switch it on! Plug the PC into the mains, along with any other devices you want to use such as your printer, scanner or external modem. Press the power switch on the PC's system unit, then switch on the monitor followed by any other devices you want to use (such as your printer).

To begin with you'll see a plain black screen with some technical-looking text. Within a few seconds, this dull screen will be replaced by something more colourful. Within about 30 seconds, the hard-disk will finish its churning and grinding, and the colourful picture will vanish to reveal the Windows desktop.

## 'Invalid system disk' message

If your computer sticks at the black screen and displays the line **Invalid system disk. Replace the disk and press any key**, this means that there is a floppy-disk in the floppy drive which doesn't contain the type of information your PC needs to start Windows. Just remove the disk and then press a key on your keyboard, and Windows will start to load.

# Shutting down Windows

When you've finished work for the day and you're ready to switch off your computer, don't press the power button yet. Just as Windows has some work to do before it can start, it has to do a few things before it stops. Instead, follow this routine:

1  Save any documents you're working on (if you want to keep them), then close any applications still running and any open windows.

2  Click the **Start** button at the bottom left of the screen to open the Start Menu.

3  Click on **Shut Down** at the bottom of the Start Menu.

4  A small window called a **dialog** will appear, like the one shown in the next screenshot, giving you several options. The dot beside the words **Shut down** means that this option is selected. This is the option you want, so click the **OK** button.

5  A large picture will fill the screen asking you to wait while Windows shuts down. After some hard disk churning, you'll see a message saying it's safe to switch off your computer. Most modern PCs will switch themselves off automatically at this point; if yours doesn't, you can turn it off using the power switch.

6  Switch off your monitor and peripheral devices such as your printer, then unplug everything from the mains.

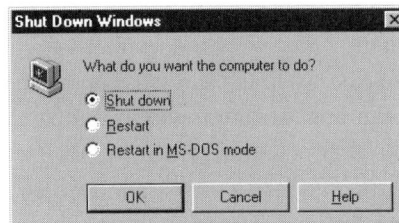

▶ The Shut Down Windows dialog: choose what you want to do, then click OK to make it happen.

# Arriving at the Windows desktop

When Windows has finished loading you'll see the **desktop**, shown in the next screenshot. At the moment it looks empty and uncluttered, with several small labelled pictures called **icons** and a grey strip along the bottom called the **Taskbar**. In the centre of the screen you'll see the pointer, which you control by moving the mouse. You'll probably see a **window** on the desktop with the title **Welcome to Windows 98**. Here's a brief explanation of what these features do.

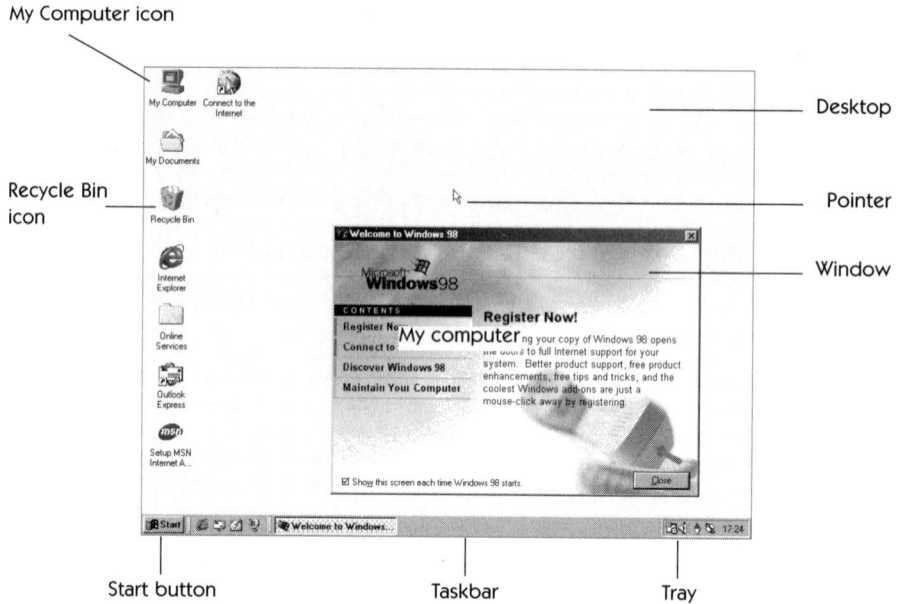

My Computer icon

Recycle Bin icon

Desktop

Pointer

Window

▶ The Windows desktop and its main features.

Start button

Taskbar

Tray

**Taskbar.** Almost everything that happens in Windows *happens in a window*. That's how the operating system got its name. A window is a box that opens on the desktop to show you the program you're using, the file you're editing and many other things. As soon as a window opens, a button will appear on the Taskbar with the same name as the window. In normal everyday work, you might have several windows open at once, putting several buttons on this bar. As well as telling you at a glance what's currently open, these buttons can be clicked to let you see a window that might be hiding behind all the others. We'll take a closer look at the Taskbar in Chapter 8.

**Start button.** This is your key to getting things done in Windows. When you click this button, a menu will appear that holds entries for all your programs along with some other useful options. Starting a program or selecting an option is as simple as moving the mouse-pointer on to it and clicking the left button. The Start button and its menu are covered in more detail in Chapter 8.

## How do I 'click' the Start button?

**GOOD QUESTION!**

Hold the mouse so that your second and third fingers are over its two buttons and your thumb is resting along its left side. Pull the mouse slowly towards you and to the left and you'll see the pointer on the screen move towards the Start button. When the pointer is over that button, press the mouse-button under your second finger.

**Tray.** This is a sunken area at the right of the Taskbar containing a digital clock and a few small icons. You might have only one icon here (looking like a small loudspeaker), or you might have several, depending upon what programs are installed on your PC. These icons usually give quick access to settings or options. For example, if you click the loudspeaker with the left mouse-button, a slider will appear to let you change the volume of your soundcard. (To make it go away again, click the mouse somewhere else.) You can also find extra information by resting the pointer over these icons for a moment: if you move over the clock, a little message will appear to tell you the date.

**Icons.** You'll find icons scattered all the way through Windows, and you'll soon start to recognise and distinguish between the different 'pictures'. Every application you use has its own distinctive icon, and any documents you create with it will be given the same icon along with any name you choose. That way, you can tell at a glance which program you used to create a particular document. You'll have several icons on your desktop at the moment, although you can add more later if you want to, to give quick access to favourite programs or documents. Later in this chapter we'll look at the most important of those icons, labelled **My Computer**.

## What's on your desk?

The layout of Windows follows a 'desktop' metaphor that's intended to make the organisation of your disks and files intuitive. The idea is that just as your desk might be covered in objects that you pick up and use, so the objects in your computer (applications, documents, printer, modem and so on) should be presented as pictures on the screen that you can 'pick up' (click with the mouse) and use in a similar way.

On your desk you have a computer, hence that icon labelled **My Computer**. Although technically *under* your desk, there's a bin for all your trash called the **Recycle Bin**, and the **Taskbar** corresponds to the jumble of papers on your desk from which you might pick something up to work with for a while (by clicking its Taskbar-button) before putting it down and looking at something else (clicking a different Taskbar-button).

# Handling the mouse

Although Windows can be used entirely from the keyboard, it wasn't designed for keyboard-only use. A little time spent getting used to controlling the mouse pays huge rewards in speed and simplicity. So before we start looking at Windows itself, now is a good time to make friends with your rodent.

First, make sure the mouse is the right way round: when you place your palm on the body of the mouse, your second and third fingers should rest lightly on the buttons and the cable should be running towards the back of your desk. Moving the pointer on the screen is simple: move your hand to the left, and the pointer moves left, and so on.

## Left-handed mouse control

If you are left-handed, the mouse buttons will probably seem uncomfortable to use. Turn to Chapter 11 and use the Control Panel's Mouse applet to switch the buttons about.

Now let's try a little exercise in **clicking**. There are three terms you'll come across: click, right-click, and double-click:

**Click** means to press the left mouse-button once (the button under your second finger). You can test this by moving the pointer on to the Start button: click once to make the Start Menu appear; click again to make it vanish.

**Right-click** means to click once using the right mouse-button. If you move the pointer to an empty space on the desktop and right-click, a menu containing options like Arrange Icons and Line Up Icons will appear. Click on a different area of the desktop to make it disappear.

**Double-click** is a knack that takes a bit more mastering. Like 'click', this tacitly refers to the left mouse-button, but you need to click twice in quick succession. To try this out, move the pointer on to the **Recycle Bin** icon, and double-click. If you're successful, a window will open on your desktop like the one in the next screenshot. You can close this window by clicking the Close button (marked with an 'x') in the top right corner. It's worth trying this routine a few times to get the hang of it.

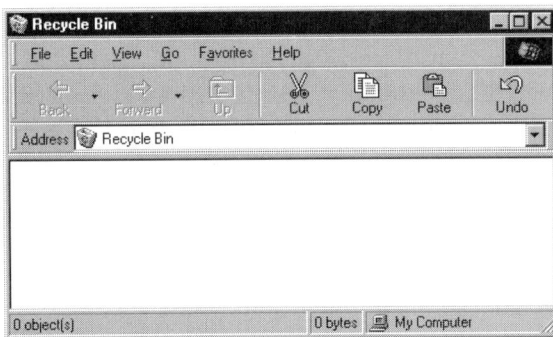

Click this button to close the window

▶ The Recycle Bin window.

# Welcome to Windows

If you can see the window titled **Welcome to Windows 98** on your desktop, now is a good time to take the 'Discover Windows 98' tour. Make sure your Windows CD is in your CD-ROM drive, and click the words 'Discover Windows 98'.

When the tour has finished loading, you'll see a choice of four tours to follow. Either click on the tour you're interested in, or type the appropriate number on the keyboard. You can follow the tour by clicking options with the mouse, or by using the keyboard.

## Why does this 'Welcome' window keep appearing?

The Welcome window can soon become an 'unwelcome window' – it appears every time you start your computer. Click on the words 'Show this screen each time Windows 98 starts' and the tick in the box to the left will disappear. Click the Close button, and you'll never see this window again.

## Drive names – learn your ABC

Whenever you want to use a particular file, you have to tell the computer what it's called. Curiously, even though the data is stored on the disk itself, you tell the computer which *drive* to look at to find the file rather than which *disk*. In fact, this isn't as odd as it may seem.

In the early days of computing, hard-disks were rare. Everyone had a floppy drive and they popped a disk into the drive to use the files it contained. A lot of people bought a *second* floppy drive in order to reduce the amount of time they spent inserting and removing disks. Over a period of time, they might collect hundreds of floppy-disks and it would be unreasonable to expect the computer to know exactly what was on each one. So they just stuck a disk into one of the drives and told the computer which drive to look at.

As the normal computer had one floppy drive, it came to be called **Drive A**. If a second floppy drive was added, it would be called **Drive B**. When the hard-drive arrived on the scene, it was automatically assigned the name **Drive C**. So on a standard PC with its one floppy drive and one hard-drive, these are called Drive A and Drive C respectively. Recently, more and more PCs have extra drives, such as a CD-ROM and backup drive, and the computer simply assigns these the next available letter name: your CD-ROM drive will usually be **Drive D** and your backup drive **Drive E**.

# Drives and folders in My Computer

So far, you've taken it on trust that there are files on your hard-disk. After all, Windows started, so there must be *something* there, mustn't there? The quickest way to take a look at what files are on a particular disk is to open **My Computer** by double-clicking its icon. When you do this, a window like the one shown in the next screenshot will open to display My Computer's contents.

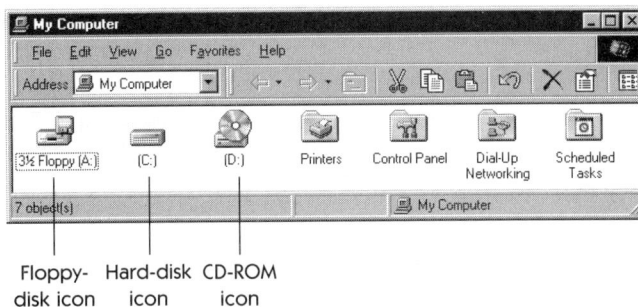

Floppy-disk icon   Hard-disk icon   CD-ROM icon

▶ You can view your drives and their contents in My Computer.

You will probably have the same three icons shown here for floppy-disk, hard-disk and CD-ROM drives, and you might even have one or two more. To look at the contents of one of these disks, just double-click its icon. The important thing to remember is that only your hard-disk is permanently attached to your PC; if you double-click the icons for your floppy or CD-ROM drive without first inserting a floppy-disk or a CD, a message will appear to tell you that the drive is unavailable.

## Creating with the keyboard

If you're finding the double-click action tricky, you can cheat: click once on an icon, which will highlight it to show it's selected, then press the **Enter** key on your keyboard to open it.

Start by double-clicking the icon for your hard-disk, labelled **C:**, and the window will change to display your hard-disk's contents as a collection of icons. Although the contents of your hard-disk will be different from mine, this window will look a lot like the one in the following screenshot, showing a mixture of **folders** and **files**.

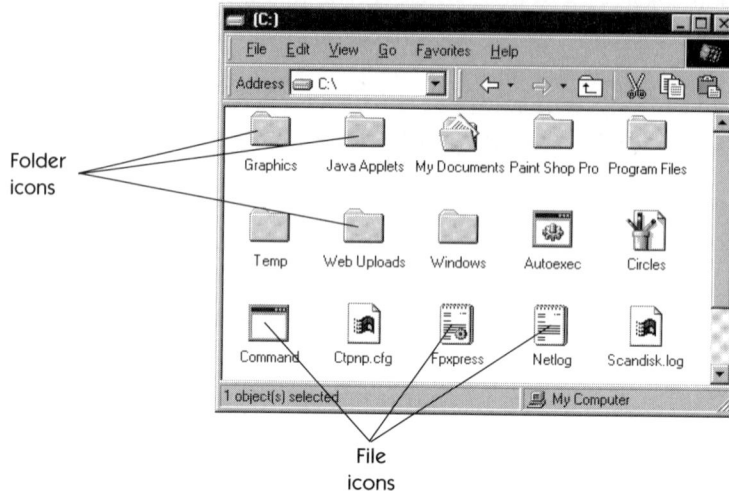

Folder icons

File icons

▶ Folders and files on drive C.

The hard-disk is best thought of as a filing cabinet. In a well-organised office, every time you start work on a new project, you grab a new folder, scribble a memorable name on the front of it, and put all the documents relating to that project inside it to make them easy to find. Then you'd store that folder alphabetically inside the cabinet with all the other folders.

The hard-disk works in a similar way: when Windows was installed, it created a folder called **Windows** and another called **Program Files**, and it placed files inside both. Most other programs you install will create their own folders in the same way, and you can create new folders yourself to organise your own files, as you'll learn in Chapter 10.

As you can see from the window you have just opened, drive C contains several folders and a small bunch of files. The folders are easy to spot – they all use the same yellow icon. Files can have many different icons according to what type of file they are, but the most important thing for now is to recognise a folder.

## Subfolder, parent folder

**JARGON BUSTER**

When one folder is inside another, it's referred to as a **subfolder** (so the System folder is a **subfolder** of the Windows folder). Conversely, the Windows folder is said to be the **parent** of the System folder.

Folders don't necessarily contain only files. If you double-click the **Program Files** folder to open it, you'll see more folder icons including **Accessories**, **Common Files** and **Plus!**, and (perhaps) some more files. If you open the **Accessories** folder, you'll see another folder and some more files inside that.

## Working with My Computer

There are two ways to look at the files and folders on your system: one way is to use My Computer, and the other is to use Windows Explorer (more on that in a moment). You can use whichever method you like, whenever you like, but most users seem to favour one method over another and use it more. Here are a few tips to help you navigate your system using My Computer:

▶ If you lose track of which folder's contents are being displayed, look at the extreme top left of the window. Beside a small folder icon you'll see the name of the current folder.

▶ If you open a subfolder and want to move back to its parent folder again, either press the **Backspace** key, or click the button on the toolbar showing a tiny folder with an upward-pointing arrow. (If you can't see the toolbar, click the word **View** on the menu bar, move the mouse on to the word **Toolbars** and click **Standard Buttons** on the menu that appears beside it.)

▶ Remember you can close any window by clicking the **Close** button (marked with an 'x' symbol) in the top right corner.

▶ You can choose between four different ways of displaying icons and information in a window. Open the **View** menu by clicking the word **View** on the menu bar, and choose from Large Icons, Small Icons, List and Details.

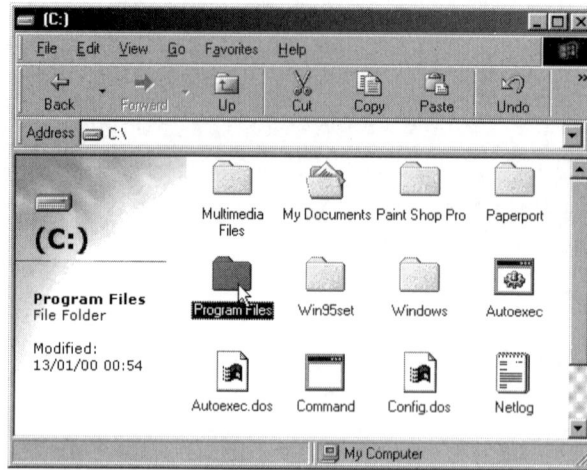

▶ The contents of drive C in Web view.

▶ You can also switch on an extra view called 'Web view' by clicking **As Web Page** on the same menu. Every time you click on a file or folder in the window, information will appear in the coloured area describing the item you clicked. With some types of file, a small preview will also be shown. (If you decide you're not keen on Web view, go back to the View menu again and click the same option a second time to switch it off.)

# The view from Windows Explorer

Windows Explorer offers another way to view the drives, folders and files on your system. One of the big benefits of Explorer is that icons for all your folders and drives remain visible while you look at the contents of one particular folder. This can make it easier to tell at a glance where you are and what you're looking at, with the added bonus that copying and moving items from one place to another is simple (as you'll learn in Chapter 10).

There are two ways to open Windows Explorer:

▶ If your keyboard has the extra Windows keys, press and hold the **Win** key (marked with a 'flying window' icon) and press **E** once quickly.

▶ Click the Start button, then point to **Programs** as shown in the next screenshot. The Programs menu will open and you can click the **Windows Explorer** entry.

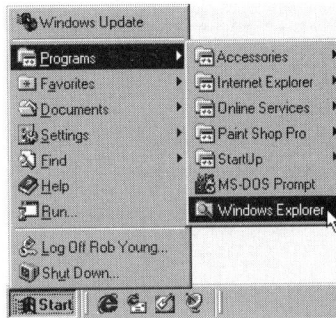

▶ Opening
Windows Explorer
from the Start
Menu.

Explorer shows a neat split-window view of your system. In the left pane of
the window you'll see icons for your desktop, My Computer, Recycle Bin
and your drives. In the right pane you'll see the contents of whatever you
select in the left. When Explorer first opens, the right pane displays the same
items you see in My Computer. In fact, if you choose to, you can use
Explorer in exactly the same way as you use My Computer: just ignore the
left pane, and double-click drives and folders in the right pane to open them.

The neatest way to use Explorer, though, is with the left pane (and you
don't need to double-click!). Every drive has a tiny '+' symbol beside it,
indicating that it contains folders. If you click the + symbol beside the icon
for your C drive, the list (or **tree**) will expand to show its folders, and the +
symbol will turn into a '−' symbol. To collapse that part of the tree again,
click the − symbol.

## Expand and open in one

If a folder has a + symbol beside it in the left pane, you can expand it and
view its contents in the right pane in a single action. Just double-click the
folder's icon in the left pane.

If a folder contains subfolders, you'll see the same + symbol beside it, and
you can expand and collapse it in the same way, as shown in the next
screenshot. Click on any drive or folder in the left pane to view its contents
in the right.

▶ Browsing
through drives
and folders in
Windows Explorer.

## Growing panes

You can choose how wide the two panes of the window should be. Move your
pointer on to the bar that splits them, and you'll see it turn into a horizontal
arrow. Press the left mouse-button and, without releasing it, drag the bar to where you want it.

# FINDING YOUR
# WAY AROUND

Whatever you're planning to use your computer for, there are three fundamental elements to become familiar with: the window, the Taskbar, and the Start Menu. The significance of the window shouldn't come as much of a surprise, given the name of the operating system. The Taskbar and Start button remain visible whatever you're working on, and these are your essential tools for working with different programs. In this chapter, you'll learn how to use these elements, and pick up the basic information you need to start working with programs and files.

## The mighty Start button

It may not look like much, but the Start button on the left of the Taskbar is your key to becoming productive in Windows. Along with a few other options we'll be looking at in Chapter 10, this is where you find quick access to all the programs on your computer. Click the Start button and the Start Menu will open. Move your pointer up to the **Programs** entry and pause there for a moment, and another menu (called a **submenu**) will pop out. On this, you'll see **program groups** such as Accessories and StartUp.

Entries for program groups all have a black arrowhead beside them and identical folder-like icons: when your pointer pauses over a group, a new submenu will open to show its collection of icons (which may contain still more groups). Entries on these menus that don't have the arrowhead and folder icon will run a program when you click on them.

If your computer came with a bundle of software, as most new computers do, you'll probably see extra program groups for those programs. Most software you install on your PC adds its own little set of icons on a separate submenu.

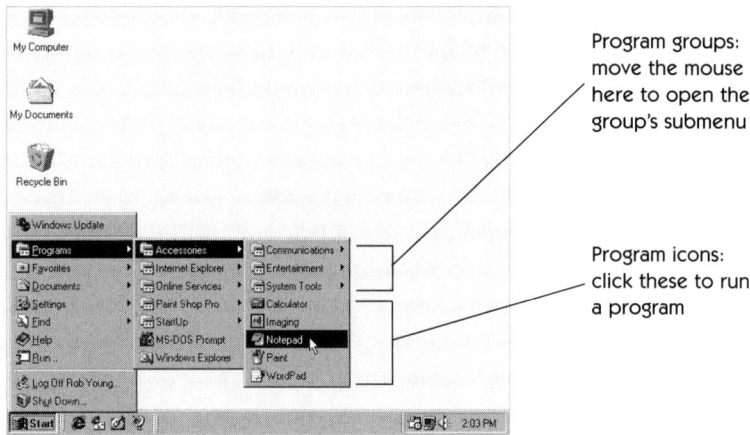

Program groups: move the mouse here to open the group's submenu

Program icons: click these to run a program

▶ Program groups and icons on the Start Menu.

# Using Windows' own accessories

Even if your new PC didn't come with a bundle of extra software, you'll still find a range of accessories supplied by Windows itself in the Accessories program group. Although most of these add-ons lack the advanced features you would expect to find in a fully-fledged (and more expensive) piece of software, they are all still perfectly useable and useful. To start one of these programs, just click it with the left mouse-button.

**Notepad**. A handy 'jotter-style' text editor for creating simple text files that can be opened in any word processor. Notepad is great for short informal notes or for storing information that you want to refer to yourself, but not the best tool for formal documents.

**WordPad**. A more advanced word-processor than Notepad, for creating longer documents using different text styles, colours and sizes. WordPad is a good choice for formal documents unless you have something better (such as Microsoft Works, Lotus WordPro or Microsoft Word).

**Paint**. A simple graphics program for viewing, drawing and editing pictures. Choose a drawing tool such as Pencil or Airbrush from the panel on the left, click a colour from the panel at the bottom, and start drawing in the white area in the main part of the window by holding down the left mouse-button and dragging the mouse around.

**Calculator**. An on-screen calculator with a choice of Standard or Scientific layouts, which you can select from its View menu. Press the **Num Lock** key until a light on your keyboard tells you that **Num Lock** is switched on, then use the numbers and mathematical keys on the numeric keypad (on the right of your keyboard). The **Enter** key in the lower-right corner acts as the Equals key.

**CD Player**. For playing your audio CDs, and creating playlists that can skip the tracks you don't like. When you place an audio CD into your CD-ROM drive, CD Player should start automatically and begin to play the disk. (If it doesn't, you can start CD Player yourself from the Start Menu.)

**Media Player**. The multimedia 'everything' player: movie files, audio CDs, animations and sound files. To listen to the sound files supplied by Windows, follow these steps: click the Start button and then click on Run. Type **media** and click the OK button. A window will open containing some icons with a picture of a yellow loudspeaker. Double-click any of these, and Media Player will appear and start playing the sound file you double-clicked.

**Internet Explorer**. If you have a modem and a connection to the Internet, this is your number one Net-surfing tool, as you'll learn in Part 4. If you haven't set up an Internet connection, this program won't do very much yet.

**Outlook Express**. This two-in-one program lets you send and receive email messages and read newsgroup messages, provided you have an Internet connection.

**GOOD QUESTION!**

## Is it okay to experiment with these programs?

Yes, go right ahead! You may not understand what each program is for straight away, and some may apparently do nothing, but it doesn't hurt to have a look around them. If you get into difficulties, click the Close button in the top right corner of the window. If the computer then displays a question in a small window, choose **No** or **Cancel** if one of those options is offered.

Along with the accessories above, you'll find a System Tools group containing utilities to keep your PC running smoothly (we'll ignore those until Chapter 12), and you may have a Games group containing a few simple computer games such as Solitaire and Minesweeper. If you can't see these games on your Start Menu, they may not be installed – turn to Chapter 11 to find out how to add them.

## Anatomy of a window

The window is the fundamental element of Windows operating systems. A window is a box on the desktop which displays a document or application, or groups of icons representing the files on your hard-disk. You might have several windows open at the same time and switch between them when you need to. For example, in one window you might have your word-processor running to type a sales report; another window could contain your spreadsheet application so that you can refer to your sales figures; a third window might display icons for all the spreadsheet documents you've created this year so that you can select which month's figures you need to look at.

In this example, the word-processor window would usually be in the foreground so that all your keyboard input would be entered into the report you're typing. The other two windows would be, quite literally, in the background: the word-processor window is covering them up like the top sheet on a stack of papers, perhaps leaving just a corner or an edge visible. When you switch to the spreadsheet window, this will move to the foreground (the top of the stack) instead, and the word-processor window will disappear behind it. The fact that you can no longer *see* this window doesn't mean it's not there, or that the report you were typing into it has been lost – you can switch it back to the foreground whenever you want to. Or you can place the windows side by side on the screen so that you can refer to one as you type into the other.

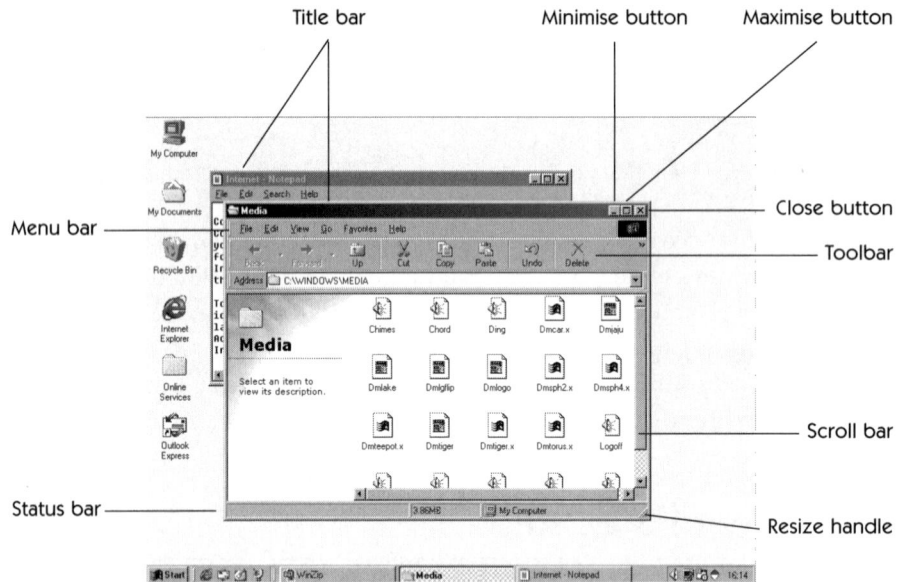

Title bar    Minimise button    Maximise button

Menu bar

Close button

Toolbar

Scroll bar

Status bar

Resize handle

▶ The window's major body parts.

Almost every window you work with will have the same features as those shown in the screenshot above. Some of these features let you change the way the window looks, such as its size and position, and others let you work with the information displayed in the window.

**Title bar**. The title bar displays the name of the folder you're looking at, or the name of the application in that window. It has an extra, useful function: you can use it to move the window wherever you want it. Just click on the bar, and drag the window without releasing the mouse-button. The colour of the title bar tells you which of your open windows is **active**. Inactive windows will have a dull grey title bar, but the active window's title bar will be blue (unless you've changed your colour scheme – see Chapter 11). The active window is the one that will react to your keyboard input, and only one window can be active at a time.

**Resize handle**. Move your pointer on to this area at the corner of a window, and the pointer will change into a double-headed arrow. Click the left mouse-button and drag the corner of the window in any direction to change its size. (With slightly more skilled mouse-positioning, you can do the same thing at any edge of the window too.)

**Close button**. We've seen the Close button before, and it does what you'd expect: click it, and the window will close. (If the window contains a document you've been working on and haven't saved, a small window called a **dialog box** will pop open to ask if you want to save it first.)

## Close Windows from the keyboard

BY THE WAY

If you prefer to work from the keyboard, holding the **Alt** key and pressing **F4** will close a window in exactly the same way as clicking the Close button.

**Maximise button**. Clicking this button increases the window's size to make it cover the entire desktop. Any other open windows will be covered too, but you can switch to them at any time by clicking the appropriate buttons on the Taskbar. When the window is maximised, the Maximise button changes into a **Restore** button: if you click this, the window will return to its original size and position.

**Minimise button**. This makes the window vanish from your desktop, making the screen less cluttered and easier to work with. It doesn't close the program and document you were working on in that window though – its button remains on the Taskbar and can be clicked to make the window reappear. You could think of the Minimise button as a 'make temporarily invisible' button.

**Status bar**. This is a simple information bar. If a window is displaying the contents of a folder, it might tell you the number of items in that folder, or the size of an item you've clicked. In a word-processor, the status bar might tell you the total number of pages in your document.

**Scroll bar**. If a window contains more information than it can display, a scroll bar will appear to let you wind the window contents up and down (rather like winding a long piece of paper through a typewriter). The scroll bar contains a long box called a scroll box, and scroll arrows at either end. To move quickly through the window contents, you can drag the scroll box up and down; for more controlled scrolling, click and hold one of the scroll arrows to move through the window a line at a time.

**Toolbar**. Not all windows have a toolbar, and for those that do you can usually choose whether to hide or display it. The toolbar contains a collection of buttons that give one-click access to some of the often-used options in a program. The same options can usually be selected from menus on the **menu bar**, but the toolbar buttons will help you work more quickly.

## A little help with the buttons

BY THE WAY

If you're not sure what a toolbar button does, place the pointer over it for a couple of seconds. In many programs, a small message called a **tooltip** will appear with a brief explanation.

**Menu bar**. The menu bar is a feature of most (though not all) windows. It's a narrow horizontal strip below the title bar containing a row of words such as **File**, **Edit**, **View** and **Help**. Each of these words is the name of a menu: clicking on the word **File**, for example, will cause a drop-down menu to open that contains options such as **New** (to start creating a new document), **Open** (to open an existing document), and **Save** (to save the document you are working on to disk), as shown in the next screenshot.

If you prefer to use the keyboard rather than the mouse, menus are just as easy to deal with. Every menu on the bar has an underlined letter. To open that menu, hold the **Alt** key and type that letter on your keyboard. To select an option from the open menu, press the option's underlined letter. For example, to select the Save option shown in the screenshot above, press **Alt+F** to open the File menu, then press **S**.

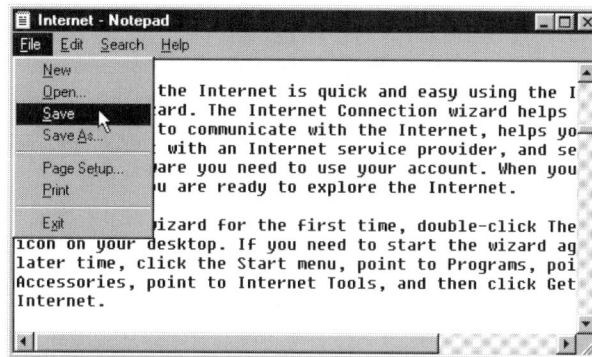

▶ Click the word **File** to open the File menu, then click the option you want.

Many of the options you see on these menus end with an ellipsis (...), such as **Open....** The ellipsis indicates that selecting this option won't carry out a command straight away, but will open a dialog box to let you provide more information. In this example, 'Open' by itself is meaningless until you tell the program what document you want to open.

# Switching between open windows

One of the things that made Windows popular was the ability to have multiple windows open and switch between them (known as **multitasking**). The Taskbar makes this not just possible, but easy. Every window you open immediately places a matching button on the Taskbar which remains there until the window is closed. Because the Taskbar stays visible, even when one or more of your windows is maximised, you can tell at a glance which windows are open, and switch to any window by clicking its button.

In the screenshot below, you can see two open windows and three buttons on the Taskbar. The Media window is active, and its Taskbar button is depressed as an indication. Behind this window you can see part of an inactive window with the words **Internet – Notepad** on its title bar and its Taskbar button. If you wanted to work with this window, you would click its Taskbar button to bring it to the front and make it active. (You could also bring it to the front just by clicking on any part of it that's visible.)

▶ A quick glance at the Taskbar tells you what's open.

The third button on the Taskbar indicates that there is a window open, running a program called WinZip, but where is it? It might be a tiny window hiding behind the other two, or it might have been minimised, effectively making it invisible. In fact it doesn't matter: to work with the WinZip window, just click its button to make it appear at the top of the stack looking just as it did the last time you saw it.

## It's still there – honestly!

Remember that you won't lose your work by minimising its window or hiding it behind another window – it's no more risky than closing your eyes! The window and the document it contains will still be there waiting for you.

If you're a keyboard fan, or you are working with the keyboard and don't want to break off and reach for the mouse, here's another couple of window-switching options:

**Alt+Tab**. Press and hold the **Alt** key and then press **Tab** repeatedly until the icon for the window you want to switch to is highlighted on the pop-up panel (shown in the next screenshot), then release both keys.

**Alt+Esc**. Press and hold **Alt** and press **Esc** repeatedly. This cycles through the actual windows themselves (rather than icons for them) bringing each to the foreground in turn. Release both keys when the window you want comes to the surface.

## Cancelling Alt+Tab

If you're using Alt+Tab to cycle through the available windows and you suddenly decide you want to just forget it and stay where you are, press **Esc** without letting go of **Alt** – the icon dialog will vanish and leave you in your original window.

These two methods can be a bit hit-and-miss. If a window has been minimised, the Alt+Esc method will ignore it. And the Alt+Tab method doesn't include dialog box windows in its list, so you can only use this to switch between programs or windows showing the contents of drives and folders.

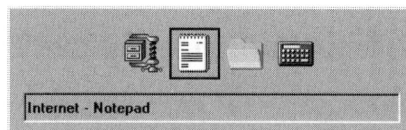

▶ The Alt+Tab panel.

## Tricks with the taskbar

As one of the main navigation tools for getting your work done in Windows, the Taskbar offers some useful customisation options:

▶ By clicking on an empty area of the Taskbar, and dragging it without releasing the mouse-button, you can place the bar at any edge of your screen.

▶ As you open more windows, the buttons on the Taskbar get progressively smaller, making their labels difficult to read. One option is to hold your pointer over a button for a couple of seconds: a tooltip message will appear containing the button's label. Alternatively, move the pointer to the edge of the bar until it turns into a double-headed arrow, then drag upwards: the Taskbar can be stretched to fill half your screen.

▶ Right-click on the Taskbar and choose Tile Vertically or Tile Horizontally to have all your open windows arranged neatly side by side. You can also select Minimize All Windows to get back to your desktop quickly. After choosing any of these actions, you can right-click the Taskbar again and choose the Undo Tile or Undo Minimize options to return to your previous layout.

▶ By right-clicking the Taskbar and selecting Properties, a dialog box will appear containing some useful options such as Auto Hide (the Taskbar will only appear when you move the pointer to the bottom of your screen), and Show small icons in Start menu. To select an option, click the small box beside it. A tick in that box indicates that the option is 'switched on'.

# Dealing with dialogs

A **dialog box** is a window that gives you information about a task Windows is carrying out, provides you with a warning or prompt when you do something you might regret later, or asks you for information.

## Prompts and informative dialogs

As dialogs go, the prompt and the progress dialog shown below are pretty straightforward. The **prompt dialog** warns you of the consequences of an action you tried to carry out – if you're happy to carry on and do it you click the **OK** button; if you'd rather not, click on **Cancel**. This dialog won't go away until you choose one or the other. A slightly different type of prompt may ask you a question, and give you three buttons for **Yes**, **No** and **Cancel**.

The **progress dialog** indicates how far the system has got in copying a file from one place to another. When the copy process has finished this dialog will disappear automatically, but until it does you can cancel the operation by clicking its single button.

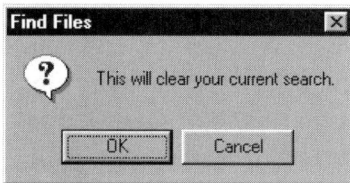

► A prompt dialog.

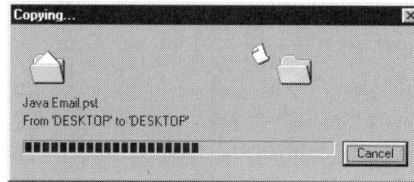

► A progress dialog.

## Save some mouse mileage

All dialog boxes have a **default** button, indicated by a dark outline (like the **OK** button in the prompt dialog). If you want to select the option indicated by the default button, you can just press the **Enter** key on your keyboard instead of moving the pointer to the button and clicking. If a dialog has a **Cancel** button, you can press the **Esc** key to cancel.

## Selection dialogs

The more involved type of dialog box is the one that asks you for information. In some cases the information required might just be the name of a file that you type into a space and then click an **OK** button, or, as in the following screenshot, there may be a range of options that you can choose from, or several pieces of information that you need to enter, with another little group of graphic objects. (The dialog box in this screenshot is a lot busier than most – it was chosen because it contains a little bit of everything!)

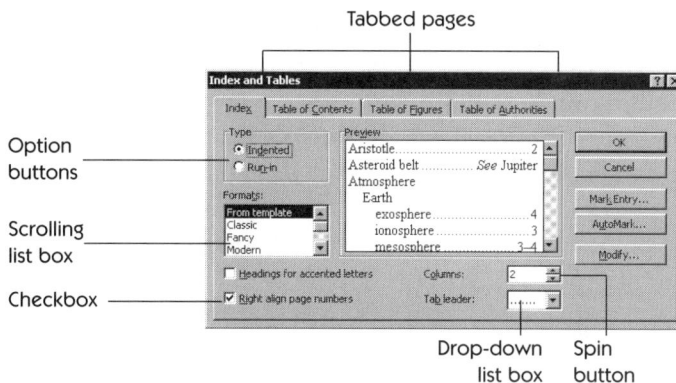

Tabbed pages

Option buttons

Scrolling list box

Checkbox

Drop-down list box

Spin button

► Common methods of making choices in dialog boxes.

**Scrolling list box**. A small box that looks like a miniature window. It contains a list of options that may be longer than the box can display, so the scroll bar to its right is used to bring the remaining options into view. You select an option by clicking its name, and the option will be highlighted to confirm your choice. Usually only one option can be chosen from the list, but you may be able to hold the **Ctrl** key while clicking several items one at a time to select them.

**Drop-down list box**. This works like the scrolling variety, but in its normal state only one option can be seen. If you click the arrow-button beside it, the box will drop downwards displaying a list of options. When you click on an option, the list will vanish, and the option you chose will be displayed in the box.

**Option buttons**. These occur in groups of two or more, and they let you choose a single option. The selected option has a black dot on its button; if you click on a different option the dot will move to that button instead. (These are sometimes referred to as **radio buttons** as well.)

**Checkbox**. These are straightforward selection boxes, and you can choose as many of these as you need to. To select an option, click on the box and a checkmark will appear; if you want to deselect the option, click it again to remove the checkmark.

**Spin buttons**. A pair of Up/Down arrow-buttons that increase or decrease the value in the box by 1 each time you click one, or you can hold a button down to spin rapidly through the values. These tiny buttons won't win any awards for being easy to use, and it's often simpler to click once inside the box, use the **Delete** or **Backspace** keys to erase the value, and just type in a new one.

**Tabbed pages**. In modern powerful applications, there are often lots of features that you can customise to suit your methods of working. All these options together could easily fill the entire screen and wouldn't be pleasant to work with, so instead they are organised into groups, with each group on a separate 'page', and each page having its own tab. Clicking on one of these named tabs will bring the corresponding page to the front. (From the keyboard, hold **Ctrl** and press **Tab** repeatedly to move from page to page.)

In addition to these objects, and the ubiquitous **OK** and **Cancel** buttons, there are several other buttons on the page whose labels end with an ellipsis (…). An ellipsis beside an option means that by selecting it you won't be committing yourself to anything just yet, but you'll be presented with another selection dialog.

# WORKING WITH PROGRAMS AND FILES

▶ **IN THIS CHAPTER**

Understand file names and the icons that go with them

Open existing files and create new ones

Learn how to save and print your files

Work with several files at once in MDI applications

Learn how to edit different types of information in your files

Unless you're a huge games or multimedia fan, the main reason you bought a computer was for storing and retrieving information – in other words, creating, opening, saving and editing files. Part of the power of Windows lies in the fact that there are several ways to do almost everything, and you can choose the one that seems simplest according to what you're currently doing. Don't feel that you have to remember all the available methods though: until you become familiar with Windows, what matters most is that you get the result you want, even if you haven't found the quickest way of doing it.

# Understanding file names

Before you start creating and saving files, it helps to know a bit about the way file names work. Any time you create a new file, you choose a name for it and select which folder you want to save it in, but a folder can't contain more than one file of a particular name. For example, if a folder already contains a file called Letter.doc and you try to save a newly-created file into the same folder using the same name, you will be asked if you want to replace the original Letter.doc with this new one, or cancel the operation. You could get around this by choosing a different name, such as Letter2.doc, or, if you're really determined to use this name, you could save the new file into a different folder.

## Different file types are allowed

You can have multiple files in the same folder with the same file name provided the extension for each is different (see below). For example, a folder could contain Letter.doc, Letter.txt and Letter.pdf quite happily.

As you can see from the file names in the previous paragraph, files are named in a particular way: a few characters, a dot, and several more characters. The characters to the left of the dot are known as the **file name**, the characters to its right are the **extension**. (If a file name contains several dots, the extension will always come after the last dot.)

## Choosing a name for your file

Unlike MS-DOS and older versions of Windows, Windows 95 and 98 use a system of long file names that makes it easy to choose names for your files. A name can be up to 255 characters long, and can include mixed upper- and lower-case characters and a few extra symbols. The symbols you can't use are \ / : * ? " < > | but you can use one or more dots in the name itself. Handy though these long file names are, if you actually tried to give a file a 255-character name, you would hardly ever be able to see this whole name because Windows just hasn't got room to display it. A more sensible length is about 25 characters, but this still gives you plenty of scope to choose a descriptive and easily recognisable name, such as Letter to Sandy or Sales Report Q3 2000.

## File extensions and icons

Most of the time, you won't have to bother about file extensions. Whenever you create or save a file, the program you are using will add the correct extension on the end of your chosen name automatically, and Windows hides these extensions from view to prevent you from worrying about them.

## Showing file extensions

If you'd like to be able to see the file extensions, open My Computer or Windows Explorer, open the View menu and click **Folder Options**. Click on the tab labelled **View** and then click on 'Hide file extensions for known file types' to remove the checkmark and click **OK**. To hide the extensions again, follow the same routine to replace the checkmark.

The function of the extension is to identify what type of file it is: different types of file have different icons so that you can tell them apart, and Windows chooses the correct icon to use by looking at the file's extension. The result is that, although you *could* look at the extensions yourself, you get the same information in a much friendlier way from the icon. Every application has its own individual icon, and the files you create with that application will be given the same icon. That way, as you look through your folders in Explorer or My Computer, you'll be able to tell at a glance which program is used to open and edit a particular file.

# Opening a file

Although you can see the icons and names of your files in My Computer and Explorer, you can't see the information they contain. To be able to view the contents of a file you have to open it in a program. This can be seen as two separate operations: first you have to start (or run) the program that can work with the type of data in your file; second, you have to load (or open) the file itself into that program, which will display the file's contents in its window in a form that you can work with. The program and the file must be compatible with each other. A paint program can't open a database file, for example, and a database program can't open a graphics file.

One of the quickest ways to open a file is to look for its icon in My Computer or Explorer, and then simply double-click it. Windows knows which program it needs to use for this type of file, so it handles everything automatically: the program will start and your file will be displayed in its window.

## Reopening recently-used files

If you've worked with a particular file recently, and you want to open it again, open the Start Menu and move the pointer up to the **Documents** entry. On this submenu you'll see the names of the 15 documents you have opened most recently. To reopen one, just click its entry.

Of course, the program you want to use might be running already: perhaps you've just finished working on a report in your word-processor and you want to finish writing a letter you started yesterday. Open the program's File menu and select the **Open...** option (or click the toolbar button containing an open yellow folder if you can see one) and you'll see the dialog shown in the next screenshot.

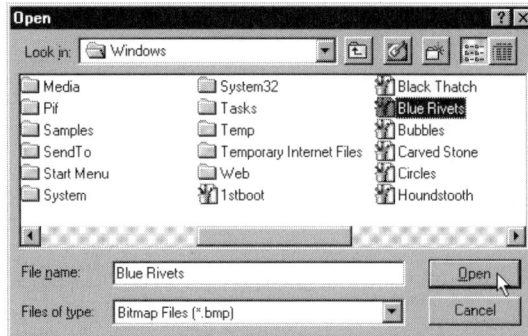

► Click the name of the file you want to open, and click on **Open**.

The main window of this dialog looks like a mini version of My Computer, and it works in just the same way. You can double-click folders to open them, click the arrow-button on the toolbar to move up to the parent folder, or open the drop-down list box beside 'Look in:' to switch to a different drive.

Most programs can work with several different types of file, but specialise in one type in particular. This will be displayed in the 'Files of type:' box, indicating that only files that match this type are being displayed in the main window of the dialog. If the file you want to open belongs to a different type, you can choose it from this box.

When you find the file you want to open, either double-click it, or click it once and then click the **Open** button. The dialog will vanish and your file will open to let you view or edit it.

## The 'recent files' list

Some programs offer a much faster way to open a document. They keep track of the names and locations of the last few documents you opened, and place them on the File menu. To reopen one of these documents, just open the File menu and click the name of the document.

# Saving an edited file

When you open a file, it isn't removed from the disk it was on. So if you use one of the options above to open a file, take a look at it, and then close the application you were using, the file will still be on the disk unchanged next time you want to open it.

If you make some changes to a file you've opened, however, you must **save** the file if you want to keep this updated version. (In fact, if you change a file and then try to close the application without saving it, a dialog box will pop up to ask whether you want to.) If you choose not to save an edited file, the changes you made will be lost forever and the file on your disk will remain as it was before you opened it. When you save a file you've edited, you can choose whether you want to replace the original version with this newer one, or keep both.

▶ To replace the original file with this edited version, open the File menu and choose **Save** (or, in most programs, just press **Ctrl+S**).

▶ If you want to keep the old file, you'll have to save this one with a slightly different name or save it into a different folder. Open the File menu and click **Save As...** (which tells the program you want to save the file as something different). The dialog that appears looks exactly like the 'Open' dialog shown above, except that the Open button is replaced by a Save button. Choose the folder into which you want to save the file (if you want to save it to a different folder from the original). If you want to save the file with a different name, type it into the **File name:** box. Click the **Save** button to complete the task.

When you save a file, the program and file remain open and you can continue to work on the file. In fact, it's advisable to save a file every few minutes so that if something goes wrong you won't lose all the changes you made to it. If you used Save As to save a file to a different location or under a different name, the program will remember these details in future, so subsequent saves can be made by selecting File, Save or pressing **Ctrl+S**.

## Automatic safety copies

Some programs offer the option of creating an automatic backup copy of a file when you save – in other words, keeping a copy of the previous version and replacing its original extension with **.bak**. This is an option well worth taking: if you muck up your document and then save it, you can open the backup copy and use that to replace it.

# Creating a new file

To be able to create a new file, you have to start the application that works with the type of information you want to use in the document. So the first decision to be made is what sort of document you want: for a text-based report or letter you need to run your word-processing software; for a drawing or picture you'll need your paint program; to enter and manipulate sets of numbers you'll run your spreadsheet application. In almost all cases, that's all there is to it. When the window opens containing the application you selected, it will start with a 'clean sheet of paper' so to speak – a large white space into which you can begin typing your letter or drawing your picture, or a grid of boxes to begin entering your numbers into.

Of course, the application you need to use may already be running. In this case, you just open the application's File menu and click on the word **New**. If you already have a document open in the window, the new blank document will replace it (although, as usual, if you have made changes to it and not yet saved it, a dialog box will first appear to ask if you want to do so).

# Saving a new file

When you create a new document, as above, it doesn't exist on disk until you save it. When you try to close the application, the usual dialog box will pop up to ask if you want to save the document: if you select **No**, this new document will be gone forever.

As usual, you should save this file every few minutes as you work on it. The first time you do so, the application doesn't know what you want to call it or where you want to store it. From the File menu, you can choose either the **Save** or the **Save As** option – both will result in the Save dialog box appearing. Choose a folder in which to save the file, and type a name for it in the **File name** box, then click the **Save** button or press **Enter**. As you continue working on the file, you can simply select File, Save (or press **Ctrl+S**) to overwrite the stored file with the updated version.

# Printing a file

Along with opening, saving and creating files, printing them is something you'll be doing pretty frequently (as long as you have a printer, of course). Print options and commands are listed on the File menu and are fairly standard from one application to another, so we'll take a look at each of the entries you're likely to come across.

The **Print** option is often followed by an ellipsis (...) indicating that it leads to a dialog box rather than printing immediately. To print a single copy of the document on the default (or only) printer, click on **OK** or press **Enter** when this dialog appears. Provided your printer is switched on and has paper, the document will print.

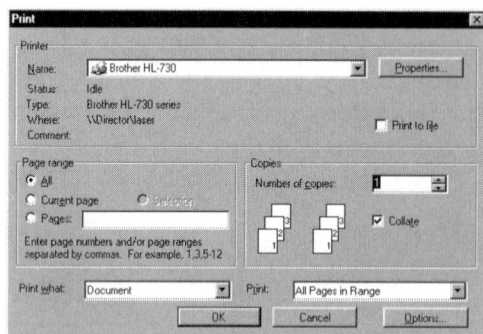

▶ A typical Windows Print dialog.

The Print dialog itself can vary slightly from one application to another, but you'll find many of the same options there somewhere. The default printer will be shown in the drop-down list box at the top. If you have more than one printer, you can choose a different one from this list. A box with spin buttons will show the number of copies to print, and there will usually be some method of specifying a range of pages to print if you don't want to print the whole document.

## Quick printing

If there is a **Print** button on the application's toolbar, clicking that will usually bypass the Print dialog, and print one copy of the document on the default printer without stopping to ask questions.

In many applications, you'll find another pair of print-related options on the File menu:

**Page Setup...** – Like the Print option, this will lead to a dialog from which you can set options such as paper size and orientation, and the sizes of margins. The settings you choose will usually be reflected in the layout of the document on screen – for example, if you increase the sizes of the margins in a word-processor document, the margin-size will be increased by similar amounts on screen to give you an impression of how the document will appear when printed.

**Print Preview** – Selecting this option displays the whole of the page you're working on shrunk to fit on the screen to let you check the overall appearance and layout of the page before printing. In some applications you may have an option to view two or more pages side by side, which involves shrinking them still further. Clicking somewhere on the page will often allow you to zoom in and out on a particular area of the page, and you can usually cycle through a multi-page document using the PageUp/PageDown keys. A Close button on the toolbar will close the preview and return you to the document you were working on.

# Working with multiple document interfaces

A handy feature found in some applications is the **multiple document interface** (MDI) which allows several documents to be open in the same application at once. Each document is given its own window inside the application's window, and you can arrange these document windows to be side by side, one above the other, or in a 'stack' so that only the top window is visible. Just as only one application at a time can be active, in an MDI only one document at a time can be active, indicated by the colour of its title bar.

▶ Microsoft Word's multiple document interface.

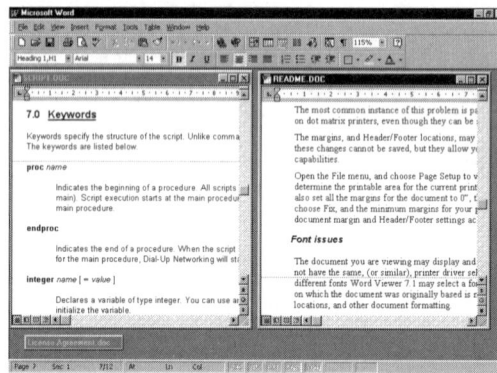

In the screenshot above, the document window on the right is active, so any keys you type on the keyboard, and any options you select from the toolbar or menus, will be applied to this document. Like any other window, document windows have maximise, minimise and close buttons: the close button will close the document (prompting you to save it if necessary); the maximise button will make the document window expand to fill the whole application window; the minimise button will reduce the document to a rectangular icon at the bottom of the application window.

To switch from one open document to another you can click the mouse in the window you want to work with to make it active (if you can see it), or hold **Ctrl** and press **F6**, or click on the **Window** menu and choose from the list of open documents. Just as you can close an application window from the keyboard by using the keystroke **Alt+F4**, you can close the active document window in an MDI by pressing **Ctrl+F4**. You can also close a document by clicking its window's **Close** button, or by choosing **Close** from the File menu.

# Editing a file

One of the main reasons for opening a file is to add to it or change it in some way – in other words, *edit* it. Since any application that allows you to create and save a document will also allow you to edit it, the **Edit** menu is as much a fixture on the menu bar as the File menu. In fact, most of the other menus you'll find are also geared towards making the editing easier, but their names, and the entries they contain, will vary widely from one application to another depending upon the type of information you're working with (for example, a database application has no need of a menu called 'Sound Effects'!). The Edit menu has its own variations too of course, but there are a few entries here that turn up in almost every application.

## Cut, Copy and Paste

These three commands form a group of the most useful editing tools you'll come across. Between them, they enable you to move or copy large chunks of a document around, saving you the tedium of repeating work you've done once already.

These commands work with something called the **clipboard**, a temporary storage place provided by Windows that any application can access whenever it needs to. The clipboard can hold any kind of data you select – a picture, a block of text, a snippet of sound or video, or even a whole document. (The various ways of selecting the data to be edited are explained in *Selection methods* on p. 108.)

▶ The **Cut** command works rather like the Delete key on the keyboard: the item you selected will vanish from the screen in the same way, but it will be placed on the clipboard rather than disappearing forever.

▶ The **Copy** command stores an identical copy of the item you selected on the clipboard. The original text, picture or document isn't affected.

▶ The **Paste** command places the item currently on the clipboard into your document. In a word-processor, spreadsheet or other text-based application the pasted item will be placed at the position indicated by the flashing cursor (known as the **insertion point**); in a graphics-based application the pasted item will usually appear surrounded by a dotted box attached to the pointer – just move the pointer until the item is where you want it to be, and click to fix it in place.

## Clipboard control from the keyboard

The Cut, Copy and Paste commands can be accessed from the keyboard using the keystrokes **Ctrl+X**, **Ctrl+C** and **Ctrl+V** respectively. You'll be using these commands a lot, so it's well worth remembering the keystrokes even if you're more of a mouse-lover.

The clipboard can hold only one item at a time, so if you cut a section of text, and then cut another one it will replace the first. Also, since there's only one clipboard for the whole of Windows to share, if you copy something with one application, then switch to another application and copy something else, the first copy will be replaced on the clipboard. However, once something has been placed on the clipboard (using either Cut or Copy) it can be pasted as many times, and to as many different places, as you like.

## Undo

As the name suggests, this is the command you head for when you do something you didn't mean to. It could be something as minor as typing a wrong letter in a word-processor (although the **Backspace** key would take care of this more easily), or something as major as accidentally deleting a paragraph or part of a picture – selecting **Undo** will make it like it never happened.

Some applications have several levels of undo. Windows' **Paint** program, for example, will let you undo your last three actions by selecting Undo three times. (An 'action' refers to the period of time between clicking a mouse-button in the drawing area and releasing it again; in this time you might have made just a single dot or you might have drawn a large and intricate freehand shape.)

## Undo from the keyboard

In most applications, you can undo your last action by pressing **Ctrl+Z** instead of sending your mouse off to the menu bar.

## Find and Replace

These are options found in text-based applications such as word-processors, spreadsheets, databases and so on. Find and Replace are actually two separate dialogs, but they work in a similar way. **Find** allows you to search a document for all occurrences of a particular word or phrase that you type into its box. When an occurrence is found you can stop and make a change to it or search for the next. A **Match case** checkbox lets you narrow down your search to occurrences using the same combination of upper- and lower-case characters you entered. Checking a second box marked **Find whole word only** ensures that the search ignores longer words containing the letters you specified – for example, if you wanted to search for occurrences of the word **rant**, checking this box would prevent the word **currant** being found.

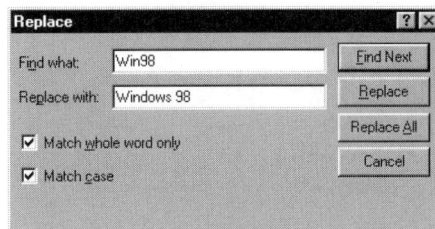

▶ Easy automated text replacement.

In the **Replace** dialog, you type a word or phrase (or just a single character) to search for and a second entry to replace it with. Clicking the **Replace All** button will automate the process, and a final dialog will tell you how many occurrences were replaced in the document. If you prefer, you can step through the document from one occurrence to the next clicking the **Replace** button to replace the text that was found or the **Find Next** button to ignore it and move to the next occurrence.

## Select All

This is another option found more often in text-based, rather than graphics-based, applications. Choosing this option (or pressing **Ctrl+A**) will highlight the contents of the entire document in preparation for some kind of global editing action. There are few occasions when this might be useful: one is so that you can copy the whole document to the clipboard ready to paste into a different document or application; another is so that you can apply a formatting command to the whole document such as changing the size or colour of the text.

## Selection methods

Whenever you want to carry out an editing action on a part of a document you first have to select that part. Otherwise the action might have no effect at all, or, worse still, it might affect the whole document. There are various selection methods, and which to use will depend on the type of document you're working on and how much of it you need to select.

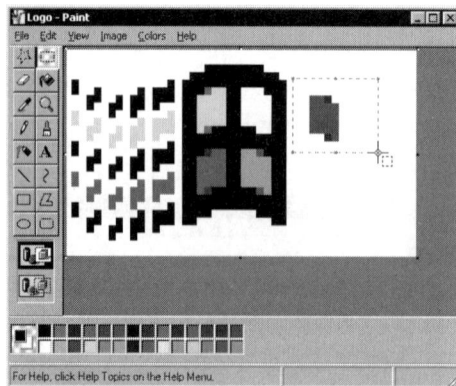

▶ Using the selection tool in **Paint**.

In a graphics applications such as Windows' Paint accessory, a selection tool called Select or Scissors is used to mark the area you want to select. After choosing this tool, click the mouse-button at one corner of the required area and drag diagonally – a dotted box will expand as you do so, as shown in the screenshot above. When the required area is outlined by this box, release the mouse-button and choose the editing action you want.

A similar method is used to select multiple cells in a spreadsheet or table: click in one cell and drag the mouse vertically, horizontally or diagonally to highlight the cells you want to work with. Another method (which is also used to select multiple files in My Computer or Windows Explorer) is to press and hold **Ctrl** and click in each of the required cells. In this way you can select cells scattered throughout the document rather than having to select a block of adjoining cells.

| UK | NZ/Au | Total |
|---|---|---|
| 34 | 22 | 56 |
| 6 | 10 | 16 |
| 21 | 14 | 35 |
| 18 | 6 | 24 |
| 30 | 8 | 38 |
| 13 | 2 | 15 |
| 4 | 2 | 6 |
| 6 | 4 | 10 |
| 19 | 2 | 21 |
| 32 | 30 | 62 |
| 21 | 7 | 28 |
| 44 | 7 | 51 |
| 6 | 3 | 9 |
| 8 | 3 | 11 |
| 26 | 2 | 28 |

▶ Drag the mouse over adjoining cells in a spreadsheet to select them.

When working with text there are several possible methods you can use, one of which is **dragging**. Move the pointer to the left of the first word you want to select, and simply click and drag along the line or diagonally down the page until you've highlighted all you want. Here's a quickfire list of other methods (some of which are limited to Microsoft applications):

▶ To select characters one by one using the keyboard, hold **Shift** and use the left or right arrow-keys to highlight consecutive characters.

▶ To select a single word, double-click it with the mouse.

▶ To select words one by one using the keyboard, hold **Ctrl+Shift** and use the left or right arrows-keys to highlight consecutive words.

▶ To select a whole line from the keyboard, move the cursor (insertion point) to the beginning of the line and press **Shift+End**.

▶ To select a whole line (as an alternative method for some Microsoft word-processors) move the text-pointer to the extreme left of the line: when it turns into a right-slanted arrow, click once.

▶ To select a whole paragraph, triple-click it with the mouse. This is a Microsoft trick requiring a whole new nimbleness from the mouse-button finger.

▶ To select a whole paragraph (another alternative Microsoft method) move the text-pointer to the extreme left of the paragraph: when it turns into a right-slanted arrow, double-click.

▶ To select all text between the insertion point and the end of the document press **Ctrl+Shift+End**.

▶ To select all text between the insertion point and the beginning of the document press **Ctrl+Shift+Home**.

▶ To select the whole document (a Microsoft alternative to the **Select All** menu-option), move the text-pointer to the extreme left margin once again: when it turns into a right-slanted arrow, triple-click.

# GETTING MORE OUT
# OF WINDOWS

The fundamental role of the computer is to help you create, by allowing you to open, edit and save files, as you learnt in Chapter 9. The next step is to organise the way you work and find ways to make the whole creation process faster and easier. In this chapter we'll explore some of the countless methods offered by Windows to help you do just that.

# Getting help when you need it

Whatever you're doing, and whatever knotty problem you're trying to solve, Help is at hand to give you a few clues. Windows itself, along with its accessories and the applications you install yourself, all come with their own help files, and they're always within easy reach:

▶ The general Windows help files can be opened by clicking **Help** on the Start Menu, or by opening the Help menu in My Computer or Windows Explorer and selecting **Help Topics**. If your keyboard has the extra Windows keys, you can also press **Win+F1**.

▶ Get help on a specific Windows accessory by opening its Help menu and choosing the same Help Topics entry.

▶ Applications have a Help menu too. It might contain the same Help Topics, or it might have a **Contents** entry (leading to its main Contents page) and a **Search for help on...** entry leading to the index page, both of which are explained below.

▶ Remember the magic key: wherever you are, press **F1** and 'context-sensitive' help will appear to explain what you're looking at and how it works.

The Contents page is usually a good place to start when you want to learn how to use a new program or carry out a particular operation such as printing a file. The different topics covered by the help file are grouped into sections indicated by a book icon, and the topics themselves have a page icon. Click a book icon to reveal its contents, then click the topic that sounds most promising.

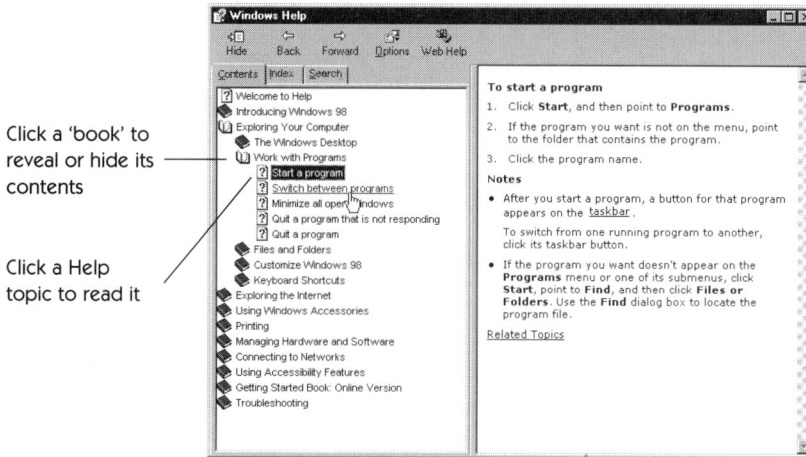

Click a 'book' to reveal or hide its contents

Click a Help topic to read it

▶ Every Windows program includes a Help file like this.

If you can't see a topic that seems to cover what you're looking for on the Contents page, click the **Index** tab and type a keyword into its topmost box. As you type, the list of possible topics below will adjust to display those that match. Pick a topic that looks relevant and double-click it. If you *still* haven't found the answer, click the **Find** tab. The very first time you do this, Windows will need to create a list of words in the Help file, which will take a minute or two. You can then type in a descriptive keyword, and the list below will show all the Help topics that contain that word.

## What's This?

Sometimes you'll find yourself wishing you could just point at something on the screen and say 'What's that?'. Well, sometimes you can. Almost all of the dialogs and tabbed pages in Windows offer this type of context-sensitive help which appears in tooltip messages.

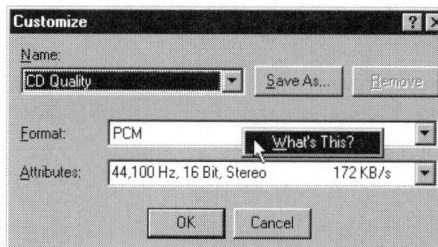

▶ The question mark button and 'What's This?' menu.

There are three different ways of opening these tooltips:

▶ If a window's title bar contains a button with a question mark icon (like the window in the screenshot above), click the button and then click the item you want explained.

▶ If there's no button (or if there is, but you prefer this method), right-click on the item and a tiny context menu will appear with the words **What's This?** on it – just click the context menu.

▶ Click the item once to select it and then press **F1**. There are times when this third method is no use: for example, if the item in question is a button, by the time you've clicked it, it will be too late to press **F1** – for better or worse, you'll have just found out what that button does!

# Working with floppy-disks

Modern floppy-disks are enclosed in 3.5-inch slim plastic cases, making them much more resistant to dirt and dust than the older cardboard 5.25-inch variety. All the same, they're still fragile devices so always keep them in a box when they're not in use and store them away from magnetic fields such as speakers and mobile phones. In one corner of the disk there's a little plastic tab called the **Write-Protect Tab**: when this is moved upwards (so that you can see through the hole it was covering) the floppy drive will be unable to write any new data onto the disk and, more importantly, unable to delete its existing data. When you know you want to store more files on the disk, or delete some, just move this tab downward to cover the hole again.

**GOOD QUESTION!**

## Which way around do floppy disks go into the drive?

Insert a disk into the drive with the sliding metal cover going in first and the label side up (or pointing away from the eject button if your drive is mounted vertically). The disk is held steady in the drive with a spring mechanism so press it firmly until it clicks into position. To eject a floppy-disk, make sure its drive light is out, then press the eject button.

The 3.5-inch disk comes in two flavours, **double-density** (DSDD) and **high-density** (DSHD), referring to the capacities of the disks. The double-density disk has a total capacity of 720 kB, the high-density disk a capacity of 1.44 MB. You can identify a high-density disk by a small engraved 'HD' symbol beside the metal shutter. The standard 3.5-inch floppy drive included as standard in all PCs can work happily with both disk capacities, but you'll rarely see the 720 kB disks these days.

You can save a file to a floppy-disk in just the same way that you save it to your hard-disk. Choose **Save As...** from your application's File menu, then open the drop-down list box marked **Look in** and click your floppy drive's icon. Click the **Save** button to save the file.

## Preparing a floppy-disk for use

Before you can use a new floppy-disk it has to be **formatted**. In its 'out-of-the-box' state, the 3.5-inch blank floppy-disk is a standard disk type that can be used by many different types of computer, and other electronic devices with disk drives. Different computers create their own format on a blank disk so that they can use it, and the PC can only use disks with a DOS format.

### Ready-formatted disks

BY THE WAY

It's quite common to buy boxes of floppy-disks ready-formatted for a PC to save you the trouble of doing it yourself. Look out for the word 'Formatted' somewhere on the box.

You can reach the Format command by right-clicking on your floppy drive's icon in My Computer or either pane of Windows Explorer and selecting **Format...** from the pop-up context menu. Choose whether you want to perform a Quick or a Full format by checking the appropriate box – a new disk will need a full format, a previously-used disk can be quick-formatted to save time – and click on **Start**. When formatting has finished, you can click **Close**, or insert another disk and click Start again. (If you've got a bunch of disks to format, you can save some time by removing the checkmark beside **Display summary when finished**.)

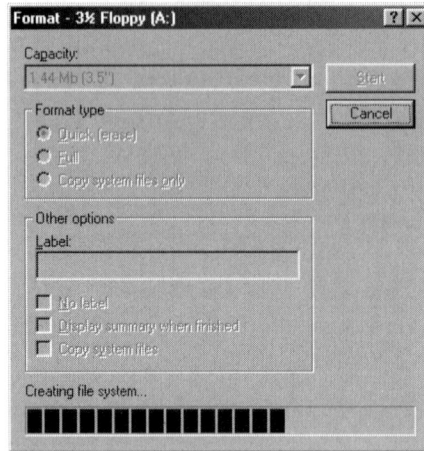

▶ To format a
floppy-disk,
choose your
Format type, then
click Start.

You can format a disk that you've already used and which still contains
data if you want to, but be warned: formatting a disk erases it completely
and (usually) irrevocably! Always make sure you've put the correct disk in
the drive before you choose the Format command.

## Copy the floppy

Windows makes it easy to make an exact copy of a floppy-disk, even if you
have only one floppy drive (as most PCs do). Put the disk containing the
data you want to copy in your drive, then right-click your floppy disk icon
in My Computer and choose **Copy Disk...** from the context menu. A dialog
will appear containing two small windows labelled **Copy from** and **Copy
to**. The icon for your floppy drive will be highlighted in both if you have
only one floppy drive; if you have two floppy drives or a backup drive,
place a blank disk in the second drive and make sure its icon is selected in
the **Copy to** window.

Click the **Start** button on this dialog to begin copying. If you're copying
from one drive to another, you can just wait until Windows tells you the
process has finished. If you have a single floppy drive, Windows will read
the data from the first disk, and then ask you to remove this disk and insert
a blank one in the same drive so that the data can be written to it.

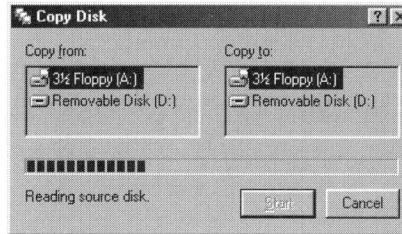

▶ Choose the drive you're copying from and the drive you're copying to (they may be the same) and click Start.

# Using audio CDs and CD-ROMs

The number one thing to remember about CDs is: don't believe the nonsense you hear about them being indestructible. They are certainly resilient, and they might survive a drop from a tall building, but a misplaced fingerprint on the silver data surface might make some of the data unreadable. Always handle CDs by their edges, and keep them in their cases when you're not using them.

**GOOD QUESTION!**

## How do I get a stuck CD out of the drive?

If a CD gets stuck in the drive and the tray won't eject, find a paper clip and straighten it out, insert it into the tiny hole in the front of the drive unit and push. The tray will slowly slide out. If the tray won't close by pushing the button after you've removed the offending CD, push it gently back into the unit and restart your PC as soon as you can to let the drive reset itself.

CD drives in computers are just like those in home stereos: in most cases, you press an eject button to slide out the disk tray, place the disk in the tray, and then press the button again to close it. If your CD drive uses a multi-disk cartridge, place the disk in the cartridge, then slot the cartridge into the drive. Bear in mind that different drives expect the disk to be inserted label-up or label-down: make sure you check the instructions for your drive.

Windows can tell the difference between an audio CD and a data CD-ROM. When you insert an audio CD, the CD Player accessory will start automatically and begin to play the disk. If you insert a CD-ROM, Windows searches the disk for a program called **Autorun** which it again runs automatically. The Autorun program may be a multimedia presentation that introduces the contents of the disk in a friendlier format than just a plain list of files, or it may start your CD-based game automatically. If the CD-ROM doesn't have an Autorun program on it, nothing will happen at all. To look at the contents of the disk, open My Computer or Windows Explorer and double-click on the CD drive's icon.

## Prevent CD autoplay

If you don't want your CD or CD-ROM to run automatically when you insert it, hold the **Shift** key when you close the drive-tray and until the drive light goes out.

# Organising your files and folders

An important key to productivity in Windows is organising your files and folders so that you know where to find everything without frantic clicking. One popular way to stay organised is to create a single folder on your hard-disk that will contain all the documents you create. In fact, this is apparently such a popular method that Windows 98 creates a folder called **My Documents** for you automatically, and you can open this by double-clicking the My Documents icon on the desktop.

When you first save a newly-created file, Windows will usually suggest the My Documents folder as a place to store it. You can store your own files straight into this folder, but it's usually best to create subfolders inside it to make different types of file easier to find. For example, you might create subfolders called Pictures, Letters, Accounts and so on. Whenever you create or save a new file, either pick the appropriate subfolder for the file, or create a new folder.

## Do I have to use the My Documents folder?

No; if you prefer to keep your files somewhere different (perhaps in lots of different folders) choose whatever suits you best. Windows will continue to offer the My Documents folder when you save a new file, though, so you'll have to click your way to your preferred folder.

Over the next few pages, we'll look at the various options for creating, moving, copying and renaming files and folders. The important thing to remember when you do this is: never move, rename or delete a file or folder that you didn't create yourself.

## Creating new folders

As an illustration, let's take the example mentioned above and create a folder called Letters in your My Documents folder.

1   Open My Documents by double-clicking its icon on the desktop.

2   Right-click on any blank space in the window (not on an icon) to bring up the context menu, and move the pointer down to the **New** entry. When the submenu appears, click on the word **Folder**, as shown in the next screenshot.

3   A new folder icon will appear in the window named **New Folder**. Type the word **Letters**. As you begin typing this new name will replace the highlighted one. Then press **Enter**.

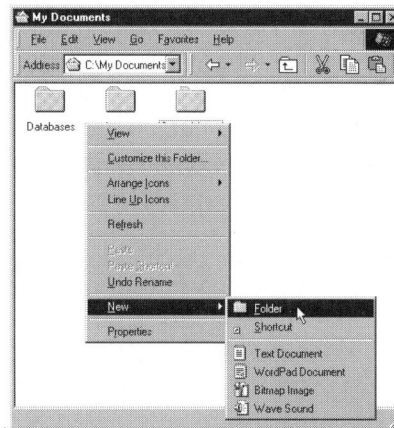

▶ Two clicks, and you have got a new folder.

You can create folders anywhere you like in just the same way. To create a new folder on your C drive, for example, open My Computer, double-click your C drive's icon and follow the same steps.

## Creating a new folder for a new file

When you save a new file from an application, the Save dialog that appears is like a mini version of the My Computer window (skip back to Chapter 9 for more about this dialog). If you're ready to save a file and realise that you want to put it in a folder you haven't created yet, you can do it from within the Save dialog.

Click on the little 'new folder' button at the top of the dialog (pictured to the left), and the usual New Folder will appear in the folder you're looking at. Type a name for the folder and press Enter, double-click the new folder to open it, then continue saving the file in the usual way.

## Renaming files and folders

There are three different ways to change the name of a file or folder, and you can choose whichever seems easiest at the time. A name can use up to 255 characters, with upper- and lower-case letters and spaces, but the characters \ / : * ? " < > | are not allowed – if you try to use them, Windows will tell you to try again.

▶ Right-click on a file or folder icon and choose **Rename** from the context menu. A box will appear around the current name. Type the name you want to use instead and it will replace the current name. Press **Enter** when you've finished.

▶ Click once on the file or folder, then press **F2** and type the new name.

▶ Click the file or folder icon, then click on the label below the icon. (Make sure these are two separate clicks, not a double-click.) The same box will appear for you to type a replacement name.

## Copying or moving files and folders

There are more ways to copy and move folders and files in Windows than you can shake a stick at. One way to copy a file, for example, is to open it in an application, choose Save As from the File menu and then save it to a different location. If you then delete the original file, you've effectively moved it!

One of the neatest ways to copy either a file or a folder is to use the Copy and Paste options. In either My Computer or Windows Explorer, right-click on the icon and choose **Copy** from the context menu. You can then casually click your way to the folder or drive in which you want to create the copy, right-click on a blank space in the window, and choose **Paste**. (If you want to create a shortcut to the item instead of making a copy of it, choose **Paste Shortcut**. See *Fast access with shortcuts* on p. 126 for more details.)

If you want to move the item rather than copy it, follow the same routine but select the **Cut** option after right-clicking the icon. You'll see the icon fade slightly, but it won't actually be moved until you choose the Paste option.

## Clipboard shortcuts

If you would rather use the keyboard than the context menu, click the icon to select it and press **Ctrl+C** to copy, or **Ctrl+X** to cut. Open the target folder and press **Ctrl+V** to paste.

Yet another option is to use the buttons shown on the left, on the toolbar in My Computer or Explorer after clicking the required icon once to select it. The three buttons, from left to right, correspond with Cut, Copy and Paste.

A final method is to use **drag and drop**, which is easiest in Windows Explorer. In the right pane, make sure you can see the file or folder icon to be copied or moved. Then adjust the left pane so that you can see the target folder or drive. Finally, right-click the file or folder icon and drag it into the left pane until it is over the target icon, then drop it by releasing the mouse-button. As soon as you let go of the file, a context menu will appear like the one in the next screenshot, asking whether you want to copy or move the item, create a shortcut to it (see p. 126) or cancel the operation: click an option to make your choice.

▶ Drag an icon to the target with the right mouse-button, then choose the result you want from the menu.

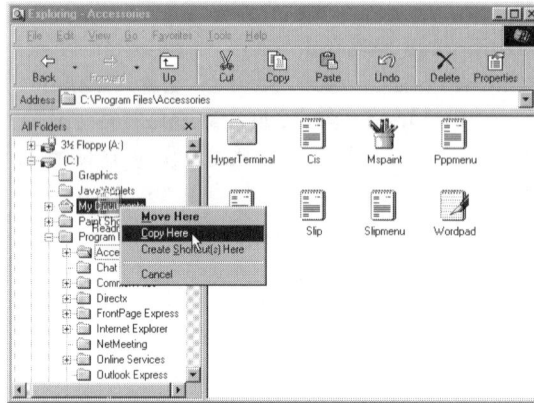

If you want to copy or move several files to the same place in one operation, you need to select each item first. To select a continuous row or column of files, click the first file you want, then hold **Shift** and click the last – all the icons in between will also be selected. To select several files from different parts of the window, press **Ctrl** as you click each icon you want. In either case, if you find you've selected an icon by accident, hold **Ctrl** and click it again to deselect it.

## Regrets, I've had a few...

If you copy, move, rename or delete a file or folder and then wish you hadn't, you might be able to undo it. Provided that was the last thing you did, click the **Undo** button on the Toolbar, or press **Ctrl+Z**.

# Recycle Bin: deleting and retrieving files

Files and folders are easy to delete: one of the simplest ways is to click an icon once to select it, then press the **Delete** key on your keyboard. You can also click the button marked with an 'X' on the toolbar in My Computer and Explorer, or right-click the icon and select Delete. Finally, if you can see the Recycle Bin icon on your desktop or in Explorer, you can drag the item using the left mouse-button and drop it on the Recycle Bin icon.

The Recycle Bin exists *because* files are so easy to delete and because people make mistakes. When you 'delete' a file using one of the methods above, the file isn't actually erased from your hard-disk. Instead, it's moved into a hidden folder. By double-clicking the Recycle Bin icon, you can see the rubbish you've thrown away and, more importantly, rescue any of it you threw away by accident.

## Deleting from floppy-disks

Be careful not to take the Recycle Bin for granted. Files deleted from a floppy-disk won't be placed in the Bin but will actually be deleted.

To **undelete** a file from the Recycle Bin, right-click its icon and choose **Restore**. The file will be replaced in the folder from which it was deleted. (If you deleted the folder that contained the file too, it will be recreated automatically.) You can find out where a file will be restored to by double-clicking it: on the properties page that appears, look at the entry beside **Origin**. If you prefer to restore a file to a different location, you can use any of the methods covered in *Copying or moving files and folders* on p. 120.

If you delete a folder, that folder and its entire contents will be moved to the Recycle Bin. Restoring the folder will automatically restore everything that was in it. Unfortunately, if you can see a folder in your Recycle Bin and can't remember what files were in it, the only way to find out is to restore it and then open it to have a look.

Here are three useful tips to bear in mind about the Recycle Bin:

▶ The Bin can expand to cover 10 per cent of your hard-disk (potentially several hundred megabytes!) if you keep deleting files without emptying it. To reclaim this space, periodically open the Bin and examine its contents to make sure there's nothing there you want to keep, and then select **Empty Recycle Bin** from its File menu. When you do this, those files are gone for good.

▶ If you're quite sure you want to delete something without the option of retrieving it later, you can bypass the Bin. Highlight the file you want to delete, then hold **Shift** as you press the **Delete** key. The file will be instantly deleted. (Note that you can't use Undo to bring back a file deleted in this way – it's really gone.)

▶ If you're tired of being asked whether you're sure when you delete something, right-click the Bin's icon, choose **Properties**, and remove the checkmark beside **Display delete confirmation dialog box**.

# Finding files and folders on your disks

However well you've organised your folders and files, there are bound to be times when you need to find something in a hurry and can't remember where it is. At times like this, the **Find** option leaps into action. Open the Start Menu, move the pointer up to **Find** and choose **Files or Folders...** from the submenu to open the dialog shown below.

The first tabbed page, marked **Name & Location**, is the important one, letting you find files or folders with a particular name and/or containing specified text anywhere on your system. Just type the name (or part of it) into the **Named** box, and either choose a drive or folder to search from the drop-down **Look in** box or click the **Browse** button and double-click the folder you want to start from. If you want to find files that contain a particular word or phrase, type it into the **Containing text** box. Click on **Find Now** and the window will expand downwards to display the list of matching items found.

▶ Type the name of the file or folder you're looking for, choose a drive or folder to search, and click **Find Now**.

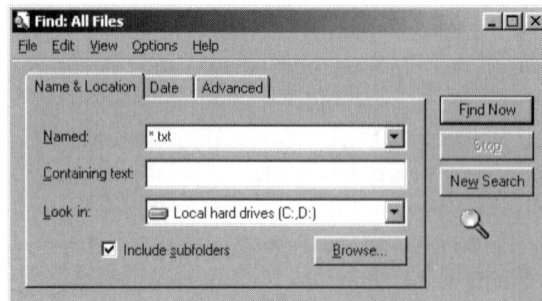

Looking at the results in the Find dialog is exactly like looking at files in My Computer or Explorer: you can double-click a file to open it, right-click it for the usual cut, copy and rename options, move or copy it to a different location, and even delete it. The Find dialog is a powerful tool, so here are a few tips to help you make the most of it:

▶ You can use the * (asterisk) symbol to replace a group of letters in the file name if you're not sure what they should be. For example, a search for **fin\*.doc** would find any files on your system called **Fines.doc**, **Final.doc** or **Finsbury Park.doc**. Similarly, searching for **\*.txt** would find any file with a **.txt** extension, and **\*.\*** finds *every* file on your system (up to a limit of 10 000).

▶ Switch off the Case Sensitive setting on the Options menu (by clicking it to remove the checkmark) if you want Windows to display all matches regardless of upper- and lower-case characters. If you enter something into the **Containing text** box, remember that the search will take longer: Windows has to search *inside* every file rather than just looking at file names.

▶ You can choose how you want the results sorted in the lower window: click one of the bars labelled **Name**, **In Folder**, **Size**, **Type** or **Modified**. Clicking **Name**, for example, will sort the results alphabetically. Clicking the same bar again will sort them counter-alphabetically.

▶ When browsing through My Computer or Explorer, press F3 to open the Find dialog with the current folder selected in the **Look In** box. If your keyboard has the extra Windows keys, you can press **Win+F** to open the dialog wherever you are.

## Using context menus

Before the arrival of Windows 95 and 98, the right mouse-button was just an unnecessary extra weight that the mouse had to drag around – it couldn't be used to accomplish anything useful. Windows 95 changed all that by introducing the **context menu** (sometimes called the shortcut menu).

When you click almost any object in Windows with the right mouse-button, a menu will appear containing a variety of options that apply to that object. The options you'll see on the menu vary according to the type of object you clicked: for example, you can click a file or folder icon to cut, copy, rename or delete it; click inside a folder window to create a new folder or change the folder view; click on selected text in your word-processor to format it, and much more. Although most of the same options can be found elsewhere, the context menu is very often the quickest way to get at them.

## Fast access with shortcuts

Over the last two chapters we've talked about organising and finding the folders and files on your system using My Computer and Windows Explorer, and you've learnt how to run programs from the Start Menu. These are vital things to know, but there's still a problem: you won't find every file you're likely to need listed on the Start Menu, and trawling through My Computer or Explorer to find a frequently-used file soon starts to get on your nerves.

This is where **shortcuts** come in handy. A shortcut is a tiny 'pointer' file that tells Windows the location of the *real* file or folder. In fact, shortcuts aren't restricted to pointing at files or folders: you can create a shortcut to a drive, a printer, a networked computer and many more objects. Not only that, you can create as many shortcuts to a single item as you want to, and keep them pretty much anywhere you like.

In effect, having shortcuts to a file is like having lots of copies of the file in different places, but while the file itself might be several megabytes in size (and you wouldn't want unnecessary copies of a file that size hanging around your hard-disk!) a shortcut is roughly 400 bytes.

The place you'll usually want to create shortcuts is on the desktop, where they are always within easy reach, and the simplest way to create a shortcut is to use drag and drop. Open the folder containing the file, folder or program for which you want a shortcut and, in one action, click its icon with the right mouse-button, drag it to the desktop and release the mouse-button. From the context-menu that appears, click on **Create Shortcut(s) Here** (shown in the screenshot opposite) and hey presto, you have a shortcut.

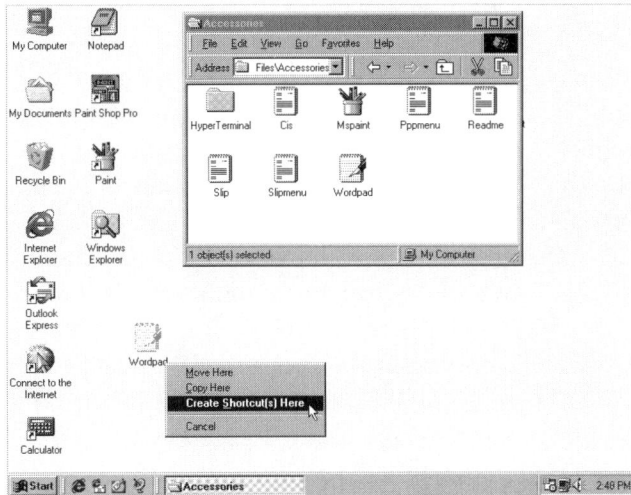

▶ Drag an item from one place to another with the right mouse-button, choose **Create Shortcut(s) Here**, and you've got a shortcut.

## Drag and drop alternative

If you're not a big fan of drag and drop, right-click on the icon and choose **Copy**, then right-click on your desktop and choose **Paste Shortcut**.

When you create a shortcut, it has two distinctive features that enable you to distinguish it from a 'real' file: the icon's label will be prefixed with the words **Shortcut to**, and its icon will gain a small black-and-white arrow. The arrow symbol can't be removed (it's there to help you avoid deleting the wrong one accidentally) but you can rename the shortcut to anything you like – turn back to *Renaming files and folders* on p. 120 for details.

Double-clicking the shortcut to an object will give exactly the same result as if you had double-clicked the object itself. The important thing to remember is that you can move, rename and delete shortcuts and this will have no effect at all on the original object. (If you delete a shortcut accidentally, you can either retrieve it from the Recycle Bin, or just create another one to replace it.)

## Customising shortcuts

Shortcuts probably sound pretty useful so far, but they have a few extra features tucked away. More than any other type of file on your system, a shortcut can be customised to suit the way you want to work with it. These options are hidden away on the shortcut's **properties sheet**. You can open the properties sheet for a shortcut (or any other file) in several ways: one of the simplest is to right-click its icon and choose **Properties**; alternatively, click the icon once, and press **Alt+Enter**.

A shortcut's properties sheet consists of two tabbed pages headed **General** and **Shortcut**. Most of the excitement happens on the second of these: the first applies to the shortcut file itself, showing its size, location and other pretty dull information. Move to the second tab (shown in the following screenshot) and it's a whole new ball game.

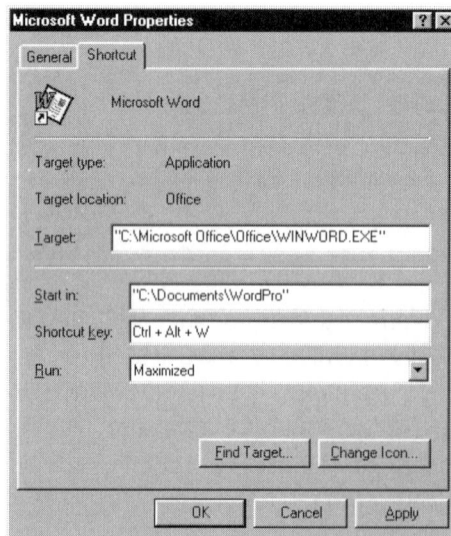

▶ The feature-packed second tab on a shortcut's properties sheet.

▶ You can choose a hotkey combination in the **Shortcut key** box. Click once in this box and type **W**, for example, and you'll be able to open this program or window simply by typing **Ctrl+Alt+W** on your keyboard, regardless of what application you're currently using. (Windows inserts the **Ctrl+Alt** automatically; if you'd prefer to use **Shift+Alt** or **Ctrl+Shift** instead, press those keys along with the **W**.)

▶ The drop-down list beside **Run** gives you the choice of **Normal Window**, **Maximized** or **Minimized**. Most of the time you'll want a normal window. Maximized will open the program or window full-screen; Minimized will open it as a button on the Taskbar that you can click when you're ready to use it.

▶ The **Start in** button is useful in shortcuts to applications. As an example, if you keep all your word-processor documents in a folder called **C:\Word-Pro**, create a shortcut to your word-processor and type the path **C:\Word-Pro** in this box. Whenever you want to open a file or save a newly-created one, the word-processor will offer you this folder in its **Open** and **Save** dialogs, saving you a lot of clicking or key-pressing to navigate to the right folder.

## Path

**JARGON BUSTER**

A path is a list of the folders that Windows has to search to find a particular subfolder or file, similar to the way you have to click through My Computer's folders to find the file you want. The path **C:\My Documents\Letters\Memo.doc** tells Windows to start at drive C, look inside the My Documents folder, then the Letters subfolder, and open the file called Memo.doc it finds there. The drive letter is always followed by a colon, and each drive, folder or file must be separated by a backslash.

## Shortcut suggestions

So what are shortcuts good for? Here are a few ideas for shortcuts you might find useful:

▶ Open My Computer and drag each of your drive icons out to the desktop. A dialog will tell you you can't move or copy them here and offer to create shortcuts – click **Yes**. You can now open your drives quickly without first opening My Computer.

▶ Open My Computer followed by your Printers folder, and drag your printer-icon to the desktop in the same way. To print a file fast, just drag it on to this icon.

▶ If you have files that you use regularly, such as an appointments file or a list of regular contacts, create a shortcut to the file on the desktop.

▶ Create shortcuts to the folders you use most often to save yourself piling through Explorer or My Computer to find them.

▶ If you find yourself using **Control Panel** a lot (see Chapter 11), drag its folder out of My Computer in the same way as the drive icons. Or, if you use just a couple of Control Panel applets regularly, open Control Panel and drag out the icons you want.

## Send it to where you want it

Windows has one more powerful feature that makes use of shortcuts, and its full potential is often overlooked by beginners. If you right-click on any file or folder you'll see a **Send To** entry on the context-menu whose submenu contains an icon for your floppy-disk drive and perhaps two or three more entries.

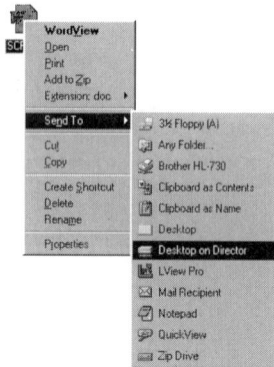

▶ The **Send To** option and its submenu of shortcuts.

The **Send To** option works like an automated drag and drop, sending the item you clicked to the drive, folder or program you chose from the submenu. For example, if you click on **3½ Floppy (A:)** the file or folder you selected will be copied to the disk in your floppy-drive. The aspect that gets overlooked is that you can customise the options that appear on Send To's submenu. Open your Windows folder, and then open its Send To subfolder, and you'll see that all the entries on the menu are actually ordinary shortcuts. To outline the uses of the Send To option, here are a few suggestions for shortcuts you might want to add to this folder:

▶ Add a shortcut to **Notepad** (C:\Windows\Notepad.exe). Anytime you come across a text-based file with an unusual extension you can open it in Notepad by right-clicking it and choosing **Send To/Notepad**. This is also handy if you *don't know* whether it's a text-based file or not – you'll soon find out.

▶ Add a shortcut to your printer by dragging it from the Printers folder inside My Computer. You can then print a file by sending it. This is useful if you have more than one printer and need to choose which one to use for a particular file.

▶ If you have certain folders that you keep moving things into, put shortcuts to these folders in Send To. If the folder is on the same drive as the item you send, the item will be moved; if the folder is on a different drive, the item will be copied. If you want to take control over whether an item is copied or moved, you can use the **Ctrl** or **Shift** keys to force a copy or a move respectively. For example, to force something to be moved to a floppy disk rather than copied, hold the **Shift** key as you click on $3\frac{1}{2}$ **Floppy (A)**.

In Windows 98, you also have a useful option to send items to the desktop as shortcuts. You can use this to create shortcuts to folders and programs you use most often, or just create shortcuts to the files you want to work with during this Windows session and then delete the shortcuts again when you've finished work on each.

# CUSTOMISING WINDOWS FOR SPEED AND STYLE

▶ **IN THIS CHAPTER**

Turbo-charge your Start Menu for quicker access

Create your own colour, sound and mouse-pointer schemes

Choose the best settings for your mouse and keyboard

Set up screensavers and power-saving features

Learn hotkey combinations for fast access to menu options

One thing that most computer users want to do is to stamp their own style on Windows. With PCs gaining new talents every few months, more and more of us are using them for many hours a week, so it's only natural that we'd like to coax as much speed and enjoyment out of the system as we can. The more you use Windows, the more tricks and shortcuts you'll find, but in this chapter you'll learn some of the most useful customisation options to get you started.

# Rearranging your Start Menu

One of the wonders of the Start Menu is that everything you need is close at hand, whatever you happen to be doing. Almost every new program you install will create its own submenu and add a new collection of icons. Unfortunately, many software-writers appear to have no control over their egos: along with the vital entry that starts the program itself, you'll often find entries for text files that you'll probably read only once, help files that are available from the program's own Help menu, links to the company's Internet site, and other paraphernalia. So let's streamline that Start Menu to make the important stuff easy to find.

The Start Menu is actually a subfolder of your Windows folder, and the Programs menu is a subfolder of that. The easiest way to view and edit the contents of these folders is to right-click on the Start button and choose **Explore** from the context menu, then double-click the **Programs** folder in the left pane to open and expand it in one go (as shown in the next screenshot). If you look at the contents of the Programs folder, you will see that all the submenus you see on the Start Menu are actually subfolders containing ordinary shortcuts to programs and documents. The folders have more colourful icons than all your other folders, but apart from that they're no different.

In the same way that you organise files and folders elsewhere on your disk, you can move or delete shortcuts and folders on the submenu to make it easier to work with. (Remember that if you delete a shortcut accidentally, you can restore it to the same location from the Recycle Bin.) Just one caveat – don't rename or delete the folder called **StartUp**. The shortcuts inside this folder are run automatically as soon as Windows starts, and Windows expects to find this folder inside the Programs folder. However, you can place more shortcuts inside it if there are particular programs you want to use every time you run Windows.

▶ The Start Menu
folders and its
subfolders.

Here are a few suggestions for ways to streamline your Start Menu:

▶ Work your way through folders added by software you have installed
and remove shortcuts to Help and text files. If you ever need to read
these files, you'll be able to find them in the folder into which the
program was installed.

▶ Create a new folder called **Control Panel** inside the Programs folder,
then open the real Control Panel folder and use the right mouse-button
to drag all the icons into the new folder to create shortcuts. This gives
much faster access to any Control Panel applet when you need it (see
*Working with Control Panel* on p. 138 for more on applets).

▶ Create a new folder called **Folders**, and create shortcuts to the folders
you need to open most often by dragging them into it with the right
mouse-button. You could also create a shortcut to My Computer here in
the same way.

▶ Inside the Accessories folder you'll find subfolders such as
Entertainment and System Tools. To make these easier to access, drag
them from Explorer's right pane with the left mouse-button and drop
them on the icon for the Programs folder in the left pane to move them.

▶ As with any shortcut, you can assign these hotkey combinations to
reduce the time you spend navigating this menu to find your most-
needed entries.

▶ For much faster access to everything in your Programs folder, select every item in the folder (apart from the StartUp folder) by holding **Ctrl** and clicking each icon in turn. In one action, click any selected icon with the left button, then drag and drop on to the Start Menu folder in the left pane. The result: your submenus will now appear on the Start Menu itself, as shown in the next screenshot, saving the need to scrabble around inside the Programs menu. (If you have so many icons that the Start Menu can't display them all, right-click on the Taskbar, select **Properties**, and choose **Show small icons in Start menu**.)

▶ In Windows 98 you can drag items around on the Start Menu itself to arrange them in a different order. In one action, click an item with the left mouse-button, drag to wherever you want it and let go. If you want to move it from one folder into another, drag it to the target folder and wait for moment; the target folder's menu will open so that you can drop the item into it. If you right-click an item on the menu, a context menu will appear that lets you cut, copy, delete or open items, and you can use the right mouse-button to drag Start Menu items to your desktop to copy or move them there.

## Start Menu problems

There's a bug (a piece of bad programming) in Windows that means it doesn't always update the Start Menu properly when you rename or delete a shortcut. For example, if you right-click an item and choose Delete, the item may not disappear. If that happens, click the desktop to make the Start Menu close, then click the Start button and have another look – you should find that the deleted item has now gone.

## Adding and removing Windows components

If your PC came with Windows pre-installed, or you chose the 'Typical' installation option, you may be missing out on a few useful accessories. To see what else is available, add extra components, or remove any you don't need, open Control Panel (in the My Computer folder), double-click **Add/Remove Programs** and click the **Windows Setup** tab.

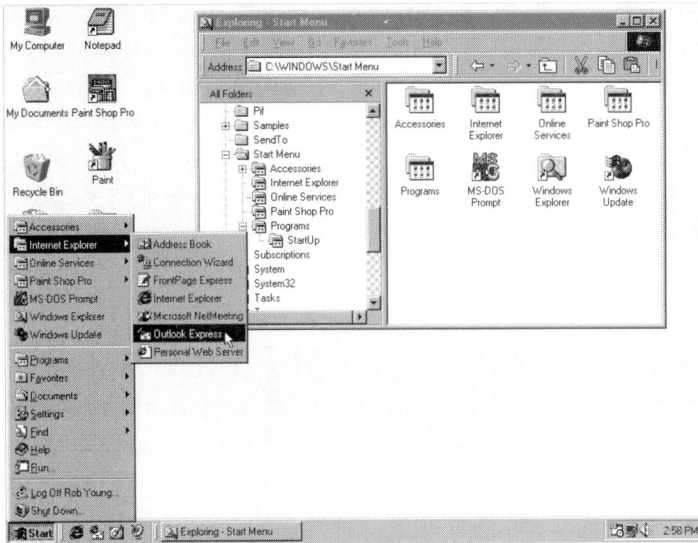

▶ Move the folders inside Programs to the Start Menu folder to place them on the Start Menu itself.

All the components are collected into groups under headings such as **Accessories**, **Communications** and **Desktop Themes**. Click one of these group names and click on the **Details** button to see which components the group contains. You can add a component from this group by checking the box beside the component's name, or remove it from your system by clearing the checkbox. When you've made all the selections you want from one group, click **OK**, then choose another group from the list to look at.

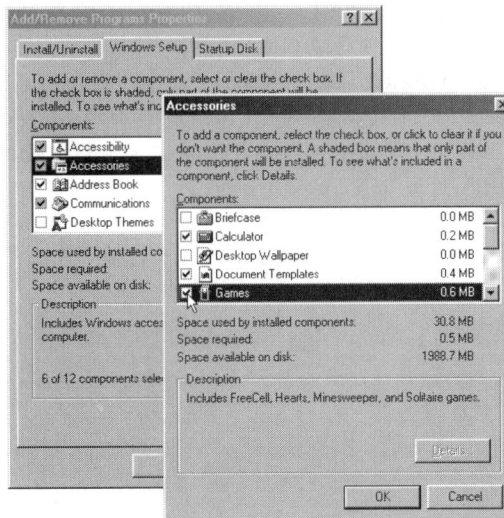

▶ Adding the missing Games to your PC from the Accessories group.

137

When you've worked your way through each group in this way, click **OK** on the main **Windows Setup** page and Windows will carry out all the additions and removals you've chosen (if you've chosen to add components, you'll probably need to insert your Windows CD into the CD-ROM drive). Depending what you selected, you may be prompted to restart Windows when all this is finished; if so, click the **OK** button and be patient – it might take a little longer than usual to restart while Windows updates the system.

# Working with Control Panel

The Control Panel is a special folder which contains a collection of separate small programs (known as **applets**) that allow you to view or change various features of Windows such as colour and sound schemes, mouse and keyboard settings, and vital system behaviour. To open the Control Panel, click on **Start / Settings / Control Panel**, or click its icon near the bottom of the tree-view in Explorer, or double-click it in My Computer. Run an applet by double-clicking its icon. Each Control Panel applet functions as a separate entity, so you can have as many of these open at once as you want to.

Because Windows gives you so much scope to customise things, tabbed pages are much in evidence in Control Panel and most applets have a daunting array of options, checkboxes and buttons. You can find out what each applet does by clicking it once and looking at Control Panel's status bar for a brief description, but when you come to navigating these pages and changing settings, use the context-sensitive Help to find out what each element on a page is for (see *Getting help when you need it* on p. 112). Over the next few pages, we'll look at some of the features of Control Panel that you're likely to need most.

## Apply changes for testing

In most of the Control Panel applets you'll see a button marked Apply. This puts into action the changes you've made without closing the applet's window – if you don't like the result, you can change the settings immediately.

# Setting the clock

The **Date-Time** applet lets you change the time and date shown by your clock, and alter your time zone (particularly useful for globetrotting notebook PC-users). To change the date, select the required year and month from the drop-down lists, and click a date in the area below. To change the time, click inside the box below the large analogue clock, then use a combination of the delete, backspace and number keys to replace the displayed time with your new time. If it all goes wrong, click Cancel and start again.

To change the time zone, click the **Time Zones** tab. Here you can either choose the new time zone from the drop-down list, or (if your geography is up to it) click on areas of the map below. When you've made all the settings you need in this applet, you must click **Apply** before clicking **OK**, or your changes will be ignored.

## Get a date quickly

A quicker way to reach the Date-Time applet is to just double-click the digital clock in the tray on the extreme right of the Taskbar.

# Personalising your mouse

The **Mouse** applet is a multi-paged epic with plenty of options to give your rodent a makeover. The first tab, labelled **Buttons**, is the practical one: from here you can switch mouse-buttons for left-handed use and set the double-click speed. The **Motion** tab lets you adjust the speed your mouse moves across the screen and gives you the option to show pointer-trails (ghost-pointers that follow your mouse around to help you see where you are) and to adjust their length.

▶ Click the Browse button to replace the current pointer with something different.

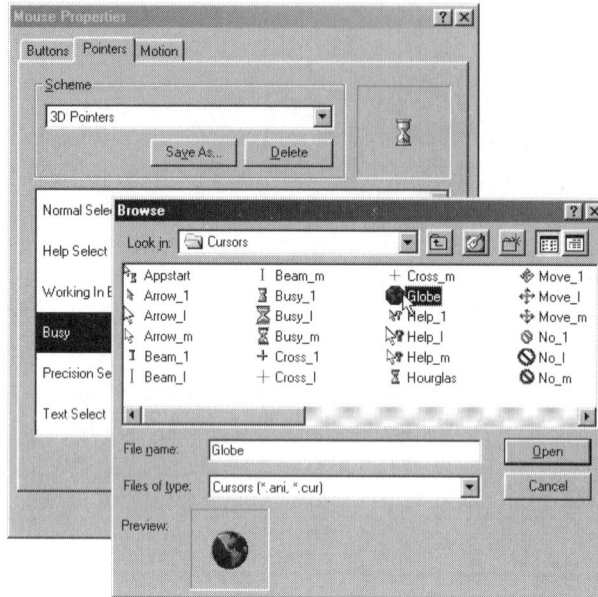

The **Pointers** tab is one of Windows 98's many 'scheme' pages: from this tab you can choose which types of pointer you want to assign for different actions, and save them as a scheme that can be recalled anytime. You can choose which scheme to use from the drop-down **Scheme** list at the top of the page, or create your own by clicking one of the pointer-types in the window and using the **Browse** button to find and select one of the pointer files in C:\Windows\Cursors. When you've chosen all the pointers you want, click **Save As...** and type your own choice of name for the scheme, which will be added to the **Scheme** list, and click **OK**.

## Adding more pointers

For maximum choice, make sure you've got the Windows cursor collection installed. Run Control Panel's **Add/Remove Programs** applet, go to **Windows Setup/Accessories**, click the **Details** button and check the box beside **Mouse Pointers**. Click **OK** to install them. (You'll need your Windows installation CD for this.)

# Getting audio accompaniment while you work

**Sounds** is a single-page applet that works in a similar way to the Pointers tab in the Mouse applet, allowing you to assign sound effects to system events and dialogs, such as maximising or minimising a window, starting or quitting Windows, or selecting a menu option. The sounds are all digitally-recorded files that have a **.wav** extension.

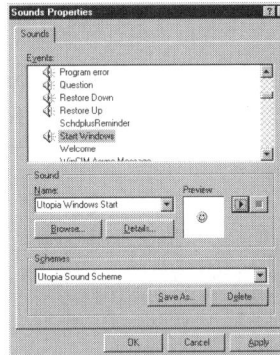

▶ Choose a sound scheme from the **Schemes** list, or create a new scheme by assigning sounds one at a time from the Browse button.

This is another 'scheme' applet that allows you to choose the collection of sounds you want to assign, and save the result to build up a list of your own Sound Schemes. To use one of Windows' preset schemes (or one you made earlier) choose it from the **Schemes** box at the bottom of the page and click **OK**. Or follow these steps to create your own scheme:

## DIY sound effects

Using the Sound Recorder accessory, you can create your own sound effects by recording from a CD or with a microphone. Double-click the loudspeaker icon in the tray to open the mixing desk and set recording levels before you start.

1 In the **Events** window, click an event for which you want to assign a sound (you don't have to assign a sound for all of them unless you want to).

2 Click the arrow beside the drop-down list labelled **Name** to display the .wav files in C:\Windows\Media. Click on one of these entries and click the 'Play' button (with the arrow icon) beside the Preview window to hear it.

3 If none of the sounds from the Media folder are suitable, click **Browse** and search your hard-disk for other .wav files if you have some. You can preview these using the same 'Play' button at the bottom of the Browse dialog. Click **OK** when you find the one you want to use.

4 Repeat steps 1–3 to assign sounds to other events. If you choose a sound file from a different folder, the contents of this folder will be listed in the **Name** box for you to choose the next from.

## Sound advice

If you don't have any .wav files, open Control Panel's **Add/Remove Programs** applet, and click your way to **Windows Setup/Multimedia/Details**. The **Sample Sounds** entry adds a small collection of sounds to your Media folder. There's also a collection of preset **Multimedia Sound Schemes**. Check off the items you want to install and click **OK**.

5 When you've selected sounds for all the actions you want, click **Save As...**, type a name for the scheme and click **OK**.

6 Click **Apply** and/or **OK** to put the new scheme into effect.

# Adjusting keyboard response

There isn't much that can be changed about the humble keyboard, but what there is you'll find on the **Speed** tab of the **Keyboard** applet. The slider for **Repeat delay** lets you choose how long Windows should wait before repeating a character when you hold down a key. The **Repeat rate** slider adjusts the speed of those character repeats. A text-box lets you test your settings before applying them. There's also a slider for **Cursor Blink Rate** which determines how fast the insertion-point cursor should flash in text-based applications.

A second tab, labelled **Language**, adds the option to switch languages and keyboard layouts quickly. Click the **Add...** button and add the languages you want to use, then highlight them one at a time and click **Properties** to change the keyboard layout for each. You can specify a hotkey combination to switch between languages, or check the box marked **Enable indicator on taskbar**. The indicator is a two-letter abbreviation of the currently selected language that appears in the tray – click once to display a menu of your chosen languages and select one to switch to, or right-click the icon and choose **Properties** to get back to this Language tab quickly.

# Changing your Windows wallpaper

At the moment, your desktop is probably the greenish colour that Windows sets automatically when it's installed. Whether you're a big fan of green or not, sooner or later you'll probably want a change, and Windows offers many ways to customise how things look. One of those is to cover the desktop with a wallpaper image or a pattern.

Open the **Display** applet (or right-click a blank area on the desktop and choose **Properties**) and make sure the **Background** tab is selected.

In the list box you can choose a bitmap image file (files with a **.bmp** extension) to display on the desktop. (By default, the list shows bitmap files from your Windows folder, but you can use a .bmp image from any folder by using the **Browse** button to locate and select it.) Choosing **Center** places the image in the middle of your screen, **Tile** uses multiple copies of the image to cover the entire desktop, and **Stretch** expands the image to cover your entire desktop. As you click on picture names in this list, the preview screen above will show how the result would look.

By clicking the **Pattern** button you can choose a pattern which adds an overlay to the desktop while keeping its current colour.

# Getting creative with colour schemes

If you prefer not to use a wallpaper image, that teal colour on the desktop is just one of many colours you can change by clicking the **Display** applet's **Appearance** tab. As in the Mouse and Sound applets, you can choose an existing scheme from a drop-down list (the default scheme is Windows Standard) and click **Apply** to see how it looks, or create your own custom scheme and save it.

▶ Pick an existing colour scheme, or create your own by selecting items and changing their colours and fonts.

To create your own scheme, start by clicking on items in the interactive preview window to select them, and then choosing colours, fonts and sizes for them from the controls at the bottom. If an option is greyed out, it can't be changed for the item you've selected. Some of the items that you can edit, such as the colour of tooltip messages, don't appear on the clickable preview, but you can select them from the **Item** list.

## Test your scheme first

Always audition colour schemes you create yourself by clicking the **Apply** button and looking at a few windows and menus before closing the applet. If you choose colours unwisely, it's possible to make some items 'invisible', which could make it difficult to find your way back to the Display applet to put things right.

# Setting up a screensaver

Screensavers are fun, but they serve a useful purpose: when you leave your computer and monitor on for long periods without using them, the image can literally 'burn' into the coating on the inside of the screen. This, needless to say, is bad news, leaving permanent ghost images on your monitor. One answer is to turn off your monitor when you wander away for a while, but on some PCs that's not possible. A more enjoyable answer is the screensaver which kicks in after a pre-determined time and keeps the image changing. When you're ready to start work again, just move the mouse or press a key on the keyboard and the saver will vanish leaving everything as it was before you left.

Windows comes with its own set of screensavers, but you can pick up many more on magazine-cover disks, the Internet, or as complete stand-alone software packages like Berkeley Systems' superb After Dark series, or Microsoft Scenes.

You can switch between different screensavers and adjust their options by selecting the **Screen Saver** tab on Control Panel's **Display** applet, shown in the next screenshot. If you choose to, you can also set a password for the screensaver by checking the box. After the screensaver has started, it can only be stopped by entering the correct password, thus preventing anyone prying into your system while you're away from your desk.

**Display Properties**                              ? X

| Effects | Web | McAfee ScreenScan | Settings |
| Background | | Screen Saver | Appearance |

Customise the way
the saver looks

Audition the saver
with the settings
you've made

Choose the saver
you want to use

Screen Saver
3D Pipes ▾        Settings...    Preview

☐ Password protected    Change...    Wait: 15 ▴ minutes

Choose how long
your PC should be
inactive for before
the saver starts

Energy saving features of monitor
To adjust the power settings for your monitor,
click Settings.

Settings...

OK    Cancel    Apply

▶ Setting up a
Windows
screensaver.

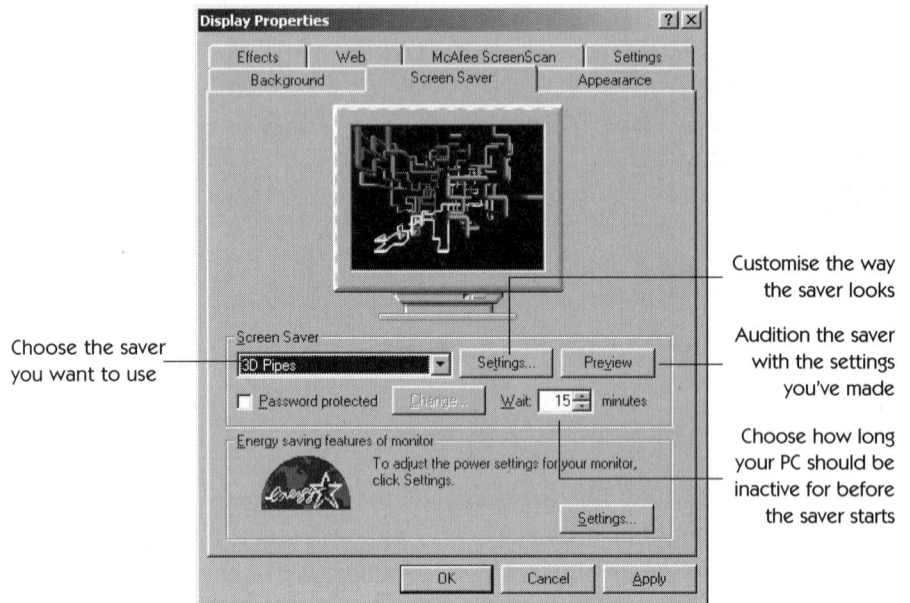

Most PCs and monitors now include power-saving features, and you can opt to use these instead of (or as well as) a screensaver. Click the **Settings** button at the bottom-right of the dialog to open the Power Management page (you can also get to this page by opening the **Power Management** applet in Control Panel). In the boxes at the bottom you can choose to put your monitor and hard disk to sleep after specified periods of inactivity. As with a screensaver, just moving the mouse or pressing a key will wake them up again. Most users will be happy to settle for a single power-saving setting, but you can use the upper section of the dialog to save and recall different power schemes by name if you want to.

**?**
GOOD QUESTION!

## Should I save my work before the screensaver comes on?

Your data, windows and unsaved documents are not affected by the screensaver starting or your monitor switching off. It's similar to the effect you have on BBC1 when you turn off your TV. It's still a good idea to save open documents if you're leaving your PC for a while, though, just in case something unexpected happens such as a power cut.

You may have another couple of options available in the Power Management window:

**Standby mode**. When your PC goes on standby, it turns off the monitor and hard disks, effectively putting itself in a low-power state. Moving the mouse or pressing a key on the keyboard brings everything back to life.

**Hibernation mode**. When your PC hibernates, everything in the computer's memory is stored on to your disk, and the computer and monitor then switch off. Next time you switch on your PC, it reads the memory-store from your hard-disk and, as with standby mode, your desktop and open windows will be just as you left them. Hibernation is the better choice when you're going to be away from your PC for a long period (such as overnight).

# Keeping track of your print jobs

You can open the **Printers** folder from within Control Panel or from My Computer. Inside this folder you'll find icons for any printers connected to your system, along with software printers such as Microsoft Fax. Double-clicking a printer icon will open a small window to display the **print queue** – the list of documents waiting to be printed. By right-clicking a document you can pause, resume or cancel printing. To change the order in which documents are printed, drag entries up or down in the queue. From the Printer menu, you can choose **Purge Print Jobs** to stop printing and remove all print jobs from the queue.

Like most objects in Windows, each printer has its own properties sheet which can be opened by right-clicking and selecting **Properties**, or clicking once and pressing **Alt+Enter**. The tabbed pages you'll find here will vary according to the make and model of your printer, but you should find options that let you choose the default paper size and orientation, print quality, and other (sometimes quite exotic) settings.

# Installing and removing fonts

Fonts are sets of instructions that tell Windows how to display text on the screen and how to print it, each font being a separate file on your hard-disk.

Some fonts are used by Windows itself to display the text on menus and tabbed pages; others are fonts that you can choose from drop-down lists in your applications for use in your own documents. Windows supplies a small set of fonts, including Arial, Times New Roman, and WingDings, but you can add your own fonts to the collection easily. (Some people find fonts irresistible and have several hundred of them!)

To see which fonts are installed already, open Control Panel's **Fonts** folder. The fonts look like any other file on your system and come in two types: the type you'll probably choose to use yourself are the **TrueType** fonts, which have blue 'T' icons. Those with the red 'A' icon are required by Windows, but don't have the flexibility of TrueType fonts for your own uses. Double-click any of these font files to see examples of the typeface.

## Delete with care

Don't delete any fonts that you didn't install yourself. If you delete a font that Windows needs, it will try to use something similar, but it may just make your dialogs, menus and tabbed pages unreadable if you're unlucky.

Deleting fonts is easy. In fact, some would say it's *too* easy! Click the font file you want to get rid of, and press the Delete key. A prompt will ask if you're sure, and the deleted font file will be sent to the Recycle Bin from where you can rescue it if you need to, but only its icon will be recognisable – the Fonts folder is a special folder that displays font files with a friendly name, but as soon as a file is moved elsewhere it reverts to its own unusual-looking file name.

To install new fonts, you must have some font files to install, of course, and there are many cheap CD-ROM packages of TrueType fonts available from computer stores or by mail order. Choose **Install New Font...** from the File menu and you'll see the dialog in the next screenshot. Use the Drives and Folders lists to navigate to the location of your new fonts (or click the **Network** button if you want to install fonts from another PC on your network). When you arrive at a folder containing font files, Windows will list the fonts it found in the upper portion of the window. To install them all, click **Select All** followed by **OK**. If you want to install only some of them, click the names of the required fonts while holding the **Ctrl** button, then click **OK**.

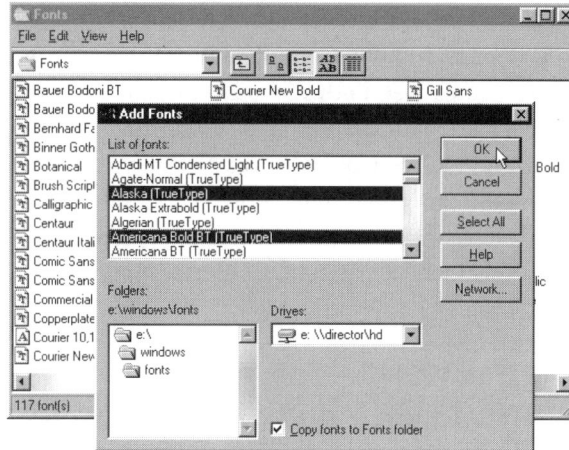

▶ You can install fonts from any drive or folder on your system or network.

# All in one – Desktop Themes

Desktop Themes are complete sets of wallpapers, icons, sounds, mouse-pointers and screensavers with names like Dangerous Creatures, Mystery, Science, and Underwater. A set of 17 themes is included on the Windows 98 CD-ROM, although they may not be installed on your system.

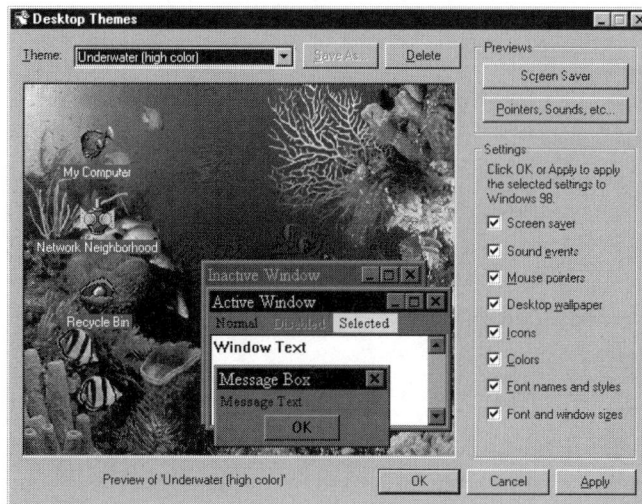

▶ Choose a Desktop Theme from the list and transform your desktop and windows.

You can use the Windows Setup tab of the Add/Remove Programs applet in Control Panel to install new themes or remove any you don't like: select the **Desktop Themes** entry and click **Details** to display the list of available themes. Bear in mind that each theme takes a hefty slab of disk space, so you probably won't want to install all of them. When you have one or more themes installed, you'll find a new **Desktop Themes** icon in Control Panel (if you can't see it, press **F5** to force Control Panel to reload its icons). Double-click this icon and pick one of your installed themes from the **Theme** box to preview it, choose whether to use all the theme's elements such as icons and colours by checking or unchecking the boxes on the right, and click on **Apply** or **OK** to put the theme into action.

**GOOD QUESTION!**

## Where can I get more themes?

One option is to buy an add-on pack called Microsoft Plus 98, which adds another 18 themes to the list (along with a few extra bits and pieces). If you have Internet access, visit some of the popular software sites such as **www.winsite.com** – you'll find plenty of free themes covering all manner of subjects.

## Accessibility help for the disabled

If you have difficulty seeing the screen clearly, hearing sounds, or working with the mouse or keyboard, Windows 98 has a range of options that can help. In fact, some of these can be useful for any Windows user. You should be able to see the **Accessibility Options** icon in Control Panel, but you may not have the additional accessibility tools. If you need those, go to the Windows Setup tab of the Add/Remove Programs applet in Control Panel, select **Accessibility** and click on **Details**, then check the box beside **Accessibility Tools** and click **OK**.

Double-click the **Accessibility Options** icon in Control Panel to choose the options you want to use from the tabbed pages.

▶ **StickyKeys** lets you type keystrokes like **Ctrl+S** by pressing one key at a time.

▶ **ToggleKeys** plays a sound whenever you press the **Caps Lock** or **Num Lock** key (something we all do by accident when typing).

▶ **SoundSentry** displays a visual message for the hard-of-hearing whenever Windows plays a sound.

▶ **High Contrast** changes the Windows screen to use easily-visible fonts and colours.

▶ **MouseKeys** lets you move the pointer using keys on the numeric keypad instead of the mouse.

The Accessibility Tools include Microsoft Magnifier, which displays an enlarged view of the portion of the screen containing the pointer (also a useful tool for anyone working on high-definition graphics), and an Accessibility Wizard that lets you tailor individual items to your precise needs, such as the size of text, icons and window elements. The Wizard also includes the options contained in the Accessibility Options applet, but presents them all in a much more user-friendly (and *accessible*) form. You'll find Magnifier and the Accessibility Wizard in the Accessories group on the Start menu.

# Get there faster with hotkeys

Even if you're a big fan of the mouse, there are times when tapping a couple of keys on the keyboard to get something done is much quicker. For those times, here's a short list of hotkey combinations for use in Windows itself or in applications you run.

| Open the Start Menu | Ctrl+Esc |
|---|---|
| Close any open menu or dialog | Esc |
| Open selected item's context menu | Shift+F10 |
| Open or run the selected item | Enter |
| Rename the selected item | F2 |
| Delete the selected item | Delete |
| Delete, bypassing the Recycle Bin | Shift+Delete |
| Open the properties sheet for the selected item | Alt+Enter |
| Open the Find dialog in a folder | F3 |
| Iconic list of open windows and applications | Alt+Tab |
| Cycle through open windows, applications and dialogs | Alt+Esc |
| Open a menu | Alt+underlined letter |
| Select a menu option | Underlined letter |
| Cycle through tabbed pages | Ctrl+Tab |
| Switch between controls in dialogs and tabbed pages | Tab |
| Close a window or quit an application | Alt+F4 |
| Open a file | Ctrl+O |
| Print the current file | Ctrl+P |
| Save the current file | Ctrl+S |
| Cut the selected item | Ctrl+X |
| Copy the selected item | Ctrl+C |
| Paste the selected item | Ctrl+V |

Here are a few extra hotkeys you can use if your keyboard has the additional Windows keys:

| Open the Start menu | Win |
|---|---|
| Open Windows Explorer | Win+E |
| Open the Find command | Win+F |
| Open the Run command | Win+R |
| Minimise all windows | Win+M |
| Restore all windows after minimise | Win+Shift+M |
| Open the Control Panel | Win+C |
| Open the System applet | Win+Break |
| Open the Mouse applet | Win+I |
| Open the Keyboard applet | Win+K |
| Open the Printers folder | Win+P |
| Open the Windows help file | Win+F1 |

# Quick Windows tips

Windows has an almost inexhaustible supply of customisation possibilities, options and shortcut methods that can make the operating system and its accessories easier, faster or more enjoyable to use. Here are a few of them.

▶ When you select the **Shutdown** command from the Start Menu, you have the option to **Restart the computer**. If you only want to restart Windows itself (which is much faster), select **Restart the computer**, then hold **Shift** as you click on **OK**.

▶ If you don't like using the right-mouse button when you drag and drop files and folders, try using these in conjunction with *left* button dragging: hold **Ctrl** to force a copy; hold **Shift** to force a move; or hold **Ctrl+Shift** to create a shortcut.

▶ If your **Send To** menu is getting too full you can turn it into a mini Start Menu. Go to C:\Windows\SendTo and create new folders inside it, then drag items into it from the SendTo folder to organise them into groups. This is useful if you've created SendTo shortcuts to lots of different folders on your system – create a folder called **Folders** and drag all these shortcuts into it to keep them separate from the other items.

▶ When viewing any list of files in Windows – whether in Explorer, My Computer, Find, or anywhere else – type the first two or three letters of the entry you want (in quick succession) to move straight to it.

▶ If you want your screensaver to start immediately when you leave your desk, create a shortcut on your desktop to one of the **.scr** files found in C:\Windows. You can double-click it to start it running or assign it a hotkey combination.

▶ Experiment with your tray icons – many have different options on their menus depending whether you click with the left or right mouse-button. The option shown in bold type is the action that occurs if you double-click the icon.

**12**

# KEEP YOUR SYSTEM RUNNING SMOOTHLY

**IN THIS CHAPTER**

Make a startup disk for emergencies

How to keep backups of your system and vital documents

Use Windows' utilities to keep your system purring sweetly

What to do when a program hangs or Windows won't respond

Computer viruses: don't panic, but do get some protection

Windows is able to look after itself pretty successfully in keeping everything working, but once in a while things may go wrong. In this chapter we'll take a look at the ways you can get everything back to normal again when a program (or Windows itself) starts misbehaving. However prevention is better than cure – if you prepare for disasters now, you should never experience anything worse than an inconvenience in future!

# Create a startup disk

When you installed Windows you were given the option of creating a startup floppy-disk to start the system in the event of a serious crash. If you didn't (or if your computer arrived with Windows pre-installed thus denying you the prompt), grab a high-density floppy-disk and your Windows 98 CD-ROM and do it now:

1   Double-click the **Add/Remove Programs** icon in Control Panel.

2   Click the **Startup Disk** tab and then click on **Create Disk**.

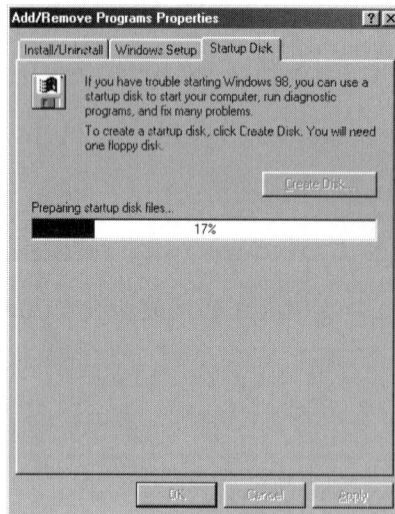

▶ Grab a blank floppy-disk, click on Create Disk, and you'll always be able to start your computer in times of trouble.

156

Once the disk has been created, you need to make sure it actually works. Shut down the computer from the Start Menu's **Shut Down** command, and then restart the computer using your PC's Reset button with this emergency disk in the drive. You should arrive at the MS-DOS command-prompt (a black screen showing the text A:\> and a flashing cursor). If you do, it works. Remove the disk from the drive and restart the computer by pressing the Ctrl, Alt and Delete keys at the same time. Write-protect this emergency disk (see Chapter 10), label it **Windows 98 Startup Disk** and keep it somewhere safe.

# Back up your system configuration

Although few computer books tell you to do this, it's something I absolutely swear by. Admittedly, I fiddle around with my system more than the average user, but these backup copies have saved my bacon on more than one occasion!

The settings for your entire system are stored in something called the **registry**: this covers your hardware settings, details of all the software you've installed, and much more. Unfortunately, the files that make up the registry are too large to fit on to floppy-disks. The good news is that Windows supplies a simple program you can use to keep backup copies on your hard-disk. Grab your Windows CD and follow these steps to install the program and make a backup:

1  Using Windows Explorer, open the **other** folder on your Windows CD, then open its **misc** subfolder, and finally the **cfgback** subfolder. You should see two files both named **cfgback** – an application and a help file.

2  Copy both files to your Windows folder, either by dragging them into the left pane or by using copy and paste.

3  Create a shortcut to **cfgback.exe** and place it somewhere handy, such as your Start Menu's System Tools folder, and rename the shortcut **Registry Backup**.

4  Run this program. Instructions will appear, so click the **Continue** button three times.

5  In the upper box, type a name for your backup to help you remember it later, and click the **Backup** button. Click **Yes** when prompted to continue, then sit back and wait a few minutes.

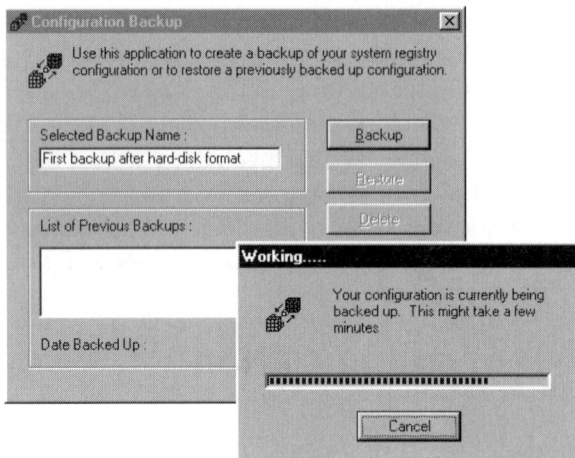

▶ Type a name, click **Backup** and a few minutes later you have a safety copy of your system settings.

This program will let you create up to nine backups in this way, and will list them all in order of date (although you should note that the date is in the American month/day/year format). Ideally you should aim to run this program every month or two so that you always have a recent backup, but only do it when you know your system is working perfectly – there's no point in creating a backup of a system with problems, is there? As time goes on, you can delete your earliest backups by selecting them from the list and clicking **Delete**.

The point of these backups is that you can restore the system if you get into problems that you can't fix (preferably after seeking some expert help too). Re-run this program, select the most recent backup that you know to be okay from the list, and click the **Restore** button. After a few minutes, you'll see a prompt to restart your computer. If that backup really was okay, the problem should have disappeared. However, if you've installed any software or hardware since making that backup, you might need to reinstall the application or re-run the setup program for the hardware so that the system knows about it.

## Check your hard-disk for lost data

Although the hard-disk is a reliable device, occasionally small errors can appear on its surface that could mean you lose small chunks of file, or that Windows can't use areas of the disk. To keep your hard-disk squeaky clean, run **ScanDisk** regularly every week or so to automatically identify and fix any errors that appear.

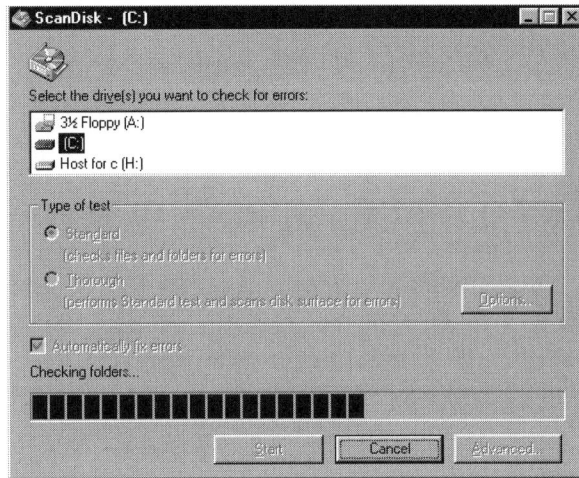

▶ Run **ScanDisk** regularly to keep your hard-disk in tip-top shape.

1 Click the shortcut to **ScanDisk**, which you'll find in the System Tools subfolder on your Start menu.

2 By default, your hard-disk will be selected and the option button beside the **Standard** test will be checked. If you want ScanDisk to fix any errors it finds without asking you first, check the box beside **Automatically fix errors**. Click **Start** to begin checking.

3 When ScanDisk has finished (usually after only a few minutes), it will display a summary of the results: what you're most interested in is the first line, which will usually tell you that no errors were found.

4 Every month or so, you should run ScanDisk and check the option button for a **Thorough** test, which checks the surface of the disk as well as the files and folders on it. This might take an hour or more, so you'll need to pick a time when you won't need to use the PC. You should also override your screensaver by selecting **(None)** from Control Panel's **Display/Screen Saver** tab.

If ScanDisk finds any lost pieces of files, it will save them to your hard disk with the names File0000.chk, File0001.chk, and so on. Take a look at these files in Notepad or WordPad before deleting them. If you recognise something from one of your own documents, check to make sure that the document is still intact, and use the text in the .chk file to put it right if necessary. If the contents of the .chk file look like meaningless drivel, it might be part of an application: run the applications you installed most recently to test them. If an application won't run, you'll need to reinstall it.

▶ *Windows 98 has a built-in task scheduler that will run ScanDisk and Disk Defragmenter for you regularly at intervals and times that you select, saving you the need to remember to do it manually. Turn to* Your PC can look after itself! *on p. 162.*

# Get optimum speed from your hard-disk

Although Windows presents your files in a friendly way in Explorer, in reality they look nothing like that on the hard-disk. Disks store files in small chunks called **clusters**, and a sort of address book on the disk tells Windows where to find all the pieces that make up a particular file. For fastest response, all the clusters for a file should be grouped together in a chain: that way, Windows doesn't have to scoot around the disk gathering together pieces of file from far and wide when you want to use one. In practice, that doesn't happen: all the clusters are the same size, so if you edit a file and make it larger, for example, it won't fit into the same number of clusters it occupied before, so some will have to be placed elsewhere. After you've worked with files for a few weeks, your hard-disk is starting to look a bit of a mess!

## Don't defragment deleted files!

Before running Disk Defragmenter, empty the Recycle Bin. If you empty it afterwards, you will undo all the good defragmentation work!

Fortunately, Windows includes a program called **Disk Defragmenter** that can group all these pieces of file back together again, speeding up your access to the hard-disk. The same program also keeps track of the programs and files you use most often, and moves those files to the fastest area of the disk so that they start more quickly. Once again, this is a program you should aim to run every week or two, and you should set your screensaver to 'None' while it's running.

You'll find Disk Defragmenter in the System Tools folder on the Start Menu. When you run it, it will automatically select your hard-disk (although you can defragment a different disk if you need to), so click **OK**. You can wander away and leave it to do the job, but it's fun to click **Show Details** and watch a graphic portrayal of all these chunks of file flying about.

▶ *You can use the Maintenance Wizard to run Disk Defragmenter automatically at regular times – see* Your PC can look after itself! *on p. 162.*

# Clear out unnecessary files

Even if your hard-disk is unusually large, one thing you don't want to do is fill it with unnecessary space-wasting files. However much you pride yourself on being organised in this area, Windows and some of your applications may conspire against you by creating temporary files on your hard-disk and not deleting them. These could easily amount to many megabytes of wasted space.

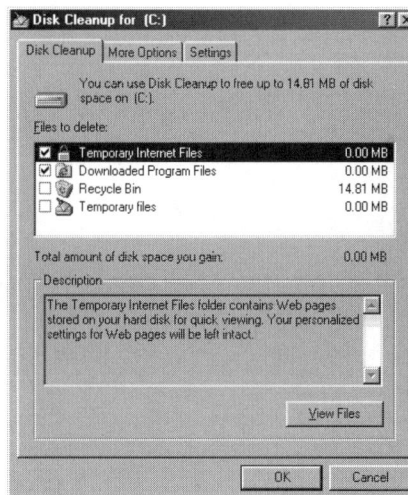

▶ Click an item to read more about it and use the checkboxes to select or deselect items.

Fortunately, Windows 98 includes a utility called **Disk Cleanup**, which you'll find in the Accessories\System Tools group on the Start Menu. Click **OK** when the dialog appears with your hard-drive selected, and you'll see the main Disk Cleanup window showing several types of file that can be safely removed and telling you how much space you can regain by doing so. Check the boxes beside the types of file you want to delete and click the **OK** button.

## Archive larger files

If you have an archive drive, you might want to move little-used files such as help files, screensavers (.scr files) and large multimedia files to it. Always try to keep at least 300 MB of free space on your hard disk.

# Your PC can look after itself!

Windows 98 has a couple of additional utilities that can automate the process of keeping your system in shape. The first of these is the **Maintenance Wizard**, found in the System Tools group on the Start Menu. Choose the **Express** option, and from the Wizard's second page choose a period when you're least likely to be working on your PC. In future, Windows will run ScanDisk, Disk Defragmenter and Disk Cleanup automatically once a week during the chosen period without bothering you.

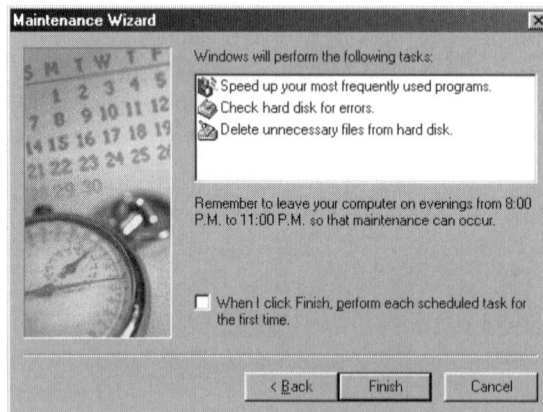

▶ Run the Maintenance Wizard once, and then leave your system to look after itself.

The second utility is **Scheduled Tasks** which you can open from the System Tools group as usual or by double-clicking its icon in the tray. The Scheduled Tasks window shows a list of the utilities that Windows runs automatically, along with their scheduled times. You can add new programs and tasks to the list by double-clicking the **Add Scheduled Task** icon, or double-click on any task to alter its settings or change its scheduled running time. If you've run through the Maintenance Wizard mentioned above, your Scheduled Tasks window will contain the items shown in the next screenshot.

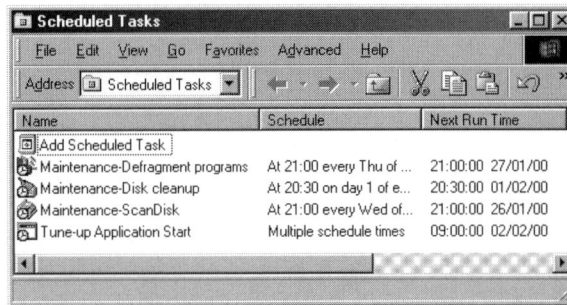

▶ Add a new Scheduled Task, or double-click to change options and schedules.

# Back up your important documents

If the worst happens and your hard-disk stops working, the thing that's going to hit you hardest is the loss of your files. Not your applications – you can reinstall those from the original disks – but the documents you create yourself. To guard against loss of irreplaceable documents, you should get into the habit making backups of your files regularly to a tape-drive or a set of floppy-disks, and Windows includes a utility called **Backup** to help you do just that. If you don't have Backup installed, open Control Panel's **Add/Remove Programs** applet and click the **Windows Setup** tab. Double-click on **System Tools**, check the box beside **Backup**, and click **OK** twice to install.

When Backup starts, you're given the option of creating a new backup job (a list of files that you want to back up), opening a list you created previously, or restoring a set of backed-up files from your archive drive to your hard-disk. Choose the option to create a new backup job, and follow these steps:

1  In the left-hand window, use the familiar Explorer layout to expand drives and folders by clicking the + signs. Click the box beside a drive or folder to add it to the list of items to be backed up. All the files and subfolders in the selected drive or folder will be added to the list. (To remove a tick from one of these boxes, just click it again.) If you want to select only individual files from a folder, click the folder itself and its contents will appear in the right-hand pane with similar checkboxes beside them.

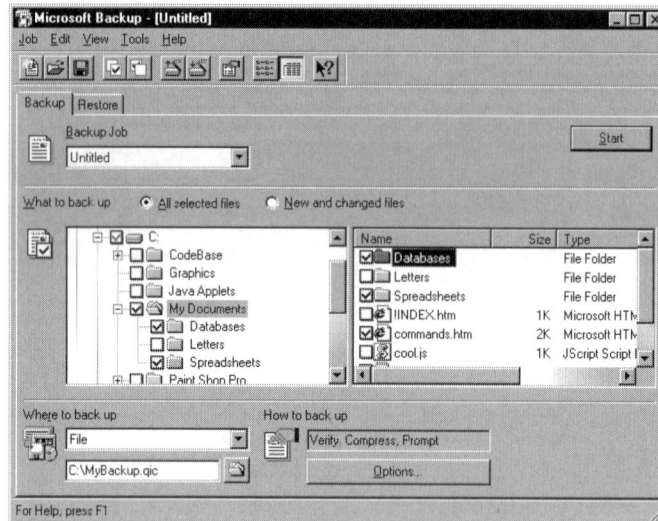

▶ Create a list of files and folders to be backed up by checking the boxes beside them.

2 Choose whether to back up every selected file or just the files that have been added or changed since you last backed them up, by clicking the appropriate option beside **What to back up**.

3 In the **Where to back up** section, choose your backup drive (if you have one and want to use it), or select **File** and enter a name and location for the single compressed backup file to be stored.

4 Click the **Options** button, select the **Advanced** tab, and check the box beside **Back up Windows Registry** (on the basis that you can never have too many backups of these vital files) and click **OK**.

5 Click the Save button on the toolbar (or press **Ctrl+S**) if you want to save this list for reuse.

6 Click **Start** to begin the backup process. Depending on the number of files to be backed up and the speed of your backup device, the process might take quite a while to complete.

You can edit the backup job file you created at any time in the future to add more files to the list or remove them. Should the worst happen and you lose one or more files from your hard-disk, click Backup's **Restore** tab, pick the file(s) you want to restore, and click **Start** to copy them to their original locations on your hard-disk. Make sure you back up your files regularly so that you won't be faced with restoring a very out-of-date copy of a lost file.

# Surviving a program crash

Very occasionally, you might do something as innocuous as clicking a toolbar button in an application, and the program will 'hang' – in other words, it will stop reacting to any mouse or keyboard input. (This is why you should get in the habit of saving the document you're working on every few minutes.) It doesn't happen often, and when it does it shouldn't stop Windows working, but your only option is to shut down that program.

To do this, press **Ctrl+Alt+Del** and you'll see the Close Program dialog, containing a list of the programs currently running. Your misbehaving program should be at the top of the list, and it might have the words **Not responding** beside it. Make sure the correct program is selected in the list, and click the **End Task** button to close it. Be patient at this point: Windows sometimes has to grapple with the program for a while before it can present you with a confirmation dialog.

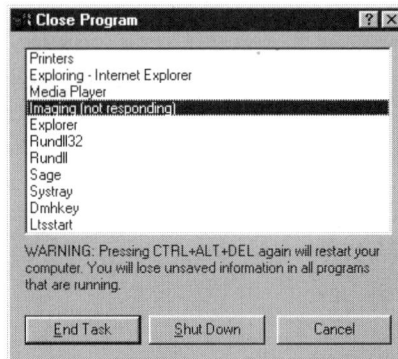

▶ The Close Program dialog – handle with care!

After the offending program has been closed, you could probably continue working in Windows, but it's best to restart the computer as soon as you can to banish any lingering after-effects. Select **Shut Down** from the Start Menu and click **Restart the computer**, followed by **OK**.

There are two important points to remember about the Close Programs dialog: first, it shouldn't be treated as an alternative to the usual ways of closing a program when you've finished work and, second, pressing **Ctrl+Alt+Del** again while this dialog is on the screen will shut down your

PC without prompting you to save open documents, and without updating Windows' own system settings, so only do this in times of extreme desperation (see below).

# How to deal with a Windows crash

In more severe situations, Windows itself may hang. If it does, your aim is to shut down or restart the computer. Begin by trying to open the Start Menu and select **Shut Down**, either by using the mouse or by pressing **Ctrl+Esc** followed by **U**. If that doesn't work, press **Ctrl+Alt+Del** to call up the **Close Program** dialog mentioned above. If a program has the words **Not responding** beside it, click its entry in the list and click the **End Task** button: once that program has been closed, the system may recover enough for you to shut down properly.

Failing that, the next thing to try is clicking the **Shut Down** button on this dialog. In many cases, this will do the trick: in a few, this dialog will then hang as well and nothing more will happen. If so, press **Ctrl+Alt+Del** twice to try to restart the computer.

If this doesn't work, the only remaining option is to press your PC's Reset button to restart the computer from scratch. This really is something to do only as a last resort. A version of ScanDisk will run before Windows restarts to check your disk for errors – this is normal behaviour that occurs whenever Windows detects that it was shut down improperly.

# Solve problems in Safe Mode

In normal everyday use of Windows, you simply switch on your computer, wait 30 seconds or so, and the Windows desktop appears. Most of the time this is exactly what you want, but there are times when it's the *last* thing you want! If, for example, you changed your display settings and the whole screen went blank, you don't want the computer to just return you to Windows when you restart – you'll still have a blank screen!

At times like this you can start the computer in a special mode called **Safe Mode**, in which Windows loads only generic driver files for display and mouse and disables any non-essentials to display a low-resolution 16-colour screen. Although the layout is unattractive and basic, it does give you the chance to put problems right and then restart the computer normally.

To start Windows in Safe Mode, follow the steps below. We'll do it the hard way, assuming you've arrived at the Windows desktop to find the screen completely blank; if you've got a different problem and you can still see the desktop, the routine will be even easier.

1 Wait until the hard-disk stops working and you know Windows has finished loading. Press **Ctrl+Esc** to open the Start Menu (although you won't see that happening if your screen is blank), press the **Up** arrow-key once to select the Shut Down option, press **R** to select Restart, then press **Enter** to confirm.

2 When Windows has been through its shutdown procedure (still invisibly of course), you'll see the usual white-on-black text of the startup process. Press and keep holding the **Ctrl** key while the computer restarts.

3 After a moment, a short list of numbered options called the Windows Startup Menu will appear on the screen, and one of its entries will be Safe Mode. Type the number shown beside the Safe Mode option, and Windows will start to load in this special mode (which will take somewhat longer than usual).

Once you've put the problem right you can choose the Shut Down option from the Start Menu again, click on **Restart**, and leave Windows to restart normally.

## Other startup options

Another thing you might need to do in times of trouble is to start the computer running MS-DOS. This and several other options can be selected from the Windows Startup Menu. As your computer starts or restarts, follow step 2 above to interrupt it and display the menu. You can then run any of its options by typing the number shown alongside, or by selecting an item using the up/down arrow-keys and pressing **Enter**. Here's what each of those options does:

**Command-prompt only**. Starts the computer in the normal way but stops at the MS-DOS prompt instead of loading Windows. (If you created a startup disk, mentioned at the beginning of this chapter, you can start the computer with that disk in your floppy drive to arrive at the same place.)

**Step-by-step confirmation**. Asks you for confirmation before processing each command in the system files Autoexec.bat, Config.sys and Io.sys to let you bypass any commands you think may be causing problems.

**Safe Mode Command-prompt only**. As the Command-prompt only option, but doesn't process Autoexec.bat or Config.sys (to skirt possible problems in those files).

**Logged**. Starts Windows in the normal way, and creates a file called **Bootlog.txt** on your C: drive listing the startup sequence.

**Normal**. Starts Windows in the usual way.

**Safe Mode with network support**. Starts the computer in Safe Mode but loads network drivers. You may want this option if you need to use files from your network to correct a configuration problem.

# Keep your computer virus-free

You've probably heard of computer viruses. Viruses are tiny programs maliciously inserted into an ordinary program which start to run as soon as you start using that program. The way viruses work and the effects they have on your system can vary: some are of the 'jokey' variety that make your PC go beep once a year; others might turn your files into meaningless gobbledegook or fill your hard-disk with trash to make it unusable.

**GOOD QUESTION!**

## Can people catch a computer virus?

You may be laughing, but I've heard this question asked many times. The answer is a definite 'no'. The term **virus** was adopted because of the way many computer viruses can replicate themselves (like the variety that attacks humans) to invade more and more of your files.

The first thing to get straight about viruses is that the threat is almost always hysterically overstated: viruses are simply not as common as some folk would have you believe. On the other hand, they certainly *do* exist, and they're commonly transferred from one computer to another in two ways: one is to run programs given to you on a floppy-disk (or some other type of removable disk), and the other is to run files from a network or downloaded from the Internet. The thing these two situations have in common is that you don't necessarily know where the program came from, or whether the computer that provided you with the program was infected with a virus.

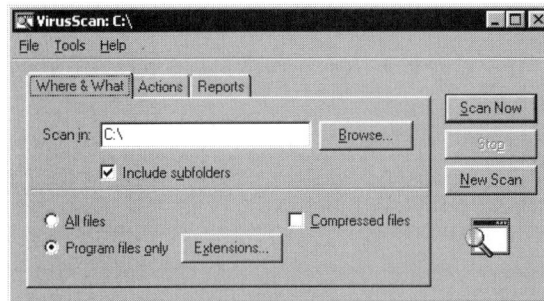

► Anti-virus utilities such as McAfee VirusScan check programs as you start them to prevent a virus taking hold.

However, viruses are easily avoidable. There are specialist utilities available such as Dr Solomon's Anti-Virus Toolkit and McAfee VirusScan (shown in the screenshot above) that can identify and stamp out viruses before they can cause a problem. These utilities check the vital system files every time you turn on your PC, and then monitor every program you run to prevent a virus being given the chance to start work. You can also select particular files or disks to scan before you start to use them.

Windows 98 users can buy an add-on software pack called Microsoft Plus 98. Along with additional Desktop Themes (see p. 149), several games and system utilities, and a very stylish replacement CD player program, you also get a copy of McAfee VirusScan.

## Keep your software updated

To work effectively virus scanners need to know what to look for – and new viruses are appearing all the time. For maximum safety, make sure you update your anti-virus software regularly following the details in the manuals.

# INSTALL AND SET UP NEW HARDWARE

Adding new hardware to your computer has traditionally been viewed as something you shouldn't do on a full stomach. It's not the physical installation of the device that causes the problems – it usually just slips into an expansion slot, or plugs into a port – it's the configuration of the thing once it's there. Windows' support for a system called **Plug & Play** has made the configuration of new devices much easier than it was in most cases, but with so many manufacturers selling so many products, instant success isn't always guaranteed.

In this chapter we'll begin by looking at the automated methods of installing and configuring hardware and lead on to some of the manual changes you might have to make in order to get everything working as it should. But first, a more pressing question …

# What is installation?

The installation of new hardware is actually two things tied up neatly in one word. The first and most obvious of these is that you have to physically *attach* the new device to the computer: with some devices this is the easy bit; with others it's more or less the *only* bit! How to attach the hardware will depend upon whether it's an **internal** or an **external** device. Once the device has been connected, the next step is to set it up properly to tell the computer what it is, where it is and how to communicate with it.

Never install a new device with the computer switched on – you might damage the PC, the device, yourself, or all three. Remember too that expansion cards and memory chips are susceptible to static electricity: only handle one of these boards by its edges, and leave it in its packing until the last possible moment.

## Fitting an internal device

Internal card devices are plugged into the PCI or ISA expansion slots described in Chapter 3. The exception is an AGP graphics card, which slots into your single AGP slot after removing the graphics card occupying that slot if necessary. You'll be able to see which type of slot is which by comparing the width of the metal connectors along one edge of the card to the width of the available slots, but your PC's manual should provide a diagram of the system unit's layout. These cards and their slots contain all the connections necessary to power the devices and pass data to them and from them.

If you're installing a new internal drive, remove the plastic cover from a drive slot, slide the drive in carefully, and then bolt it to the restraining brackets to hold it firmly in place. Drives will also need at least two cables to be connected. First, they need to be connected to the computer's power supply, and there are usually several spare power connectors in the system unit for this purpose. Second, they have to be connected to the main bus in order to send or receive data. (The 'bus' is the computer's equivalent of a motorway system, moving data quickly from one place to another.) You'll see a 4-cm wide grey ribbon inside the case (called the **interface cable**) with several plastic connectors on it: one of these connectors needs to be attached to the new device. If the new device plays sounds (as with a CD-ROM or DVD-ROM drive, or a TV/radio card) you'll also have to connect its Audio Out cable to your soundcard's Audio In to be able to hear those sounds.

## Take your time over installation

Don't install more than one piece of hardware at a time. If you install several and your PC doesn't work properly next time you start up, it might be difficult to tell which device is causing the problem.

## Hooking up an external device

External devices are very simple to connect: they usually have just one cable that has to be connected to a port (or socket) at the rear of the system unit. That, and a mains cable, is all there is to it.

Well, that's *almost* all there is to it. You have to make sure you plug it into the correct socket, some of which are known as **ports**. Ports are similar to the sockets you'd find on just about anything, in the sense that you plug something into them, and they're usually labelled. The main difference is that the PC's sockets are configured in different ways to enable them to deal with different types of data doing different things at different speeds. There are three common types of port:

**Serial ports**. Your PC will have at least two serial ports, called **COM1** and **COM2** (short for 'communications port'). The mouse may be connected to COM1, and the external modem (if you have one) to COM2. Serial ports are still not standardised and you see both nine-pin and 25-pin connectors (you can tell which type you've got by counting the pins in the socket or the tiny holes in the plug). If your device and your computer use different types you can buy a very cheap adapter to get around the problem. Serial ports transmit and receive data in a one-bit series, the format needed to send data over a telephone line.

**Parallel ports**. You'll usually have only one of these called **LPT1** (line printer port), although some computers offer two or three. To the LPT port(s), unsurprisingly, you attach your printer(s). The connectors for parallel ports *are* standardised but few devices other than printers and scanners are ever connected to them. The parallel port sends data in eight-bit chunks, and is able to check that the printer is ready to receive more data.

**USB ports**. This is a new type of port found on recent PCs, designed to make installation and use of new devices quick and simple. Unlike other devices and ports, you can plug a device into a USB port with the computer switched on and Windows running; Windows should spot the device immediately and you can start to use it straight away. The device must be specifically designed for plugging into a USB port, and up to 127 devices can be connected to a single port by linking them in a chain with cables. If your PC has a USB port and you can find a USB version of the hardware you want, buy it! If you do, you should never need to look at the rest of this chapter. The USB port should gradually make serial and parallel ports things of the past.

## Drivers: making everything talk

With almost any new device you add, you'll also have to install something called a **device driver** to go with it. This is a program that helps the PC to talk the same language as the new device, and it will usually be provided on a floppy-disk or CD bundled with the hardware itself.

## Keep up to date

Try to make sure you're always using the most recent drivers for all your hardware to get the best out of each device. These can usually be downloaded free of charge from a company's World Wide Web site (see Part 4), or you could phone the company and pester them to send you a copy if you're sure an updated version exists.

How you install the driver will vary from one device to another, and indeed from one manufacturer to another, but in general there are two methods. The neatest of these is that the manufacturer supplies a small program on disk that will copy the driver to your hard-disk and make sure the computer knows where to find it when it needs it. The second method is less automated, but not particularly difficult: the **Add New Hardware** applet in Control Panel will help you install a driver in step-by-step fashion, as we'll see later in this chapter.

## IRQ (interrupt request line)

Whenever a device is called upon to do something (for example, your soundcard needs to play a sound), it has to **interrupt** whatever the processor is doing at that time. So it sends a request for processor time (an **interrupt request**) down a line to the processor, and these lines are numbered. The lower the number assigned to a particular device, the higher its priority in the queue when the processor is busy.

# Installing with plug and play

The idea of Plug & Play is that the first time you start your computer after connecting the new hardware Windows will notice this new device, determine what it is, and add the necessary drivers for it automatically. If all goes smoothly, you should see just a brief on-screen message as your desktop appears announcing that a new device has been detected and is being configured. As well as installing driver files, the Plug & Play system covers the allocation of resources for the device, such as assigning correct and non-conflicting DMA channels and IRQs if necessary.

## DMA channels

These are numbered channels rather like IRQs. A DMA channel is a direct line to the computer's memory which bypasses the processor. This means that a device can respond faster when something needs to be done, with the added bonus that the processor is left alone to get on with other things.

Microsoft supplies its own drivers for a huge range of hardware: you might be prompted to insert your Windows installation CD so that the required files can be copied to your hard-disk. If Windows detects a Plug & Play device but can't provide a driver for it, you'll be prompted to insert the disk containing the driver-files that was packaged with the hardware.

## Do as you're told!

Although Windows might automatically install its own driver as soon as the system restarts, make sure you follow the device manufacturer's instructions. If they recommend running their own setup program from a CD after restarting, do that anyway. Their own driver might well provide you with more features for your new hardware than the Windows driver does.

Full Plug & Play support relies on having a Plug & Play BIOS (see Chapter 3) as well as Plug & Play hardware. Nevertheless, if one or both of these items are not Plug & Play compatible, Windows will still have a brave stab at identifying the new device. If neither are Plug & Play compatible, however, you may have to get your hands dirty in the system settings to sort out the problem. Turn to *Appendix D: Dealing With Hardware Problems* for some help with this.

# Changing hardware drivers

Despite its name, the **Add New Hardware Wizard** in Control Panel lets you *change* hardware-drivers as well as install drivers for new hardware. If Windows didn't manage to detect your device, or you want to install an updated driver that doesn't have its own installation program, go to Control Panel and run the wizard, then follow these steps:

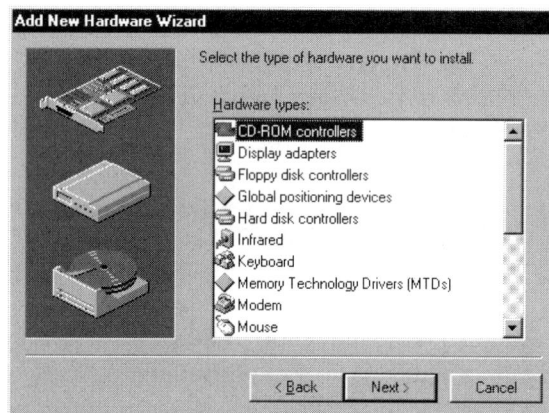

► Choose the type of device you want to install and configure.

1 Click **Next** in the first dialog to begin the process. In the second dialog click the **No** button to prevent Windows searching for the device.

2 On the next page, shown in the screenshot above, click the type of hardware for which you want to change or install drivers and click **Next**.

3 If Windows failed to detect your new hardware after you started your PC, look at the **Manufacturers** and **Models** lists to see if the device is listed. If it is, select it and click **Next** to install it. If you want to install an updated driver, or the driver that came with the software, click **Have Disk...** and direct Windows to the location of the files.

4 Installing new drivers will always require that you restart the computer for the change to take effect.

# Installing an unrecognised device

Sometimes Windows just hasn't got a clue what your device is: it can't detect it, and doesn't list a driver for it. If the manufacturer didn't package a driver with the hardware, all is not lost! Many drivers will work with different devices, so use the **Add New Hardware** wizard to try a few. It's a trial and error process, so it could involve a lot of starting and restarting of your computer, but you'll usually get there in the end.

If there are devices of the same type as yours listed by the same manufacturer, start by trying those, following steps 3 and 4 above. If none of those work (or your manufacturer isn't listed at all), try the range of generic drivers supplied for most device types: after clicking the **No** button as in step 1 above, double-click **Other Devices** in the **Hardware types** list. You'll see a list of bracketed entries in the left pane such as **(Standard display types)** and **(Standard mouse types)**. Click the correct type and choose what you think is the closest match in the right pane, then click **Next** to continue the installation.

# Adding extra RAM

The most common upgrade in recent years has been extra memory, as a result of a huge reduction in the price of RAM chips. It's a safe bet that memory will be top of the shopping list for some time to come as applications and operating systems get greedier with the amount of memory needed to make them run happily.

Depending upon your PC, the memory you have already may be in the form of SIMM chips (in which case you'll have four or six RAM slots divided into banks of two) or the more recent DIMMs (usually with three RAM slots). The big difference between the two types is that SIMM chips must be installed in matching pairs to fill a bank, so if you can only afford to add 32 MB of memory you'll need to buy it as two 16-MB chips, whereas DIMM chips can be installed singly.

You'll also need to know two more things:

**How many connecting 'pins' your computer's memory chips must have**. For SIMM chips the norm is 72-pin; with DIMMs the standard is 168-pin.

**The memory speed**. Most PCs will use DIMMs with a speed of 100 MHz, but slightly older PCs may use 66-MHz DIMMs. SIMM chips will have a speed of either 60 or 70 ns (nanoseconds).

Always check your PC's manual (or the manual for your PC's motherboard, but this won't be such a friendly read) to find out exactly what you need before getting your chequebook out.

Finally, of course, you need to decide on the capacity. RAM prices have fallen so much in recent years that 64-MB RAM has become a realistic target, and this should be enough for most uses. If you frequently open very large files or run a number of professional-level applications at the same time, you may want to play safe and go for a (still affordable) total of 128 MB.

## Battering RAM

RAM chips are extremely fragile and can be damaged by static electricity and careless handling. Always be gentle when touching these chips, hold them only by their two short edges, and leave them in their packing until you're ready to slot them into the PC.

Memory chips are installed in the same way as expansion cards (see *Fitting an internal device* on p. 172): place the edge of the chip against the memory slot, and push gently while rocking the chip up and down slightly. In most PCs the RAM slots have small plastic clips that slot into holes in the edges of the chip to hold it securely – if yours does, make sure that the clips are in place.

The good news about memory is that the physical installation is all that's needed. Provided you've installed the chips correctly (and it's not a foregone conclusion, even if a chip seems to be firmly seated) your PC should find it and start using it immediately. When you start your computer, watch the screen carefully: as the initial tests take place, you should see that the total RAM displayed on the screen has increased. (If your PC uses SIMMs, remember that two chips are needed in each bank: if one chip has been installed incorrectly, neither chip in that bank will be recognised.)

# HELP! WINDOWS Q & A

Shifting into quickfire mode, this chapter contains a collection of answers to recurring questions, problems and Windows curiosities.

## Where has the Taskbar gone?

It may have jumped to the left, right, or top edge of your screen, or it may have apparently vanished altogether. If it's moved to a different edge of the screen, click the left mouse-button on a blank grey area (not a button or icon) and drag straight down. You can move it to any edge by dragging it around like this.

If it seems to have disappeared, you've probably resized it. Move the mouse down to the very bottom of the screen, moving fairly slowly when you get there. When the pointer turns into a double-headed arrow, click the left mouse-button and drag upwards about an inch or so. This will stretch the Taskbar back to its usual height.

▶ The Taskbar can sit at any edge of the screen – just drag it to where you want it.

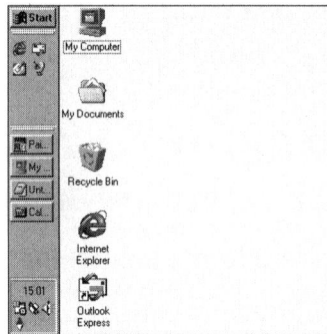

If the Taskbar suddenly reappears when your mouse reaches the bottom of the screen, you've set it to **auto hide** – in other words, it slides out of sight when it's not being used, and reappears when the mouse moves over it. To switch off auto hide, click the Start button, go to **Settings** and choose **Taskbar & Start Menu** and click in the **Auto hide** box to remove the checkmark.

# What and where is the Tab key?

The Tab key is at the extreme left of the keyboard, above the Caps Lock key and beside the letter 'Q' key. In a word-processor it acts as a type of indent key, moving the cursor from one tab stop to the text (the tab stops should be visible in the ruler at the top of the word-processor window). This is known as **tabulation**, and it makes it easy to organise text or figures into neatly-aligned columns.

Elsewhere, the Tab key is used to move from one item to the next. In a spreadsheet, use the Tab to move to the next cell. In database forms and Windows dialogs, use Tab to move from one button or text field to another.

# Why have my desktop icons jumped to the left of the screen?

This is a trick called auto-arrange. If you right-click a blank part of the desktop and move down to **Arrange Icons**, you'll see an **Auto Arrange** entry at the bottom of the submenu, and it probably has a tick beside it. Click it again (the tick will have gone next time you look) and you'll be able to drag your icons wherever you want them. When you have everything roughly in position, right-click the desktop and choose **Line Up Icons** to make them snap into neater rows and columns.

Although they tend not to be popular on the desktop, the various Arrange options are useful in folder windows and Explorer. Choose **By Name** to sort icons alphabetically; **By Type** to group different types of file together (useful if you want to find all the picture files in a folder, for example); **By Size** to show the smallest files at the top of the window and the largest at the bottom; or **By Date** to show the newest files at the top of the window.

# Why does Disk Defragmenter keep restarting?

The quick explanation is that the contents of your hard-disk changed while Defragmenter was running. This could be because your screensaver started, or because you opened, saved or deleted a file. It's best not to continue working while Defragmenter is running (your PC will be rather slow anyway – the defragmentation process keeps it busy). You should also set your screensaver option to **[None]** in Control Panel's Display applet, then set it back to your chosen screensaver once Defragmenter has finished.

▶ Use Print Scrn to take a snapshot of your desktop or active window.

# What is the Print Scrn key for?

The Print Scrn key (or, more usefully on some keyboards, Print Screen key) takes a snapshot of your desktop and stores it as a picture on the clipboard. (If you hold the **Alt** key when you press Print Scrn, it takes a shot of the active window instead.) Open a graphics program such as Windows' own Paint accessory and choose the Paste option (Ctrl+V), and you'll have a screenshot similar to the ones you can see throughout this book.

## Better screen capture

You'll probably never need a screenshot of your desktop, but if you do, there are programs that can provide far better ways of doing it. Popular graphics programs like Paint Shop Pro have screen capture options built in, and there are dedicated screen capture utilities around, all of which offer a range of extra features.

# Why have my icons changed?

Sometimes you'll be cheerfully working away, and you'll notice that icons on your desktop or Start Menu (and sometimes in My Computer and Control Panel) have been swapped with others – they may be even using icons you've never seen before. The bad news is that there's no quick and easy solution to this. The good news, though, is that it isn't something you did wrong, and it isn't permanent. It's just the result of a little glitch in the Windows system: next time you start up, the icons will all be back to normal.

# How can I type the euro symbol?

You should be able to use the keystroke **Ctrl+Alt+4**. If that doesn't work, Windows includes an accessory called **Character Map** that gives easy access to the euro and dozens of other symbols and foreign characters. You can install Character Map from the Windows Setup tab in Control Panel's Add/Remove Programs applet. Although I call Character Map an accessory, Microsoft inexplicably calls it a System Tool, so that's where you'll find it on the Windows Setup page and on your Start Menu after installation.

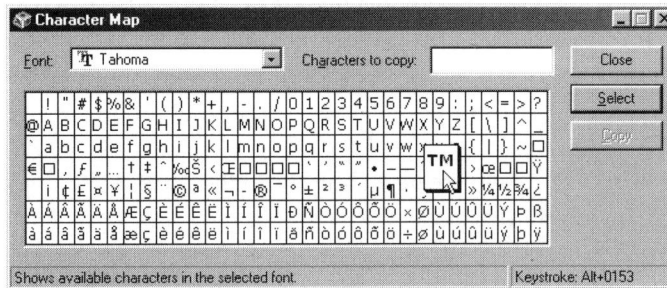

▶ Character Map gives you access to extra symbols and foreign alphabets.

Click anywhere (or move around using the arrow keys) to see larger examples of the characters. There are two ways to use Character Map: one is to click the character you need, click the **Select** button, then the **Copy** button, and then return to your application and choose Paste. The other is to note the text beside the word **Keystroke** in the lower right corner (such as **Alt+0153**). Return to your application, make sure the Num Lock key is switched on, then hold the **Alt** key and type the four-figure number on the numeric keypad. When you release the **Alt** key, the symbol will appear in your document.

# How do I make CDs play automatically?

Audio CDs should start to play almost as soon as the drive tray closes, and some data CD-ROMs (although not all) will automatically run a CD-based game or setup program. If that isn't happening with your CD drive, follow these steps:

1   Open Control Panel and double-click the **System** icon.

2   Click the **Device Manager** tab.

3   Double-click the **CD-ROM** entry to view its contents, and then double-click your CD-ROM drive's entry below.

4   Click the **Settings** tab, and check the box marked **Auto insert notification**.

5   Click **OK** in all the open dialogs to close them.

# Can I start a screensaver when I leave my PC?

If you've set a password for your screensaver (see p. 145) to protect your data while you're away from your PC, you'd usually want the screensaver to start as soon as you leave your desk. On the other hand, you don't really want to set the screensaver to start after a one-minute interval – it'll keep coming on during short pauses for thought while you work.

The solution is to create a shortcut to the screensaver on your desktop by following these steps:

1   Open My Computer, find your Windows folder, right-click it and choose **Find**.

2   In the **Named** box, type *.scr, then click on **Find Now**.

3   From the resulting list of screensaver files found, use the right mouse-button to drag one to the desktop, and choose **Create Shortcut(s) Here**. Whenever you leave your desk, just double-click this icon.

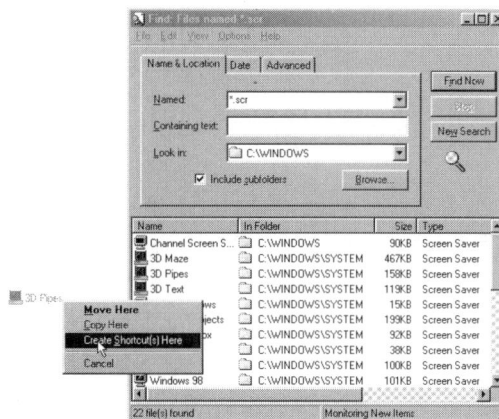

▶ Use Find to locate screensaver files, then drag with the right mouse-button to create a shortcut.

The password you set up applies to any screensaver you use, so you could create shortcuts to several of your favourites and pick and choose which to start each time.

# How can I get rid of Web View?

The Web View option for folders (selected from a folder's View, As Web Page option) isn't the most popular of layouts for folder windows, and it's switched on automatically when Windows is installed. Although you can turn it off by clicking that menu option to remove the tick, it won't be turned off for every folder.

Here's the solution: open any folder and turn off Web View. While you're doing this, you might like to choose other options such as **Auto Arrange** from the Arrange Items submenu. Next, choose **Folder Options**, also on the View menu, and click the **View** tab, then click the button labelled **Like Current Folder**. In future, any folder you open will have the same look and layout as this one.

# CHOOSING AND USING SOFTWARE

# 15

# SELECTING AND INSTALLING NEW SOFTWARE

In theory, you already know exactly what software you need. After all, you knew *why* you needed a computer and it's the software you choose that determines what this machine can do. In reality, though, it rarely works out that way: we get so bogged down in the technicalities of picking the right computer that the reason for buying the PC in the first place often becomes a last-minute 'Oh yes, I need a word-processor.' It's a fact of computer-buying life, but it's one to watch out for: a single graphics application, for example, might cost nearly half the price of your PC, but you may never use more than a quarter of its features. Conversely, you might find you have to replace software soon after buying it because it can't do what you need.

The aim of the following chapters is to provide a basic introduction to some of the common types of software – what they do, how they do it, what's available and what's popular – to help you choose wisely.

# Software buying checklist

Before you splash the cash, it's vital to make sure you're buying the right tool for the job. It's a good start to know you need a word-processor, but it doesn't narrow the field much: word-processors range from simple £40 jotters to feature-packed £200 applications with advanced formatting and layout tools. Here are a few questions worth asking yourself before you making any final decisions:

### Will it do what you need it to do?

The fundamental question that could save you both money and aggravation. Check this one carefully by reading reviews and comparing features with other applications. Try to get an in-store demonstration and a few minutes to explore it on your own.

### Will it do more than you need it to do?

Given the alternative, it's better to buy something that does more than you need, but the heavy-weight professional applications can swallow chunks of system resources, and you might find the plethora of toolbars and menus distracting.

### Will Windows' own accessories do the job?

Another case for some experimentation. These add-on accessories aren't intended to rival full-blown applications, but if your word-processing requirements are limited to short letters, memos and faxes, you might find that WordPad could handle them for you comfortably.

### Will file formats be compatible with your colleagues' applications?

For business users this can be an important consideration. If you need to pass the files you create to a colleague, make sure you can save files in a format compatible with your colleague's software. If you already use a particular application on your office PC, it makes sense to buy the same for your home or portable computer.

### Can a different type of application do this job?

Modern word-processors such as Microsoft Word and Lotus WordPro have built-in drawing tools that might make a separate drawing package redundant. A good spreadsheet application can make a very capable database. Draw up a list of the things you need to do with your PC and see how far you can reduce the number of separate applications required.

### Would an office suite be a better buy?

If you need two or more heavy-duty applications, such as a word-processor and a spreadsheet, you'll probably save money by buying an office suite (covered in Chapter 21) and get two or three more applications thrown in for good measure.

### Will it run on your PC?

Take a look at the back or side panel of the software pack for the specifications needed to run the software. Above all, remember that these are *minimum* requirements: the program may seem rather sluggish if your PC matches those specifications exactly. Even recommended specifications can be somewhat optimistic.

### Are you on the upgrade path?

If you bought an application and you now need something more powerful, find out if you qualify for an upgrade price rather than having to buy the full product. In many cases, if you have a competitor's product installed, or a 'light-weight' version of the product you want, you can save 35–50 per cent by buying the upgrade version. (But beware – this version checks your hard-disk to make sure you weren't kidding before it goes very far!) These upgrade prices apply even if the original software was supplied 'free' with your PC.

# Understanding version numbers

Software changes as quickly as the hardware it's designed to work with, so software producers add version numbers to the names of their products to help you ensure you're buying the latest version, or the version that works with your operating system. A new product will be called version 1.0; minor changes will lead to versions 1.1, 1.2 and so on. When a major change in design takes place they'll call it version 2.0. Very often the minor changes are the result of finding bugs (unexpected errors) in the previous release and putting them right.

Microsoft have adopted a slightly different way of naming products in recent years. Although products like Windows and Office still have version numbers, they're not prominently displayed. Instead they add a year number to the name, giving us Windows 98, Office 2000, and so on. This is simple enough to follow when buying a product – just look for the most recent year number. This year, of course, there probably isn't a software company under the sun who has resisted the temptation to add a '2000' to their product's name.

# Installing new software

Installation of software means making sure that all the files needed to run the program can be found by the computer when needed. This usually involves placing the files in particular folders on your hard-disk, but a few programs are small and simple enough that you can run them from a floppy-disk with no formal installation required. Other types of software, such as games or multimedia titles, may be several hundred megabytes in size and supplied on CD-ROM; copying this lot to your hard-disk would be pretty impractical, so installation involves copying a few small files to your hard-disk and leaving the rest where they are.

The most straightforward type of installation simply involves copying a few files around manually. For example, a small program supplied on a floppy-disk, or downloaded from the Internet, may just need you to create a new folder on your hard-disk, copy the program files into it, and create a shortcut so that you can start it easily.

## One at a time

Don't install more than one application at a time. If you install five in one session and your PC goes into a sulk next time you start it, it'll be no fun at all trying to track down the culprit. Install one, restart your computer, and check everything is okay before installing the next.

## Automated installation

The most common type of installation, particularly with today's large applications, involves a semi-automated installation procedure. The software is supplied on a CD-ROM, and the installation is handled by a program often called **Install.exe** or **Setup.exe** which you'll find on the CD-ROM. Running this program will lead you through the procedure step by step, asking you questions. This may vary in complexity: some software will just ask if you're sure you want to install and then start copying the files to your hard-disk when you say Yes. Other programs will give you an opportunity to choose which drive and folder you want the software installed into.

## Close your program first!

Before installing new software, close down any programs that are running. The installation procedure sometimes needs to alter some of your existing files, and if they're in use by another program it won't be able to do this, which could botch the installation.

Larger software packages such as operating systems and top-level applications often require a lot of disk space and include a collection of optional files, so they usually prompt you to choose between a **Minimal** installation (leaving out most of the optional utilities and accessories to conserve disk space), a **Typical** installation (including the options most users will need), or a **Custom** installation. The Custom installation allows you to choose which elements of the software you want to install, usually giving a brief description of each one and keeping a running tally of the disk space required as you check off the items you want.

## Customise your installation

For all but the computing novice, it's worth taking the Custom option and choosing which elements you want installed. But whether you do this or not, you can run the Setup program again in the future and easily add or remove elements.

The necessary files will then be copied to various folders on your hard-disk, and changes may be made to your system files so that the computer is made aware of this new software's arrival and the whereabouts of its files. In some cases you'll have to restart your PC after installation so that the computer can read these updated system files into memory. You may also be asked if you'd like icons to be added to the program groups on the Start Menu: if you agree to this, you can delete the icons at any time if you want to; if you turn down the offer, you can still add the shortcuts manually later.

# Uninstalling software

**Uninstalling** software means removing it (and, in theory at least, all traces of it) from your computer. The method of doing this will usually reflect the method of installation: if you created a new folder and copied the files into it yourself, uninstallation is as simple as deleting the files you copied and deleting the folder. If you created a shortcut to the program on your desktop or Start Menu, you'll need to delete that too.

Most software that has its own automatic installation program, as described above, usually has an automated method of uninstallation too. This may involve running the **Setup** program again and clicking a button marked **Uninstall**, or you may find an uninstall program in the folder the software was installed into. This program should remove any files that were copied to your hard-disk as a part of the installation, and reverse any changes made to your system files (again requiring you to restart the computer). It may or may not remove the icons it added to your program-groups, and it usually won't delete any folders it created. This last point is actually good news: you may have saved documents of your own into these folders which you wouldn't want to lose. Deleting a folder deletes its entire contents including any subfolders, and any files in those subfolders.

## Don't use Delete to uninstall!

BY THE WAY

Never uninstall a program by just deleting its folder unless you created that folder yourself when you installed it. You'll usually be leaving other files scattered elsewhere on your system, along with some orphaned settings that could cause your system to act strangely.

## Let Windows uninstall it for you

Most of the software you install will add itself to a list of programs on the **Install/Uninstall** page of Control Panel's **Add/Remove Programs** page, shown in the next screenshot.

Despite the name of the page and the details on it, there's no need to use this page to install software: just follow the instructions included with the software itself. But if you need to uninstall the program, and you can't see an uninstall option for it anywhere else, take a look at this page to see if the program was logged here. If it was, click its name in the list, then click the **Add/Remove** button and follow any instructions that appear.

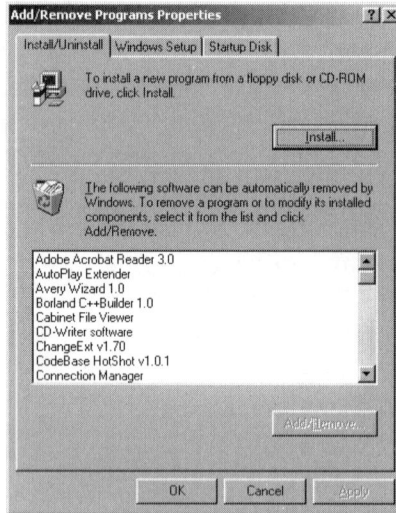

▶ Select the program to be removed, and click the **Add/Remove** button to kiss it goodbye.

# GET WRITING WITH A WORD-PROCESSOR

It sounds like something that could only have been named by a committee, but it's actually one of the simplest types of program you'll come across. Essentially, a word-processor is the computer equivalent of a typewriter, letting you type and print text-based documents, but the differences between the two are immense. How many typewriters let you change the size, colour and style of the typeface, insert drawings and pictures, or add a few lines to page 20 while you're writing page 54? Better still, there are no ribbons to change, and you don't need to cover your screen with correction-fluid.

## Word-processor basics

When the program opens you'll see a wide expanse of white space in the middle, which is your 'paper', and you can start typing immediately. A flashing vertical line (known as the **cursor** or the **insertion point**) indicates where you are in the document – any text you type will appear immediately to the right of this line. You can move the insertion point to anywhere in the document using the arrow-keys, or by clicking the left mouse-button. Whenever the mouse is positioned over the 'paper', it turns into a shape called an **I-beam** (shown in the next screenshot) to help you position the insertion point more easily between two adjacent characters than the ordinary pointer would allow.

Another important difference about a word-processor is that you don't need to press the keyboard's carriage-return key (the **Enter** key) when you reach the end of a line. Instead, the text *wraps* automatically on to the next line, and this key is used only when you want to start a new paragraph or insert blank lines.

**JARGON BUSTER**

### Text editor

A text editor (such as Windows' Notepad) is like a word-processor with no flashy features, used to create plain text (**ASCII**) files that have no font styles, formatting or layout detail. Text editors work with files with a .txt extension and are useful for creating short notes, memos and so on, being quick and easy to use. In effect, all word-processors are text editors – any word-processor will be able to open and save files in this format.

Finally, of course, a word-processor doesn't commit you to anything you've typed. You can make all the spelling mistakes you want to and sort them out later; if you change your mind about the order of the paragraphs you can use Cut and Paste to rearrange them. Most importantly, you can use a huge range of features to **format** the document, including fonts, tabs and paragraph alignment, line spacing, and text-colours. A top-level application will also include options to create graphs and tables, add logos and graphics, place text in shaded boxes and so on.

▶ *Common editing facilities found in word-processors such as Cut/Copy/Paste, Find and Replace, together with the methods of selecting sections of text, are explained in Chapter 9.*

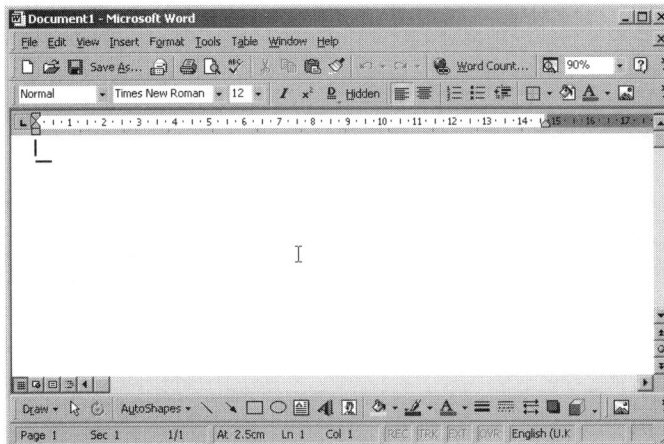

▶ Microsoft Word ready for work, with the cursor in the corner of the document window and the I-beam in the centre.

# Moving around a document

As you type text into your word-processor and your document gets longer, the text scrolls upwards and gradually disappears off the top of the screen as if you'd threaded an everlasting roll of paper into your typewriter. The text is still there, of course, and you can move backwards and forwards through the document to view or edit your work any time you like. Here are some of the methods you can use:

▶ Use the arrow-keys to move around one character or line at a time, or in conjunction with **Ctrl** to move back and forth one word at a time.

▶ Use the **PageUp/PageDown** keys to move up and down one screenful at a time. A 'screen' will be smaller than a complete printed page.

▶ Use the **Home** and **End** keys to move to the beginning or end of a line, or together with **Ctrl** to move to the top or bottom of the document.

▶ Use the scroll bar on the right of the screen to bring a portion of the document into view, then click the mouse at the position you want the insertion point to appear.

▶ If you have a wheel-mouse, just roll the wheel back and forth to move downward or upward in the document.

**JARGON BUSTER**

## Headers and footers

Small margins at the top and bottom of each page in a document that might contain the name of the document, or chapter titles. You would normally enter these once, perhaps with different entries for odd- and even-numbered pages, and they'll be automatically added to every page when you print the document. Page numbers can be inserted in the same way and the software will keep them updated as you add and delete text.

# Working with fonts and formatting

Many word-processing, spreadsheet, database and presentation applications have a toolbar like the one shown in the next screenshot containing the primary text-formatting options. From this bar you can select a font from the drop-down list box, choose the size of the font (measured in **points**) from another list-box, and pick styles and effects such as bold, italic, underlined and coloured text in any combination from buttons that can be toggled on and off. In some high-level applications, there may be extra buttons on the toolbar or a **Format** menu offering even more text-formatting options.

▶ The standard text-formatting toolbar.

| Times New Roman | ▼ | 10 | ▼ | **B** | *I* | U | 🖉 |

These controls are very simple to use: if you're typing a document in a word-processor and you know the next portion of text you want to enter should be Times New Roman, 12 point, and bold, just select the font and point-size from the two drop-down lists, click the **B** button, and start typing. To type a word in 'normal' print (i.e. not bold), click the **B** button again to turn it off. (Saving the need to keep reaching for the mouse, you can usually switch bold, italic and underlining on and off using the hotkeys **Ctrl+B**, **Ctrl+I** and **Ctrl+U** respectively.)

**JARGON BUSTER**

## Point size

Points are the units of height measurement for fonts, in which 72 points equals one inch. (This would often be abbreviated to 72 pt.) Body text, the typographer's name for standard paragraph text, is usually 11 pt or 12 pt.

You can also edit text you've already typed in just the same way. Let's say you want to underline a section of text – first select the portion of text you want, then click the **U** button. You can change the font or point-size (or both) for selected text by choosing from the drop-down list-boxes.

| | |
|---|---|
| **Bold** | ~~Strikethrough~~ |
| *Italic* | Superscript Superscript |
| ***Bold Italic*** | Subscript Subscript |
| **D**rop Cap | Underline |

▶ Some of the common, and not-so-common, text-formatting features you can use with TrueType fonts.

## Setting margins and alignment

One of the fundamental needs in document formatting is the ability to set page margins. When you first start your word-processor, the margins will be preset to defaults, but these are easily changed and the changes are saved together with the document. Margins are usually set from a **Page Setup...** entry on the File menu, and contain boxes for Top, Bottom, Left and Right into which you type a size for each margin in centimetres. You can usually type in a size for the header and footer too, and some top-level applications let you specify different inside and outside margins for documents that are to be bound, such as books and reports.

As well as changing the settings for the whole document, you can set margins for individual paragraphs. With the insertion-point placed somewhere within the paragraph you want to change, open the **Paragraph** dialog which is usually found on the **Format** menu. Here are a few of the options you might find, and what they mean:

**Indent**. The distance in centimetres that the selected paragraph (or its first line) should be moved from the left and right margins.

**Spacing**. Changes the spacing between paragraphs. You'll have simple options like **double-spaced**, and you might also be able to specify exact spacing in **points**.

## Preview before printing

To make sure your document layout looks okay before printing, choose **Print Preview** from the **File** menu to view one or more complete pages on the screen.

**Left Aligned**. This is the usual alignment option, in which each line of text will follow the line of the left margin and be ragged at the right. Your application will left align your text automatically. (Instead of opening the **Paragraph** dialog, you can often just use the hotkey **Ctrl+L**.)

**Right Aligned**. Text will follow the line of the right margin and be ragged at the left (used only for effect, usually for single lines, dates and addresses). The usual hotkey combination is **Ctrl+R**.

**Justified**. Each line of the paragraph will be forced to follow both the left and right margins to give a completely 'square' look; extra spaces are added between words to make the lines the correct length. Justified text can be difficult to read and is now used just in short bursts for effect, or to prevent narrow columns of text looking messy. You can usually press **Ctrl+J** for this one.

**Centred**. Places the paragraph centrally between the left and right margins, and used mostly for headings or unusual effects. The common hotkey is **Ctrl+E**.

## JARGON BUSTER

## Widows and orphans

Many word-processors have an option to prevent widows and orphans in their paragraph formatting dialogs. A **widow** is the last line of a paragraph printed by itself at the top of a new page; an **orphan** is the first line of a paragraph printed at the bottom of a page.

# Using the spellchecker and thesaurus

These are two common features built into word-processors more and more often, but it pays to check the box before buying – although users regard them as essentials, some software producers still don't. The thesaurus is a doddle to use: any time you're stuck for a word, type a word with a similar meaning, then start it up and see what suggestions are listed. If nothing appears that's quite right, look up one of the suggestions to see some synonyms for that. When you find what you want, you should have a **Replace** button that will enter it into your document for you.

Much as you'd expect, the spellchecker checks your spelling by looking through the document and prompting you when it finds a word not listed in its own dictionary. You can take the spellchecker's suggested word, edit the word yourself or add the word to your own **user dictionary** which the spellchecker uses in tandem with its own. The effectiveness of a spellchecker depends largely on the size of its dictionary, but it's important to make sure it can distinguish between American English and UK English.

Some spellcheckers come with a bundle of foreign-language dictionaries which might be useful.

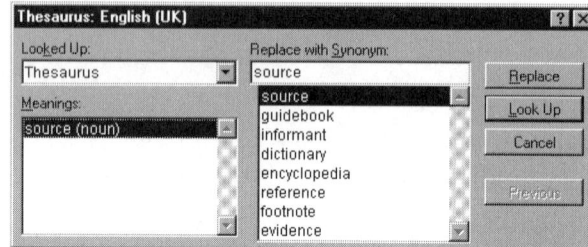

**Thesaurus: English (UK)**

Looked Up:
Thesaurus

Meanings:
source (noun)

Replace with Synonym:
source

source
guidebook
informant
dictionary
encyclopedia
reference
footnote
evidence

Replace
Look Up
Cancel
Previous

▶ Ever needed a synonym for 'thesaurus'?

## Prepare your spellchecker

When you start using a new word-processor, create a document containing your name and address, and those of friends and colleagues, lists of technical terms and jargon you use regularly and so on, and then run it through the spellchecker to add these to the user dictionary. It makes the spellchecking of future documents a much quicker process when you're trying to get some work done!

# Hot features in top word-processors

Here, in brief, are a few of the clever features found in the top-end word-processors:

**Styles**. Type and format a heading, for example, choosing a particular font, size, colour, alignment and so on, and assign it a style-name such as *Chapter Title*. You can than select any other text you type and apply this style to it with a single click rather than carrying out all that formatting each time. If you need to change a style, all the text in your document that uses the same style can be updated automatically.

**Columns**. Split your page into multiple vertical columns, newspaper style.

**Drawing tools**. Switch on the drawing toolbar and add pictures, logos and designs to your document without needing a separate draw or paint program.

**Frames**. Traditionally the domain of desktop publishing, you can place text or drawings into frames and drag them wherever you want them in the document, force text to flow neatly around them or even place them *behind* the text like a watermark.

**AutoCorrect**. Automatic correction of words you commonly misspell. Enter your incorrect spellings into a list together with their correct spellings and the application will keep watch for these as you type and correct them automatically.

**Group support**. If you work on documents in a team, your colleagues can enter their own corrections and annotations without removing the original information, letting you choose whether to incorporate their suggestions or not.

**Indexing**. Automatic creation of indexes, tables of contents and cross-references which can be updated with a mouse-click or two as the document's contents change.

**Web page design**. Save ordinary documents in a format that can be published on the World Wide Web, or work from custom templates that include preset graphics, layouts and colour schemes.

# Choosing a word-processor

Top of the heap in the word-processor world are **Microsoft Word** (the long-time best-seller) and **Lotus WordPro**. Either of these will require a bare minimum 8-MB RAM to run under Windows, and 16 MB is a more realistic minimum. To use them in conjunction with other heavyweight applications such as spreadsheets or presentations, 32-MB RAM will help things to run faster and more smoothly. Sitting well behind these two in the popularity stakes, though still with a good set of features, is **Corel WordPerfect**.

Before buying a word-processor, take a look at Chapter 21 – you might be able to save money by buying an all-in-one office suite or an integrated application.

# CRUNCH YOUR NUMBERS WITH A SPREADSHEET

It sounds like something technical that you'd run a mile to avoid using, but a spreadsheet is just a collection of boxes used to keep track of numbers. The numbers can be anything you like – your car mileage, the state of your bank account, a home-insurance valuation. But a spreadsheet lets you do much more than create lists of numbers: its speciality is to add, subtract, average, and generally crunch those numbers in any way you want them crunched, and to update the results automatically whenever you change or add an entry.

## Why use a spreadsheet?

The primary use of a spreadsheet program is to enter lists of numbers and perform calculations on them. For example, you might use a spreadsheet to log sales of a product, budget your money, manage your income tax accounts, or chart the progress of your favourite football team. Once the numbers are entered, the spreadsheet can perform anything from simple addition of figures to a complicated statistical analysis of a selection of these numbers – the kind of stuff that would take hours with a calculator and years off your life.

However, spreadsheets are more than just number-crunchers – you can view these figures as colourful charts and graphs (shown in the next screenshot), import them into word-processed reports or presentations, and create finished documents such as invoices and receipts by adding company logos and graphics. In fact, you don't have to use numbers at all – the spreadsheet's **Find** and **Replace** facilities mean that you can use it as a database for any text-based information you want to keep track of.

## Finding your way around

On first opening a spreadsheet you're presented with a large grid of boxes; each of these boxes is a **cell**, and it's into these you'll enter text, figures and formulas. Each cell has its own **address** consisting of a column letter and a row number. For example, the cell in the top-left corner of a worksheet is called **A1**.

**Lotus SmartSuite - 1-2-3 - [C:\WINDOWS\Desktop\1999 Sales]**

File  Edit  View  Create  Range  Sheet  Window  Help

A:G11          1529

| | 1st Quarter | 2nd Quarter | 3rd Quarter | 4th Quarter | Total |
|---|---|---|---|---|---|
| **WORLD SALES 1999** | | | | | |
| Canada | 63 | 79 | 72 | 60 | 274 |
| North America | 115 | 134 | 137 | 123 | 509 |
| South America | 82 | 86 | 80 | 47 | 295 |
| Europe | 103 | 121 | 119 | 103 | 451 |
| *Total* | 363 | 420 | 408 | 338 | 1529 |

**1999 World Sales**

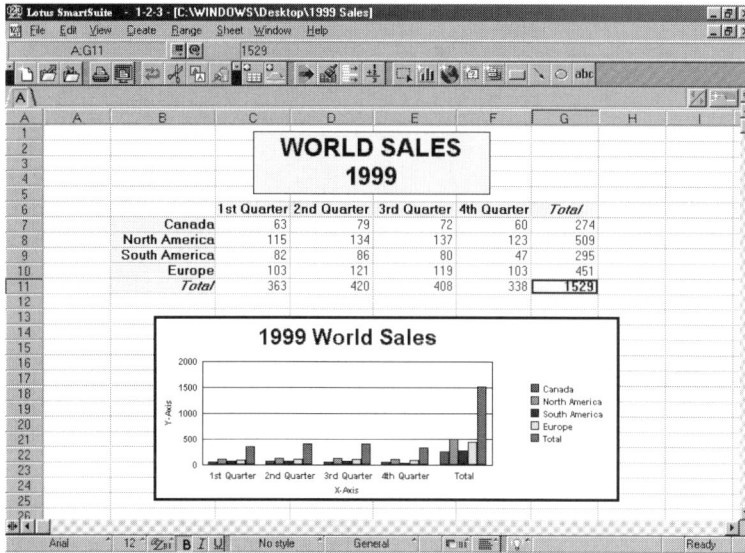

▶ Figures and chart in **Lotus 1-2-3**.

## Worksheet

**JARGON BUSTER**

A spreadsheet application usually lets you create lots of sheets all in the same file, each of which is called a **worksheet**. You'll see tabs across the top or bottom of the window marked **Sheet 1**, **Sheet 2** and so on. Click on a tab to switch to it, or double-click to give it a more informative name. For example, you might keep your year's accounts in a single file with separate worksheets named **January, February**... .

When you start up the spreadsheet application you'll see a thick box around cell A1 – this is the **cell selector** and lets you see where you are on the sheet (rather like the flashing text-cursor in a word-processor). You can move to a different cell using the keyboard's arrow-keys or by clicking a cell with the mouse. If the cell you select contains an entry, this entry will be displayed in the **formula bar** just above the column headers, shown in the screenshot below. Here's a quickfire list of things you should know about spreadsheets:

| SUM | ▼ | ✗ ✓ = | =SUM(D24 + E24 - C24) |
|---|---|---|---|
| | A | | B |
| 1 | | | |
| 2 | | | |

▶ The all-important
formula bar.

▶ To enter text in an empty cell, move the selector to it using the arrow-keys or by clicking it, and start typing. When you're done, you can press **Enter** to confirm, or click the ✓ button on the formula bar, or move to a different cell.

▶ To delete an entry in a cell, click the cell and then hit the Delete key.

▶ To cancel an entry you've typed wrongly, click the ✗ button on the formula bar. You can then either type in something different or hit **Enter** to finish and leave the cell blank.

▶ To change an entry in a cell, just click it. If it contains data you entered yourself you can replace the data by typing something new – there's no need to delete the original data first. If the cell contains the result of a calculation, the function or formula you used will be displayed in the formula bar and you can edit it there.

▶ You can select a whole column for editing by clicking its letter button, or a row by clicking its number button.

▶ Select a group of cells by clicking in one cell and dragging to highlight the cells you want to work with.

▶ Select cells scattered around the sheet by holding **Ctrl** and clicking on each cell you need.

▶ You can use Cut, Copy & Paste to move or copy the contents of cells from one part of the worksheet to another, or to a different worksheet. You can also paste (**embed**) them into a different type of document such as a word-processor report, or link them so that the word-processed document always shows the latest changes to the cells.

The usual way to begin creating a spreadsheet is to enter a list of names or labels in column A and along row 1 (making the columns wider if necessary) and then to enter all your values in the appropriate cells. Spreadsheets are intelligent – they can tell the difference between words and figures without you having to do anything special. However, if you intend certain figures to be dates or currency, you'll need to *format* the selected cells correctly so that the spreadsheet knows to treat them that way:

in most applications, you'll be able to click a button on the toolbar to set the most common number formats, or select them from a Format menu.

## Missing cell contents?

If you see the entry ***** in a cell, it indicates that the column isn't wide enough to hold the cell's contents. Move the pointer to the right-hand side of the column button and drag it slightly to the right to widen the column.

The next step is to enter the formulas needed to make the necessary calculations. Check the results of formula cells carefully to make sure they're doing what you want before you start to rely on their output – it's easy to miss out a data cell you meant to include or enter the wrong symbol by mistake. Finally, add any formatting you want to make the whole thing look good

# Formulas: doing the maths

Getting all the data into the spreadsheet (and making sure you've typed it correctly) is a good start, but it's still just lists of numbers – nothing clever there, you could do that in a word-processor. The 'clever' comes in the form of instructions entered into a cell that tell the application what you want to know about particular sets of figures. These instructions are known as **formulas** and consist of cell addresses and the standard mathematical symbols + (add), – (subtract), * (multiply) and / (divide). A formula will always start with the = (equals) sign to indicate to the software that what you're entering is a formula rather than more data.

As an example, let's say you've entered a pair of numbers into cells A1 and A2 and you want to add them together. Click in A3 and type:

=A1+A2

and press **Enter**. The formula you just entered will vanish to be replaced by the result of that calculation. Any time you click on A3 the formula you entered will be displayed in the formula bar, but A3 itself will continue to show the result. If you now change the number in A1 and press **Enter**, the total shown in A3 will immediately update – the application doesn't care *which* numbers are in the cells, it just knows it's got to add them together.

## Save yourself some typing

Instead of typing the cell addresses into the formula, you can just click the cell you want each time. (You've still got to type the mathematical symbols though.)

Make sure you enter the separate calculations into a formula in the order you want the application to perform them. For example, **=A1*B1+D4** would multiply A1 and B1 and then add D4 to the total, whereas **=A1*(B1+D4)** would multiply A1 by the sum of B1 and D4. You can use as many parenthesised entries in a formula as you like.

# Making the maths easier with functions

Although all formulas involve typing to some degree, there are ways to minimise the amount of keyboard bashing you've got to do. Typing **=A1+A2**, as in the example above, isn't too painful, but what if you had entries stretching down to A38 that needed to be added together? All those numbers, all those + signs! For this reason, spreadsheet applications include **functions**, predefined formulas that make the whole thing a lot quicker. Some of the most used functions will be represented as buttons on the toolbar; other more exotic functions will be selected from a dialog such as Microsoft Excel's 'Function Wizard'.

The most commonly used function is **SUM**, which adds together the contents of cells making it unnecessary to enter + signs. You can use the SUM function by typing **=sum** in an empty cell, or by clicking the toolbar button marked $\boxed{\Sigma}$, and then selecting the cells you want to add together. Here are a few examples:

▶ To add together A1 to A38, type **=sum(a1:a38)** and press **Enter**. You must enter the parentheses, and make sure you don't enter any spaces. Sets of sequential cells like this are referred to as a **range**. A range can cover multiple columns and rows – for example, the range **(a1:c16)** would cover A1 to A16, B1 to B16 and C1 to C16, a total of 48 cells. To select this range, you'd click in A1 and drag the pointer diagonally to C16.

## Colonic irritation

Save yourself the Shift key hassle of typing in the separating colon – you can usually use a dot instead and the software will understand what you mean and convert it to a colon for you automatically.

▶ Another way to total A1 to A38 with no typing at all is to click the $\Sigma$ button, click in cell A1 and drag the pointer down to A38 to highlight all these cells (although A1 will remain un-highlighted) then press **Enter**.

▶ To total cells scattered all over your spreadsheet, such as A3, C19, B7 and D11, click the $\Sigma$ button, then hold **Ctrl** and click each of these cells in turn. After clicking the last one you want to select, release **Ctrl** and press **Enter**.

▶ To total the entire contents of a row or column, click the $\Sigma$ button then click on the header button for that row or column. Once again, you can select multiple headers in this way if you hold **Ctrl** as you click each one.

## Avoid circular references

If you total an entire row or column by clicking the header button, make sure the cell into which you're entering the formula isn't in the same row or column: it will try to add itself to the calculation and end up going around in circles (known as a **circular reference**).

# A spreadsheet example

The screenshot below shows the quarterly income generated by two sales teams, and the expenses incurred by each team over the year. Rows 8 to 11 contain some of the calculations you might want to make from data such as this. Let's look at the formulas and functions you should enter to arrive at these results.

|  | A | B | C | D |
|---|---|---|---|---|
| | D11 | ▼ | =SUM(B8:C8) | |
| | | **Sales Team 1** | **Sales Team 2** | |
| **1** | | Sales Team 1 | Sales Team 2 | |
| **2** | 1st Quarter Income | 50,000 | 62,000 | |
| **3** | 2nd Quarter Income | 45,000 | 75,000 | |
| **4** | 3rd Quarter Income | 65,000 | 40,000 | |
| **5** | 4th Quarter Income | 30,000 | 37,000 | |
| **6** | Expenses | 28,000 | 36,000 | |
| **7** | | | | |
| **8** | Total Income | 190,000 | 214,000 | |
| **9** | Total less Expenses | 162,000 | 178,000 | |
| **10** | Average per Quarter | 47,500 | 53,500 | |
| **11** | Total Company Income | | | 404,000 |
| **12** | | | | |

▶ Typical spreadsheet data and calculations.

▶ To calculate the **Total Income** for Team 1 in B8, use the function **=sum(b2:b5)**. The total income for Team 2 in C8 would be calculated with **=sum(c2:c5)**.

▶ Calculate the **Total less Expenses** for Team 1 in B9 using the formula **=b8-b6**. To do the same for Team 2 in C9, you'd type **=c8-c6**.

▶ You could calculate the **Average per Quarter** of Team 1 (cell B10) with the formula **=(b2+b3+b4+b5)/4**, but you should have a function that does this more easily: type **=average(b2:b5)**. For Team 2 in C10, enter **=average(c2:c5)**.

▶ The **Total Company Income** in D11 is calculated with the function **=sum(b8:c8)**.

# Defining ranges for quick reference

Entering SUM functions in the example above is pretty easy – there are only two sales teams and the data is broken down into quarters. However imagine what the spreadsheet would look like if you had 30 teams and you were tracking their performance weekly – 30 columns by 52 rows of data!

To set up calculations based upon each team's performance in particular months would involve a lot of careful typing or mouse-dragging to enter the correct ranges.

To make it easier and quicker to work with large amounts of data, spreadsheet applications allow you to assign a name to a bunch of cells you've selected in advance (look for the **Name** entry on the **Insert** or **Range** menu). For example, you might select the cells relating to Team 1's sales in March and assign them the name **T1Mar**. You can then type this name into your formulas and functions rather than having to work with individual cells.

## Keep track of range names

BY THE WAY

For this to be useful you need to keep the names short – it is supposed to be a timesaver after all – and these names might not be easy to understand next time you look at your spreadsheet. Consider using a separate worksheet as a reference by typing in the names you've defined and an explanation of what data they refer to.

# Adding colours, formatting and graphics

Although the spreadsheets you create are obviously supposed to be functional, spreadsheet applications include formatting facilities to make them look more attractive than just a plain grid of black text. In fact, formatting *adds* to a worksheet's functionality – for example, if all the cells containing the results of calculations are in bold type, or have a coloured border around them, you can find the information that matters a lot faster. You'll find all the formatting options in dialogs reached from a **Format** or **Style** menu, but some of the more common features will usually be gathered together as buttons on a toolbar.

Let's start with a quickfire list of the cell-formatting options you can use. These are applied to the selected cell or cells. To increase the font size of several cells, for example, there's no need to format each cell individually – drag over the range with the pointer, or click all the cells you want to change while holding **Ctrl**.

217

**Text formatting**. You have similar text-formatting options to those found in a word-processor. You can change the font and size, underline text, or add effects such as bold, italic or colour. In addition, you can often rotate text by 90 degrees or place the characters vertically in a column.

**Cell shading**. You can change the background colour of selected cells from the default white to one of a range of more interesting colours. This can be handy for distinguishing different types of data – in a sales-related sheet, for example, you could use a different background colour for cells relating to each of the four quarters.

**Borders**. You can insert lines of various colours and styles around a cell or a group of cells. Each of the four edges of a cell can be a different colour.

**Text boxes**. It's usually possible to create a text box into which you can type a heading for the worksheet and move it wherever you want on the sheet. In this way you could create forms such as invoices with separate text boxes for your company name, company address, client details and so on.

**Graphics**. You can usually insert graphics files into spreadsheets and position them where you'd like them, perhaps to add your company's logo to the top of a form.

Apart from the standard cell-formatting features, you may have other options that can be applied to the whole sheet:

▶ You can remove the column and row header buttons from the sheet, as well as the dotted gridlines.

▶ Top-level spreadsheet applications offer a range of preset styles that include cell-shading, borders, text colours and formatting which you can apply to your worksheet once you've finished adding all the data and formulas you need.

▶ Most applications include preset templates such as invoices, purchase orders and budgets. All you need do is insert personal or company details and add your data.

## Printing cell borders

The column and row header buttons and gridlines are included just for guidance – whether you choose to hide them or not they won't be printed when you send your worksheet off to the printer. This is a good reason for putting borders around blocks of cells using the formatting tools.

# Creating charts and graphs

For sheer accuracy, numbers do it every time. But sometimes you don't really want to examine figures in a spreadsheet, no matter how accurate they are. Particularly in the case of business presentations or printed reports, it's often far more meaningful to illustrate the point you're making with a chart than to provide reams of figures. A well-chosen chart can convey the information that matters with little more than a glance.

To this end, spreadsheet applications build in features that can create charts and graphs from your worksheet (or a selected portion of it) quickly and simply. Select the cells you want included in the chart, click the dedicated button on the toolbar, drag the pointer diagonally over an empty section of the worksheet to create a box for the chart and that's about all there is to it. In Microsoft Excel the **ChartWizard** will appear and offer you simple choices about style and layout. In Lotus 1-2-3 you can double-click the chart to bring up the customisation dialog.

As long as the chart remains on the worksheet, any changes to the data within the cells will be reflected by the chart. In the same way, as the values in the cells increase, the chart will automatically increase its scale so that none can 'go off the end'.

# Choosing a spreadsheet

The undoubted king of spreadsheets, in terms of popularity and number of users, is **Microsoft Excel**, which has become the spreadsheet standard in corporate computing. Although most users will barely scratch the surface of its capabilities, it's as easy to work with as many 'lighter' applications. Its two competitors are **Lotus 1-2-3** and Corel's **Quattro Pro**, which can't match Excel's market-share but still offer similar features and power.

Top-level applications such as these will need 16 MB of RAM to run at a reasonable speed, with 32 MB a better bet if you expect to run another application such as a database or word-processor alongside it. For heavy-duty use (large, formula-laden sheets) a faster-than-average processor is an advantage. A 17-inch or larger monitor will let you see more information at once, lessening the need to scroll through the window contents.

Excel, 1-2-3 and Quattro Pro are bundled in office suites **Microsoft Office**, **Lotus SmartSuite** and **Corel Office Professional** respectively (see Chapter 21). If you need two or more office-quality applications, it's worth considering the suite. All three companies mentioned here also include a spreadsheet in their integrated (Works) applications that can satisfy all your number crunching and formatting requirements without terrifying you with complex options you feel you're supposed to be using.

**18**

# DATABASES: INSTANT STORING AND SEARCHING

You've worked with databases. A phone book is a prime example: most of us keep a book of names and numbers by the phone and flick through it when we need to call someone. The principle of a database is straightforward enough – an expanding collection of information – but the difficult trick is to find the one tiny piece of information you need quickly, and this is where the computer's ability to search vast amounts of data quickly really pays dividends.

But the computer database can do much more than simple storing and searching. Want to see your phone numbers displayed in numerical order? Easy. (Though perhaps not useful, but it's *your* database!) How about a list of all the people you know aged over 35? No problem. As long as you provide the information to begin with, the database can search, sort, store and organise it in any way you choose.

# Different flavours of database

Almost any text-based application you use could be thought of as a type of database: provided it will let you save and edit files, and it has a Search or Find option, you can use it to store and retrieve information. However, your options for sorting and searching will be very limited. An application that dares to call itself a database will let you view the information you've entered in a variety of formats, and conduct searches for all the entries that meet your criteria. Databases work with information in three different ways:

**Freeform databases**. Data can be entered anywhere, and in any order rather, like a jumble of papers on a desk. When you search for particular information, the whole database will be searched for any instances of the word or number you requested.

**Flat-file databases**. The standard type of database. Information is entered in an organised way, using **field names**. As a result, you can retrieve the information in an organised way too.

**Relational databases**. The relational database still uses fields to sort particular types of information, but the application can work with multiple databases and can find and present information spanning all these databases. Many relational databases are programmable – if you understand the language you can build your own database applications tailor-made for specific information and uses. The screenshot below shows a relational database that stores information about a company's products and customers in two mini-databases. When a sale is made, details of the customer, product and price can be selected from drop-down lists read from those two databases and stored in a third database.

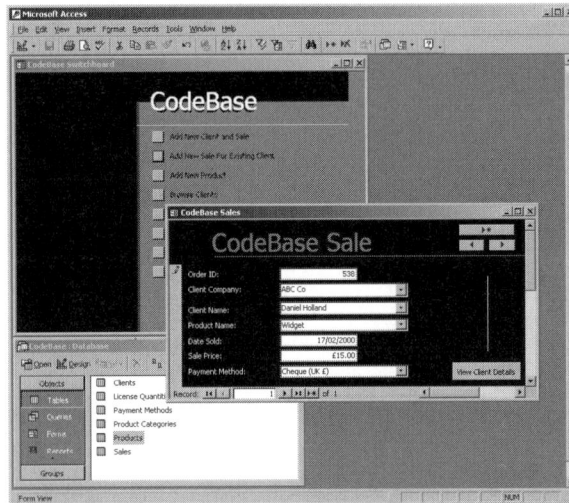

▶ A relational database in Microsoft Access.

## Files, records and fields

There are three separate elements to a database:

**Fields**. A field is a single piece of information such as someone's first name, or phone number. A field consists of a **field name** such as *Address* and a blank box into which you would type the corresponding information.

**Records**. A record is like a single card in a Rolodex or card file with multiple fields, perhaps containing all the relevant information about a single person. A single database might contain hundreds or even thousands of records.

**Files**. A database file holds a collection of records in the same way that a spreadsheet file can contain multiple tabbed worksheets.

Relational databases also use a fourth element, **Tables**. A table is a mini-database in its own right, and the Microsoft Access database shown above uses separate tables for customers, products and sales. The contents of all these tables can be linked together, so that the record for a single sale contains the customer's details taken from the first table and the product name and price taken from the second.

**GOOD QUESTION!**

## Why use multiple tables instead of storing everything in one record?

If you have to type in the customer's details from scratch every time that customer buys something, it takes a lot longer and you're likely to make mistakes every so often. Those mistakes could mean that when you search the database to find all the sales made to that customer, a few could be missing from the list.

# The first step: constructing a form

There are two distinct steps to creating a basic database. The first is to create a form that contains all the fields you need on each record, such as names, addresses, phone numbers and so on. When the form is complete, you use it as the template for entering all your information.

In recent applications you can choose from a range of preset templates designed for different uses such as employee records, music and video collections, mailing lists, recipes, and all kinds of exotica. You can then alter the field names if you need to, add and remove fields, and the first part of the job is done.

If your database application doesn't offer preset templates, or you can't find a template that works for you, you can create your own by starting from a blank sheet and adding fields to it. As you add a new field name, you'll see a box appear beside it into which you'll later type the relevant information – in most programs you'll have to specify how many characters you should be able to enter in each field.

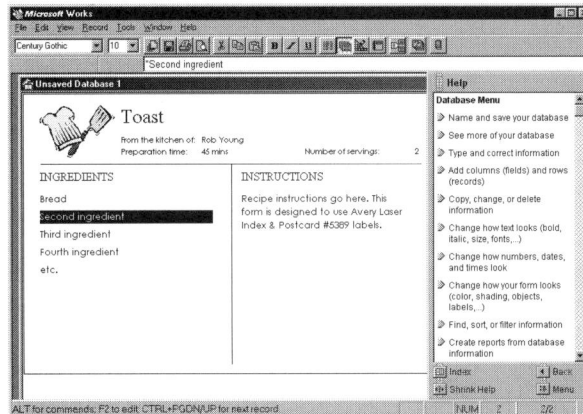

▶ A simple database record in Microsoft Works.

Split your records into as many fields as possible to make searching for information easier. For example, if you create three separate fields for day, month and year of birth it will be easy to find details of anyone born in 1964. If you want to use your database for mail merges, make sure you've split the information into the fields you'll need to enter in the template letter. For example, using separate fields for Title, First Name, Middle Initial, and Last Name will let you extract just title and last name, so that your mailshots can begin *Dear Mr Wilson* or *Dear Mrs Jones*.

You can move the fields around the sheet by dragging them to create a sensible and attractive layout, and apply various types of colour and style formatting to personalise the database. In many applications you can import pictures (perhaps to include photographs of your employees on their records), and add simple selection buttons for either/or fields such as Male/Female or CD/Tape.

## Mail merge

JARGON BUSTER

Good word-processors allow you to create a fill-in-the-blanks letter, replacing personal information like the name and address with the names of fields in a database. You can then 'merge' the database and the template together, creating personalised letters to everyone in the database.

# Filling in the blanks to create records

The second step in creating a database is to actually enter the information into your fields and build up a set of records using the template form you created. When you've typed information into one field, press **Tab** to move to the next, and so on until you've completed the first record. You can then click a button on the toolbar to add a new record and start filling the blanks in that. In most applications, the status bar at the bottom of the window will keep you informed about how many records you've created, and usually has buttons to let you step forwards and backwards from one record to the next, or jump to the first or last.

In some cases, if you already have the information entered in another type of file, you may be able to **import** it. For example, if you've been keeping a block of information in a spreadsheet, your database application may be able to lift the information straight from the spreadsheet by matching column or row headings to field names. If that doesn't work, you'll probably still be able to save some typing by dragging the text from the spreadsheet to the database.

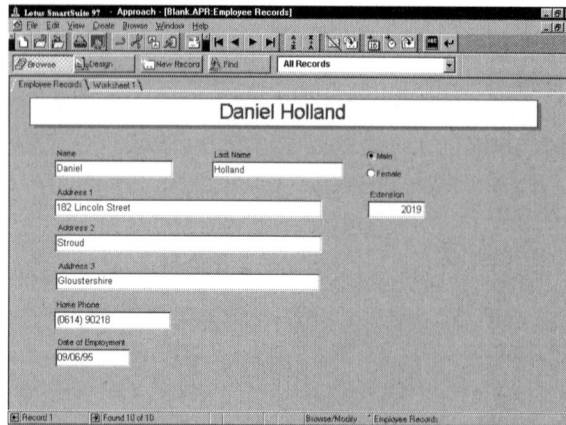

▶ A single record in **Lotus Approach**.

# Sorting records: choose your views

When you add new records to a database they remain in the order you entered them, so as you browse through the records using the buttons on the status bar you won't see any particular order to them. In fact, in some low-end applications the only way of organising records in alphabetical order is to actually *insert* them alphabetically. However, mid-to-high-end applications make this a lot easier by providing comprehensive sorting options: simply choose an alphabetical or numerical field to sort by, choose whether to view the records in ascending or descending order and the software will juggle your records around for you.

Most databases can also present the records in a list view that looks and functions very like a spreadsheet, with each field having its own column and each record being in its own row. This can be useful for viewing and comparing a large number of records at once or making quick changes to the same field on every record.

## Protection

**JARGON BUSTER**

Databases often use two types of protection (neither of which is designed to stop them having lots of little databases, in case you were wondering). **Form protection** prevents you accidentally mucking up field names and layout that you've carefully entered in your template. **Data protection** keeps the information safe that you've entered into the records themselves. Turning on one of these forms of protection is known as **locking** the form or data, and it's well worth doing even though you'll have to unlock the data every time you want to enter something new.

# Running queries to find information

One of the most common things you want to do with a database is to look at one particular record. Select the **Find** option from a menu or toolbar and you'll see a blank copy of your form layout. Type details into as many of the fields as necessary to locate the record you want. For example, if you want to see the record of an employee called John you'd type **John** in the *First Name* field; if you have several employees called John you'd fill in the *Last Name* field as well.

The database really comes into its own when you need to perform more complicated searches (known as **queries**). Instead of typing fixed entries into the fields you can use a variety of wildcards and symbols to find records that meet a number of criteria. The common wildcards ? and * can be used to replace single or multiple characters respectively (so entering **J*** in the *First Name* field would find the record of anyone called John, James, Jim or Jan; entering **J??** would find Jim or Jan). The other symbols you have available will vary according to the application you're using, but here are a few of the common ones:

| Query format | Result |
|---|---|
| <75 | Finds records with any value lower than 75 in this field. |
| >=100 | Finds records with values greater than or equal to 100 in this field. |
| 75...100 | Finds records with any value between 75 and 100 in this field. |
| Jim,Jan | Finds any records with Jim or Jan in this field. |
| Jim&Jan | Finds any records with both Jim and Jan in this field. |

## Choosing a database

At the top of the tree are the programmable databases, the list headed by **Borland Paradox** and **Microsoft Access**. Both combine power with ease of use, but unless you really need a professional-level application you'll be paying extra for features you're unlikely to use. **Access** is bundled with the more expensive Microsoft suites, **Office Professional** and **Office Premium**, but missing from the Standard and Small Business editions.

Both **Lotus Approach** and **Claris FileMaker Pro** offer similar features to the big guns, with hoards of templates and preset applications at a lower price. Both are relational (see page 222). **Approach** is included as part of **Lotus SmartSuite** (see Chapter 21).

Each of the major integrated Works applications includes a basic flat-file database suitable for the casual or less demanding user. Simple preset templates are included but querying and sorting features are usually limited.

Do you need a database at all? If you have a spreadsheet application you can create a great looking, and totally searchable, database on a worksheet. If flashy presentation doesn't matter, you could even create a free-form database by typing details into a word-processor document and using the **Find** and **Find Next** features to search for what you want. You won't be able to use advanced querying and sorting, but if you simply need to keep lists of information and find an item from them quickly, either option will let you do that with ease.

# 19

# GET ARTISTIC WITH GRAPHICS SOFTWARE

When it comes to adding artwork to text-based documents, or creating stand-alone graphics, there's very little you *can't* do on a PC. In this field of computing, more than most others, the variety of software available is immense and the features you'll find cover most points between 'incredibly basic' and 'full multimedia capabilities'. But this is also an area in which the computer can do little to automate the creation process – an expensive graphics package won't make an artist of you if there's no raw material there to start with, it'll just give you more to learn about while you're struggling! So, as a gesture of support to the artistically-challenged, before we examine graphics programs themselves, let's take a look at another way you can add attention-grabbing graphics to your documents.

## Easy art: clip art collections

One of the main funds of graphics is the **clip art** collection. 'Clip art' is a term used for pictures created by somebody else and sold (or given away!) in collections. Many office-suites and integrated applications come with their own library of clip art (sometimes termed a **gallery** in a burst of self-indulgence). The clips are usually grouped into categories such as Travel, Buildings, People, Sport and so on, to make it easier to find what you want among the hundreds or even thousands of pictures in the collection, and there's usually a bunch of utilitarian signs and symbols such as maps of the world, road signs, backgrounds, decorative borders etc.

### Yes, but is it art?

Clip art is notorious for varying in quality from bright, professional-looking drawings to ugly, smudgy black and white efforts. Make sure you're getting a quality collection before you part with hard cash. Remember they put some of their best stuff on the back of the box, so if you don't like that, it's odds-on that you'll hate the rest!

How you work with clip art will depend how it's organised: most of the many collections available on CD-ROM will have a viewer program included which loads the clips in the category you choose. When you've selected a clip, just use Copy (**Ctrl+C**) to copy it to the clipboard and Paste (**Ctrl+V**) to paste it into your document. Applications such as Microsoft Office and Microsoft Works come with their own clip art collection and viewer to which you can add your own images to keep all your graphics and multimedia files catalogued.

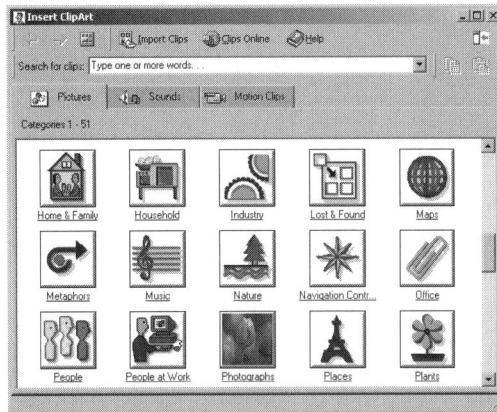

▶ Cataloguing and inserting clip art with Microsoft's clip art gallery.

# Do-it-yourself graphics software

If you prefer to create your own designs and images, there are inordinate amounts of software available, ranging from full-blown graphics suites and applications, to smaller editing and retouching utilities, plus additional tools and filters to create effects. These fall loosely into two categories: **paint** programs and **draw** programs.

**GOOD QUESTION!**

## What's the difference between bitmap and vector graphics?

Imagine that you create an image by drawing different pieces of the picture on to clear plastic, and then put all those layers into a pile to see the entire picture. That's vector graphics, and it has the benefit that you can remove a layer, or reshape and resize it (though that doesn't quite fit our metaphor). With bitmaps you have just one layer, so individual sections can't just be removed – you have to paint over anything you did wrong. Although paint programs work with bitmaps, some do allow you to create a picture in layers and flatten them to a single layer when you're done.

## Paint programs

Let's start with the simplest. The Windows operating systems give you **Paint**, a basic example of a paint program with tools for drawing lines, squares, circles and freehand shapes, choosing colours, and for erasing any part of the picture that didn't turn out quite right. As a scratch-pad for ideas or uncomplicated diagrams, Windows Paint does the job, but as a serious graphics application it doesn't come close. Professional-level applications can cost hundreds of pounds, but at the cheaper end of the market you'll still get all the tools you need to create some stunning results.

One example is the massively popular Paint Shop Pro from JASC (shown in the next screenshot). Like most graphics applications, Paint Shop Pro lets you edit multiple images at once and save them in any popular graphics format. You'll find similar drawing tools to those in Windows Paint, but with far greater capabilities: lines and joins can be smudged and blurred, irregular shaped areas can be selected for editing or copying, and a range of colour tools make it easy to swap colours in an image, apply tints, or adjust brightness and contrast.

▶ Comprehensive drawing tools and a range of special effects in Paint Shop Pro.

Although almost any graphics application will have scanner support, letting you scan an image straight into the program from a magazine or brochure, more expensive applications such as Adobe PhotoShop and Corel Photo-Paint are designed for photo editing and manipulation, and often include an exotic collection of tools for retouching scanned photographs. Most will also have a range of built-in filters that let you apply weird treatments to photographs or to your own artwork.

## Text as a picture

Although you can add text to your creations in paint programs, the text size will not necessarily be identical to the same TrueType font used in a word-processor because the program has to convert the text to a bitmap. For the same reason, once the text is there it's just another part of the picture and can't be edited – the best you can do is to delete and retype it.

## Draw programs

Rather than working with photographs and creating photo-quality artwork, draw programs offer a slightly different method of creating drawings and pictures from scratch. Although you can create similar results in a paint application, draw programs offer much greater editing flexibility and are more forgiving to work with.

Draw programs load, create and save **vector graphics** formats. Each element of the picture is a separate shape, such as a circle, square or freehand outline which can then be filled with colour, and each of these shapes remains an individual object. You can click on any object and drag it somewhere else, rotate it, or change its shape, without affecting any other part of the picture. The result of this object-oriented approach is that you can build complex pictures from the ground up by layering one object over another.

Because draw programs work with vector graphics formats, any object in the picture can be resized using the **grab handles** that appear when you click the object. Here are a few of the features you'll find in a draw program:

**Send Forwards/Backwards**. Because pictures are created by layering smaller sections, it's sometimes necessary to move items in front of or behind other items. These options are usually coupled with *Send To Back* and *Bring To Front*.

**Grids and snapping**. To help in precise drawing you can add a grid overlay to the 'canvas'. Snapping is a useful option to ensure that objects (especially squares) are perfectly aligned with each other by forcing them to jump on to the nearest gridline as if magnetised.

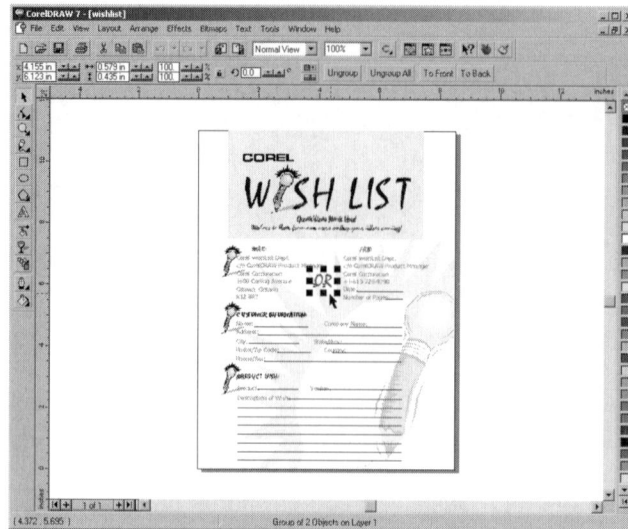

▶ The popular and powerful **CorelDRAW**.

**Full text editing**. Because these are not bitmapped graphics, text can be entered and edited freely as if in a word-processor. Some draw programs even go so far as to include proofing tools for text such as a spellchecker and thesaurus!

**Object grouping or linking**. You can create groups of two or more objects in a drawing that will respond as a single object when cut, copied, moved or resized. This is usually done using a selection tool to draw a dotted box around the objects you want to select, but another option is often to hold **Shift** and click each object separately.

# Graphics filters and effects

Together with complete graphics creation applications, you can also find smaller utilities aimed at creating advanced effects or just having fun. A popular example is Kai's Power Goo, which lets you do unwholesome things to photos with tools such as smear, smudge and bulge, or even combine pieces of one photo in another. The results can be saved as a single image, or you can create multiple cartoon-like 'frames', and save the finished masterpiece in .avi video format.

For the more serious graphic designer, most graphics applications support **filters**. These are software add-ons, available from a variety of companies, that add extra processing and effect options to your application. Once installed, you can select the filter you want to use from a drop-down menu. Popular filter collections are Alien Skin's Black Box and Kai's Power Tools.

One final oddity in the field of graphics is **WordArt,** which lets you do weird things to perfectly innocent text while it's looking the other way. WordArt is a Microsoft applet that comes bundled with both Office and Works, although **Serif TypePlus** has similar capabilities as a stand-alone program.

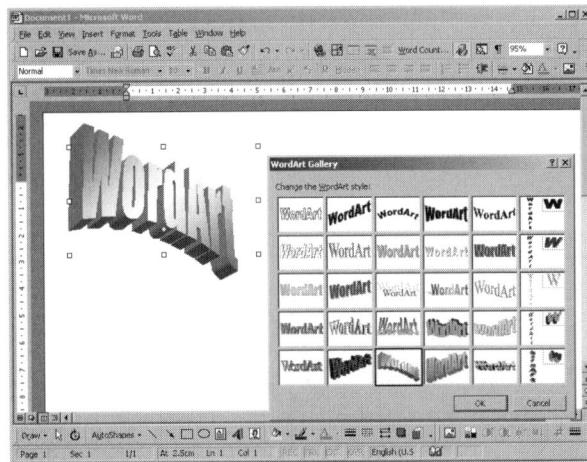

▶ Create stylish banners and headings in Microsoft Office documents with WordArt.

You can insert a piece of WordArt into a document by selecting **Insert/Object** and choosing **Microsoft WordArt** from the list. A new toolbar will appear together with a small text box. Type your chosen text into the box and then start getting creative. From the drop-down lists you can choose a font and size, and apply one of various shapes to the text. Toolbar buttons let you add outlines and shadows to the characters, stretch or compress them, tilt or swivel them, and add coloured or patterned fills.

# Choosing a graphics application

The market leader in draw programs is **CorelDRAW**, though to refer to it simply as a draw program is a bit unfair – in addition to its drawing facilities, CorelDRAW can handle 3D image rendering, 3D animation, multimedia presentations, frame-by-frame video editing, and includes sound and animation clips together with a 25 000-strong clip art library and the excellent Corel Photo-Paint. If you're serious about computer graphics, this package is worth its serious price-tag. Giving CorelDRAW a run for its money are Macromedia Freehand and Adobe Illustrator.

At the cheaper end of the draw programs market are **Serif DrawPlus** and the modestly-titled but fuller-featured **Corel Graphics Pack**.

JASC's **Paint Shop Pro** is a hugely popular paint program, offering advanced editing and creation tools with a good array of filters and special effects. **Adobe PhotoDeluxe** is slightly less versatile, but friendlier for the beginner. In the higher price bracket, **Adobe PhotoShop** is widely regarded as the 'must-have' graphics application, although **Corel Photo-Paint** may be a more beginner-friendly way to get your hands on similar features.

To create and work with images of any format and enjoy gratifying results you'll need a display that can handle at least 256 colours, but if you're working with photographs or you want to create photo-realistic artwork you'll need a 64 000 colour (**high colour**) or 16.7 million-colour (**true colour**) display. For intensive work with large graphics, 96 MB of RAM should be regarded as an absolute minimum, with 128 MB being a better bet.

**20**

# DOCUMENT PUBLISHING WITH DTP

Desktop publishing packages (or DTP in geek-speak) are the applications that bring you newspapers, magazines, books, brochures, flyers and so on, the common link being an amalgamation of text and graphics in the same document. The main curiosity of DTP software is that text editing and image editing facilities are usually poor. This isn't as paradoxical as it seems; rather than aiming to replace the word-processor and paint or draw program, DTP's role is to act as a receptacle for previously-composed text and graphics, and to provide the necessary tools for final formatting and layout to construct a finished document.

# Getting started with desktop publishing

The first move is to write your text. This can be done in a simple text editor such as **Notepad**, but make sure you turn on the Word Wrap option – if you don't, you'll be tempted to insert carriage-returns at the end of a line to keep from scrolling too far across the screen, and these will appear as separate paragraphs in the DTP document. Preferably, use a more advanced word-processor with a spellchecker so you can be sure the text is correct before you copy it to the DTP page, but save it in plain text (.txt) format.

## Story

Text you import into a DTP document is referred to as a **story**, and a document can contain as many different stories as you want, just like a newspaper or magazine.

If you need to create graphics (other than basic lines, rectangles and circles), do these too but make sure you save them in a format your DTP program can open.

## Adding your text to the page

The big difference between DTP programs and basic word-processors is that text and graphics are placed in **frames**, rectangular dotted-line boxes. Text requires a text frame, pictures need a graphics frame. The tools for drawing these frames are frequently used so you'll normally find buttons for them on the toolbar.

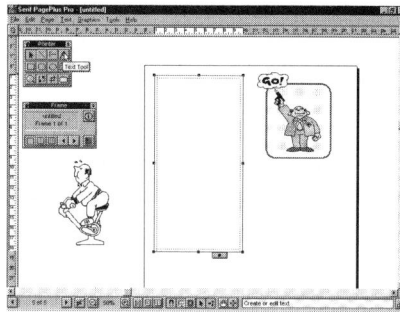

▶ A text frame waiting for text, and a graphic waiting on the paste-up board.

To import your text, create a text frame like the one shown in the screenshot above. You can create a single-column frame or choose to split the frame into two or more columns across the page and the text will flow from one to the next automatically. Then select the **Import Text** command and find and double-click on the text file you created. If your frame isn't large enough to hold all the text, move the pointer on to one of the grab-handles and stretch it.

If you're importing an especially long story, create a number of text frames and link them together using the **Link** option. When frames are 'linked', the software knows it can use these frames for that story and will automatically **flow** the text from one frame to the next. If you have only one small frame and a very long story, it'll seem that most of your text has vanished until you create more frames!

## Paste-up board

**JARGON BUSTER**

When you look at your DTP document in full-page view, the space you see around the document is known as the **paste-up board**. You can use this space to store imported stories and graphics to help you keep track of what you want to add, and drag them into the document itself when you're ready for them. In the same way, you can drag sections out of the document and on to the paste-up board if you want to do a rethink on layout.

As it appears in your document, the text looks pretty dull (and in full-page mode it looks tiny too). The next step is to zoom in so that you can read the text comfortably and to start formatting. The formatting options are similar to those found in any word-processor – fonts, sizes, colours, bold, italic and so on – but there are fewer shortcuts to selecting text. Although it's possible to type *all* your text directly into the document, it's this lack of flexibility that makes the import method preferable. In some DTP applications, you can double-click a block of text and format it in a fairly normal-looking window instead.

## Importing pictures and graphics

In a similar way to importing text, you'll usually have an **Import Picture** option on the File menu for bringing in graphics. First you'll have to create a graphics frame for the image: in some applications the imported image will expand or contract to fit the size of the frame and look pretty distorted until you resize it; in others the box will be automatically resized to fit the image.

The idea of having separate text- and graphics frames is a good one: you can move a graphics frame on to a text frame and (in most applications) the text will shift out of the way automatically and skirt around it, as in the next screenshot. This is known as **text-wrapping**; in some cases the application will handle it automatically, but in others you'll have to make the settings yourself for each graphic separately. You can usually choose whether the text surrounding the picture should form a square edge to it or follow its contours, and you may have extra options to let you choose how much space there should be between picture and text.

JARGON
BUSTER

## Serif and sans-serif fonts

In a serif font, the characters have small hooks or ornaments (called **serifs**) which add a slightly informal air; this sort of font is commonly used for block text. Sans-serif fonts don't have these ornamental flourishes and are used most in headings.

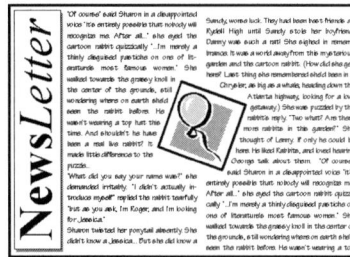

▶ Some of the formatting options available, including text-wrapping and drop-shadows.

Drawing tools are usually basic, but you have the full range of colours to work with (including 'Clear' to make text or a graphic object transparent) and a few DTP applications support the Pantone colour chart for precise colour-matching.

# Hints for successful DTP-ing

When laying out your document it's important to keep your eye on the ball. Although you can do all kinds of clever stuff with rotated text, coloured boxes and frame outlines, text-wrapping and so on, a page overloaded with interesting effects becomes very difficult to read. In other words, less is more! That being said, here are a few tips and effects you can use:

▶ Place headlines or pictures in a box with a thin black outline and add a **drop-shadow** to it by placing a grey rectangle underneath it shifted slightly downwards and to the right or left. This has the effect of pushing the text box towards the reader.

▶ Add shadows to text by making a copy of the text frame, changing the colour of the copied text and placing this behind the original but slightly off-centre.

▶ Place a small amount of justified text inside a circle (created using the circle tool) and use text-wrapping to wrap it to the inside edges of the circle. You can heighten the effect by making the circle and its border clear so that all you can see is the text itself.

▶ Choose your fonts carefully and try to stick with a maximum of four in a document. A serif font such as Times New Roman makes an easy-to-read body-text typeface; headlines often work well with sans-serif fonts such as Arial, but a more fancy font adds an informal air if it doesn't appear too often on the page.

▶ In brochures intended to sell a product, rotate pictures of the product a few degrees (between 6 and 10 degrees should do it) rather than keeping them square on the page to make them look friendlier and more appealing. Use the Crop tool to remove any large expanses of distracting background, and use a paint or draw program to improve photographs (by adding the clear blue sky always found in holiday brochures, for example).

▶ If you want each page to follow a similar layout (for example, four columns with your company logo at the top), you can create a **master page** with each item in position which will be used as a template for each document page to save you repeating all the same moves for each page.

## Leading and kerning

**JARGON BUSTER**

Two typesetting terms that pop up a lot in DTP. **Kerning** is adjusting the space between two characters. This is often used in headlines to tidy up irregular-looking spacing, but you can use it to great effect to give a headline or subhead a much tighter look. **Leading** (pronounced 'ledding') is the vertical distance between lines of type (measured in points).

## DTP vs word-processor

Modern top-end word-processors are becoming more like desktop publishing programs all the time: you can flow text into columns, create drawings, import graphics, place pictures or text into frames and put the frames anywhere on the page, and much more. So why not just use a word-processor instead?

In fact, there's no reason why you shouldn't. If you've already got an application like Microsoft Word or Lotus WordPro that includes drawing tools and frames, you can create remarkably sophisticated documents by placing everything into frames and moving these where you want them. Here are a few of the major differences and additions you'll find in a dedicated DTP program – if these don't matter to you, and you've got a good word-processor already, stick with it.

**Grouping**. Once you've placed multiple frames, pictures and objects where you want them and juggled around with the *Send To Back* and *Bring To Front* commands to layer everything correctly, you can group these items together as one to ensure you can't move one frame accidentally and ruin all your careful work. Word-processors treat frames and drawing objects as separate items.

**Snapping**. Precise alignment of frames is made simple with **snapping**, which forces the edges of a frame to jump to the nearest gridlines. You may even be able to type in exact co-ordinates and sizes for each frame.

**Stacking**. You can stack as many frames and objects as you like one on top of the other, regardless of their contents. A word-processor will give you little choice about how different items can be stacked and which will remain visible.

**Crop and rotate**. DTP programs allow you to crop pictures – chop out unnecessarily large areas of background and so on – and to rotate frames a degree at a time. (Watch out for programs that allow rotation only in huge 90-degree increments!)

# Choosing a DTP application

At the professional end of the market, you'll find **Quark Xpress** on most publishers' computers. Slightly cheaper is **Adobe PageMaker**.

There's a huge price difference between the best and the rest: in the more affordable price-bracket are **Microsoft Publisher**, and the amazingly full-featured **Serif PagePlus**. The **Serif Publishing Suite** bundles PagePlus with DrawPlus and TypePlus (mentioned in the previous chapter) as a self-contained graphics and DTP package and is well worth a look.

Successful DTP is harder to achieve on a standard 15-inch monitor: ideally you want as much as possible of your page to be visible while you work on it, without zooming out so far as to make the text unreadable. If DTP is your thing, regard a 17-inch monitor as the minimum and a 20-inch monitor as a safer bet.

As with any graphics-related application, the more RAM you have the better. You could find the going a bit slow with less than 48 MB.

# OFFICE SUITES: THE ALL-IN-ONE SOLUTION

After reading the last few chapters you might have built up a list of two or three or more types of software you'd like. If so, this is a good time to pause and look at another option – the works application or office suite. Instead of buying a bundle of separate software titles, you might be able to buy a single package that contains everything you need at a significantly lower price.

## What's an office suite?

Office suites are often recognisable by the use of the word 'Office' somewhere in their names (and an extra digit in their prices!). These are collections of fully-featured applications, all of which are also available separately. The main selling point of office suites is that the total package costs a lot less than you'd spend buying each item individually; but a few extras are thrown in for good measure. Office suites have added features that help you organise your work, share information between the different programs, and start or switch between each application easily.

A **works application** is a slightly different idea: rather than being a collection of separate programs bundled together, this is a single program built to fill a variety of roles. The works application contains the same basic ingredients as an office suite – a word-processor, spreadsheet and database – but they're not as feature packed, and should be easier to understand and use.

## Office suite pros and cons

The main plus-point in buying an office suite is price: if you need two or more professional-level applications you'll probably save money by buying the suite and gain another couple of applications and a few handy extras into the bargain. The second benefit is that each application will be carefully integrated – throughout the suite, the menus and toolbars follow a common layout to make the learning easier. This integration also helps you work with several applications at once. For example, you can quickly import names and addresses from the database into the word-processor to create personalised letters from a template, or copy a chart from the spreadsheet into a business presentation.

On the negative side, office suites are huge beasts: a typical installation will take over 150 MB of hard-disk space, and the power of these applications requires a lot more resources than a Works package. If you only need one top-level application (such as a good word-processor) and you can make do with simpler spreadsheet and database features there's no point in wasting money and hard-disk space on the full suite.

# Works applications pros and cons

There are several simple reasons for the popularity of works software: the package is compact, light on disk-space and resource requirements, easy to use and gives great-looking results. Like the office suites, each element is tightly integrated with all the others and uses common tools and menus. Although a works package is a single application, it has a multiple document interface (MDI) so it's easy to have a database open in one window and a spreadsheet in another to compare or copy information between them. Finally, of course, there's the price: integrated applications are a good deal cheaper than office suites. However, with the price of office suites dropping all the time, the number of good works packages available has dropped to just one: Microsoft Works.

## Start small

If you buy the works software and later decide you need the office suite, you should be able to buy the **upgrade** version rather than paying full price, so you're usually not risking much money by picking the smaller of the two to learn with.

There's not much to be said against works packages – because they're cheap it's not really a disaster if you decide you need something more powerful six months later. Indeed, you may decide you just need to buy a more powerful word-processor, but continue to use the other elements of the works application. However, you may want to consider the issue of compatibility: if you use an office suite at work, you won't usually be able to open the same files in your integrated application.

# Which office suite?

The two big players in the office suite league are **Microsoft Office** and **Lotus SmartSuite**. In both cases, the applications provided are powerful and feature-filled, but generally are easy to understand and use. Here's a closer look at what each contains.

## Microsoft Office

This is the top-selling office suite, which helps to explain why most of its constituent applications also hold the top spot. The current version, Office 2000, is available in four flavours: **Small Business Edition**, **Standard**, **Professional**, and **Premium** aimed at different types of user with varying requirements.

All four editions contain **Word** (word-processor), **Excel** (spreadsheet), and **Outlook** (personal organiser). To these essentials, the Small Business Edition adds the **Publisher** desktop publishing package and **Small Business Tools** for preparing financial reports, forecasts and accounts, and the Standard edition adds **PowerPoint** (business presentations). The Professional edition also includes PowerPoint and Publisher, and adds **Access** (programmable, relational database). Finally, the Premium edition includes all the above, along with **FrontPage** (designing and managing Web sites) and a high-level graphics application named **PhotoDraw**.

▶ The Microsoft Office shortcut bar.

Each program can be accessed from the **Shortcut Bar** (shown in the above screenshot) if you choose to install it. This docks at one edge of the screen and works just like the Windows Taskbar, or can act like an ordinary window and be dragged to wherever you want it. You can add your own shortcuts to any program or folder as buttons on the bar, and choose whether the bar should slide out of the way when not in use. You can also install **Camcorder**, a clever little program that can record all your mouse movements, key-presses and screen actions and play them back as a movie, ideal for creating software tutorials or demonstrations.

You'll need upwards of 150 MB of disk-space to install the Standard version, and a minimum of 64 MB RAM. To work with two or more Office applications at the same time with reasonable speed, 128 MB RAM is a more realistic target.

▶ **Lotus SmartSuite**'s SmartCenter bar with drop-down 'drawers'.

## Lotus SmartSuite

SmartSuite Millennium comes in one all-in version. Applications consist of **WordPro** (word-processor), **1-2-3** (spreadsheet), **Freelance** (business presentations), **Organizer** (personal organiser), **FastSite** (Web site design), and **Approach** (relational, programmable database). In a similar vein to Microsoft's Camcorder, SmartSuite includes **ScreenCam**, along with a separate ScreenCam Player.

SmartSuite has a similar shortcut bar to that used by Office, which follows a file-cabinet metaphor: various 'drawers' open to display shortcuts to applications, shortcuts to documents, help-file icons, an address book and an appointments calendar. Another quick-start option is **SuiteStart** which places icons for each application in the tray on the Windows taskbar, though it may take you some time to learn which is which!

▶ The optional SuiteStart icons give you one-click access to the Lotus programs.

251

A typical installation of Lotus SmartSuite will take around 135 MB of hard-disk space, although there's a useful option to run the applications you need from the CD-ROM rather than installing them on your hard-disk, if you don't mind them starting and running a little more slowly than they should. As with Microsoft Office, 64 MB RAM is a recommended minimum for anything other than occasional use.

## Microsoft Works

When you first start Works, you're presented with a simple dialog from which you can choose the type of document you want to open or create. Works includes a word-processor, spreadsheet, calendar and flat-file database, all of which are easy to use and give good results.

Like all office suites and integrated applications, Works offers a huge collection of templates that you can use to get started on particular types of document, or you can use a **WorksWizard** which asks you simple questions about the design, layout and content of the document you want to create and puts it together for you. You also get several extra applets including **WordArt** and **Draw** to add graphics to your documents.

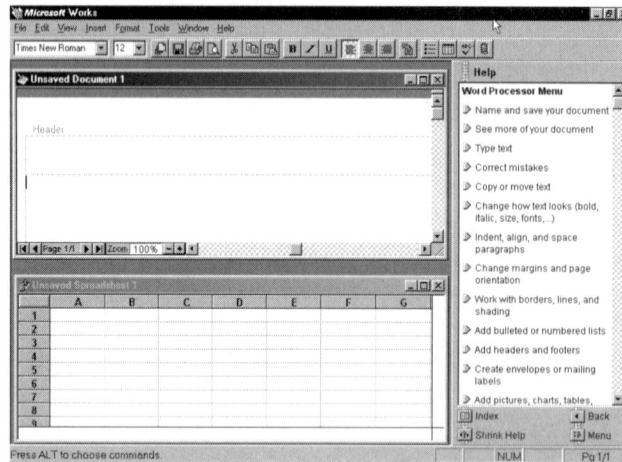

▶ Works lets you view and create different types of document in a single window, with one-click links to the things you'll want to do most often.

Just to complicate things, the current edition of Microsoft Works comes in three editions. Along with the basic **Works 2000**, there's the catchily-titled **Works Suite Basic 2000** which adds copies of Microsoft Money and the Microsoft Encarta multimedia encyclopaedia, and **Works Suite 2000**, with the same two extras plus Microsoft Word, Microsoft Home Publishing and a photo-editing program called Picture-It! Express.

# Choosing office suites and works software

If you need two or more powerful, full-featured applications, an office suite is a sensible and cost-effective choice. It'll take a large chunk of disk-space, but if these are the applications you'll spend most of your time using, this shouldn't matter too much. Make sure you've got a bare minimum of 64 MB RAM to keep things moving at a reasonable speed.

**Microsoft Office** is the clear winner in terms of popularity and sales, and it's neat, fast and easy to use. However if you need a database you'll have to pay extra for the Professional or the Premium edition (or buy one separately). **Lotus SmartSuite** grabs extra points for including a high-quality database as standard, and one that's easier to use than Microsoft Access. Another contender is **Corel WordPerfect Office**, available in Standard, Professional and Voice-Powered editions. As with the Microsoft offering, you'll need the Professional edition if you want a database, but this really consists of the Standard edition plus several products from other companies. Finally, Corel offers the **WordPerfect Family Pack**, consisting of a word-processor, spreadsheet and two graphics applications at a price similar to that of a works application.

Works applications are thin on the ground these days, and Microsoft really have it all sewn up with **Microsoft Works**. The main question is, which edition of Works do you need. An extra benefit of Works is that it gets you on to the upgrade path for Microsoft Office if you have a sneaky feeling that's what you might need at some point in the future.

# QUICKFIRE SOFTWARE

Over the last few chapters we've looked at some of the most common types of software found on the average computer. But in the PC world, as elsewhere, if there's a market for it, there's a product to meet that market – the list of software categories is almost endless. So, moving into quickfire mode, here's a brief rundown of some of the other tricks your PC can do if you feed it the right software!

# Personal organisers

The software personal organiser is the computerised version of those little leather binders you can carry around that contain diaries, addresses, notes and so on. The big differences are that the software version is usually cheaper (no leather involved!) and isn't as easy to lose. In geek-speak, the software organiser is known as a **PIM**, short for personal information manager. One of the best (and coincidentally the cheapest) is Starfish Software's **Sidekick**, closely followed by **Lotus Organizer** (included in the SmartSuite office package) which follows the FiloFax metaphor right down to animated page-turning.

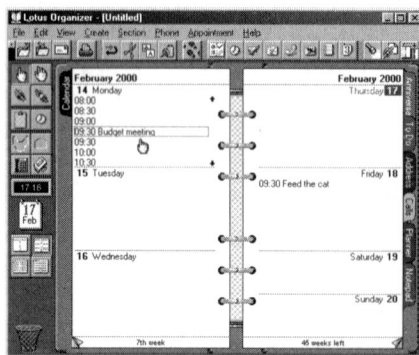

▶ Separate tabbed book-sections in **Lotus Organizer**.

The features you'll find in these programs include an appointments diary, address and phone book, To Do lists with priority planning, year planners, and automatic phone dialling. You can also set an alarm to sound at a pre-set interval before appointments to remind you, and print out your appointments in organiser-sized pages to carry around in your leather-bound version.

Microsoft produces Outlook, which it inexplicably calls a DIM (for desktop information manager). Leaving aside the obvious 'dim outlook' references, the program itself is a powerful combination of contact manager, appointments calendar and reminder system, task manager, and email/fax utility. Outlook is available as a stand-alone program, but it also comes bundled with Microsoft Office and integrates well with other Office applications to help you organise your projects and files.

# Accounts software

For simple accounting, just adding up lists of income and expenditure, a spreadsheet program can do just fine. However if you have monthly and quarterly standing orders, income paid directly into your bank account, loans and other complications, it's easy to lose track of your finances between one statement and the next. Accounts packages allow you to enter all these details once and will then keep the totals balanced for you automatically – your only job is to remember to enter everything that's necessary.

The two biggest players in accounts software are Intuit's **Quicken** and **Microsoft Money**. Both are cheap, and can track a variety of bank, building society and credit card accounts, as well as loans and investments. For professional accounting, one of the most popular programs is **Sage Instant Accounting**.

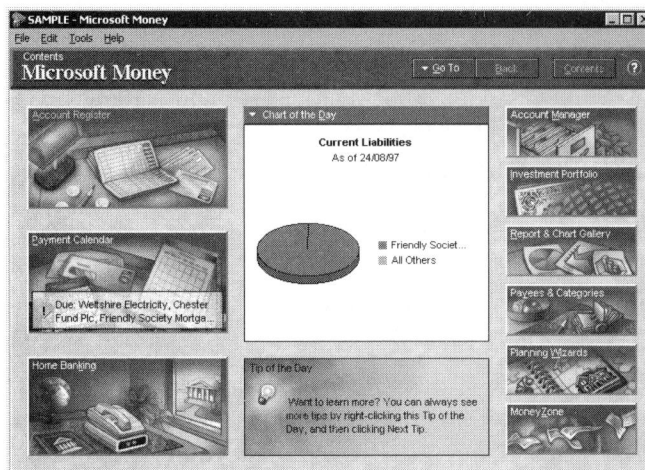

▶ Account management and online banking with **Microsoft Money**.

One major advantage of Microsoft Money is **online banking**. If you have a modem and your bank provides this service, you can simply dial-in at any time of the day or night and pay bills, check your balance, download a statement, and transfer funds from one account to another.

## File compression utilities

Once in a while you'll come across files with the extension **.zip**, particularly if you download files from the Internet. These are known as **archives**, and they contain one or more files compressed to take up less space (and thus download faster). There are actually several other types of archive, less frequently encountered, with the extensions **.cab**, **.lzh**, **.arj** **.tar** and **.arc** but each works in a similar way.

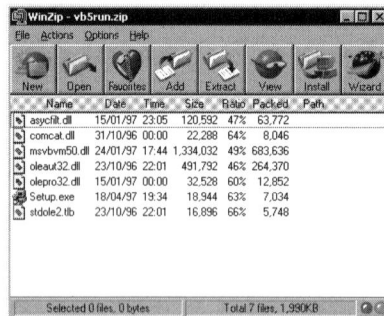

▶ **WinZip** displaying the contents of an archive.

In order to decompress (**extract**) the files from an archive, or create new archives you need a program capable of working with these files, and the undoubted leader in this field is the shareware utility **WinZip** from Nico Mak Computing (shown in the screenshot above). This can create and open many different types of archive and integrates itself neatly with Windows for single-click archive extraction.

## Multimedia titles

Over the last decade or so, PCs have been transformed from dull office machines to all-singing, all-dancing entertainment centres: they've gained sound capabilities, incredible graphics and video, and high-capacity CD-ROM or DVD-ROM drives. With the arrival of these multimedia talents, a new type of software began to appear that took advantage of them. These titles are supplied on one or more CD-ROMs or a single DVD-ROM, and (unless you have a huge hard-disk) you usually install a small number of files and then insert a CD into the drive whenever you need to use the software.

The most popular type of multimedia title is the encyclopaedia, and as usual it's Microsoft that holds the top spot in the popularity stakes with **Encarta**. There are many others available, including **Hutchinson's** and **Compton's**, but they all have one thing in common: alongside the textual articles, there are pictures, sounds, animations and movie footage to help illustrate the topic.

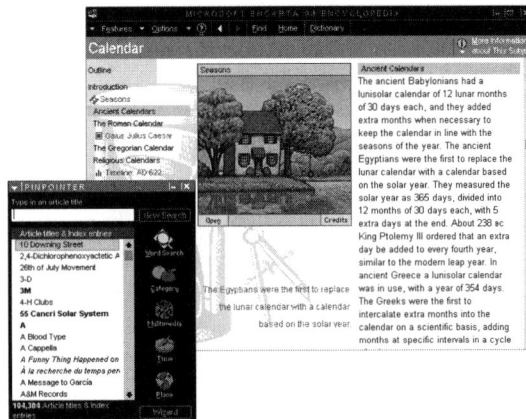

▶ The massively popular Microsoft **Encarta** encyclopaedia.

You can find topics quickly by typing in descriptive words, searching through an alphabetical list, or selecting a category to learn more about, such as Sports, History or Performing Arts. Encarta also includes an interactive atlas that lets you zoom in and out of continents, countries and cities, and a timeline allowing you to find topics covering particular periods in history.

# CD-writing software

Copying files from your hard-disk to a floppy-disk is something the PC has been equipped to do for years, but the arrival of recordable CDs has caught it by surprise, and specialised software is needed for the job. Any CD-R or CD-RW drive you buy will come bundled with the software you need to use it, and it's likely to be the top name in CD writing, **Adaptec Easy CD Creator**, shown in the next screenshot.

## Wizard

A wizard is a type of dialog box you'll see a lot in Windows. It gathers information from you in a friendly step-by-step way using a series of pages. After answering each question, you click the **Next** button to advance through the steps until the job is done. At any point, you can click the **Back** button to change an answer.

When you start CD Creator, you have a choice between creating a data CD (a CD containing computer files for reading on another computer) or a music CD that can be played in any audio CD player. If you choose to follow it, a simple wizard dialog will lead you through the steps needed to create the CD, but it's not rocket science: to create a data CD, for example, you can simply drag files and folders from the top section of the window to the lower section, keeping an eye on how much disk space they'll occupy, click the **Create CD** button on the toolbar, and sit back and wait.

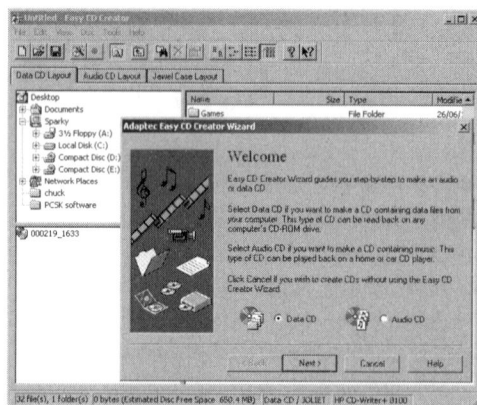

▶ Create new CD-ROMs or audio CDs in minutes by following a few simple steps.

Easy CD Creator also lets you create CD inserts by adding text and graphics in desktop-publishing style and printing out the finished result. For even more professional results, you can design a label for the CD itself, though you'll need a special disk printer connected to your PC to handle the printing.

# Troubleshooting utilities

We looked at the system utilities included with Windows 98 in Chapter 12, which between them handle the essential maintenance of your PC. But once in a while, something may happen that the Windows software can't help with: your printer or modem stops working, you don't hear any sound when playing audio CDs, or your PC starts running slowly.

At times like this you need troubleshooting software such as **First Aid** or **Nuts & Bolts**. These programs work in a semi-automated way by asking you questions about what's wrong, suggesting things you should check, and most importantly, examining and fixing errors in system settings that mere mortals would rather not delve into.

▶ The friendly main screen of **First Aid '98** – just click the item that's causing problems.

# Uninstall utilities

Although most of the software you install has its own uninstall program or routine in case you change your mind, the results of an uninstall are not always perfect. Some files may be left behind even if no other program uses them, folders and shortcuts may not be removed, and orphaned entries in the Windows Registry may remain that slow down your system.

Programs such as Quarterdeck's **CleanSweep** do a much better job by watching your system during software installations and noting every change that takes place. If you later decide to uninstall a program, just click the **Uninstall Wizard** button. You can view logs of all the files and settings to be removed, and the program will back up all removed files in case you change your mind a second time and want to put the program back again.

▶ CleanSweep monitors software installations to make thorough removal easy.

All the removals that CleanSweep and similar programs carry out are **intelligent**: files that are required by another program on your system will be left alone, along with any documents you created yourself and saved into the program's folder.

## Shareware

Rather than being a type of program, the shareware concept is a way of selling software. Because the cost of packaging, advertising and distributing programs is sky-high, many software programmers and companies allow their creations to be distributed on magazine-cover disks, bulletin board services or the Internet.

The benefit for the consumer is that you get the opportunity to try out the software before you pay for it. A secondary benefit is that the software is usually a lot cheaper than a similar commercial product would be, but the understanding is that you *should* pay for it if you choose to continue using it beyond the specified trial-period – this is known as **registering** the software.

In return for registering you'll normally receive the latest version plus a manual, and be entitled to free upgrades as they become available. Here are a few variations on the shareware theme:

**Postcardware**. Instead of actually paying for the software you send the author a picture-postcard of your town. The author still retains full copyright.

**Freeware**. Once again, the author retains copyright, but this time it doesn't even cost you a postcard to continue use!

**Nagware**. Every time you use the software, a dialog will appear that has to be clicked to make it vanish. This may appear every few minutes, forcing you to either give up or register.

**Time-limited**. This is a common method employed by larger companies eager to generate sales of more expensive applications. You have full use of the program for a period of around 30 days, after which time it will cease to run.

**Save-disabled**. The software has no nag-screens or time-limitations, but you won't be able to save or print any of the documents you create.

**Beta versions**. As new software is developed it goes through various phases. Beta versions are early, but working, versions of products given away free for anyone to use at their own risk. The benefit for the user is that of having the very latest software; in return, you're expected to report any bugs or problems you experience with the software in some detail to help the company identify and eradicate them. This is known as **beta-testing**.

# 4

# SURFING THE INTERNET

# MEET THE INTERNET

▶ **IN THIS CHAPTER**

Find out what the Internet *really* is

Discover some of the great things you can do on the Net

Meet the five most popular areas of the Internet

What do you need and what does it cost?

One of the great motivators for buying a computer over the last few years has been the prospect of getting on the Internet. Although it was hyped out of all reality in the mid-1990s, the dust has finally settled and people are starting to treat the Internet as an ordinary, but useful, part of daily life. In fact, for many of us an Internet connection is as much a necessity as a telephone.

Over the next few chapters, we'll take a look at what the Internet is all about, and how you can get online to surf the World Wide Web and exchange email messages with other users. I don't have space to cover more than the basics, but if this brief introduction gives you a taste for the Net, you'll find all you need to know in another of my books, *The UK Internet Starter Kit* also published by Prentice Hall.

Before you can get really excited at the idea of getting on the Internet, it helps to have some idea of what it really is, what you can use it for, and (I hate to say it) how it works. So let's kick off by looking at how the Internet is organised and at some of the ways you can use it. I'm also going to introduce most of the technical-sounding stuff you'll need to know in this chapter.

# What is the Internet?

The technical explanation is that the Internet is a giant, worldwide computer network made up of lots of smaller computer networks. As with any network, these computers are connected to one another so that they can share information. *Unlike* most networks, though, the vastness of the Internet means that this information has to be passed around using modems and telephone lines rather than an office full of cables.

But all that's just hardware, and it's probably not making your mouth water. Instead, let's zoom in on that word 'information', the key to the *real* Internet. The types of information these computers can share covers a huge (and expanding) range – pictures, sounds, text, video, applications, music and much more – making the Internet a true multimedia experience. Anyone can connect their computer to the Internet and gain instant access to millions of files, browse around, or search for some specific item, and grab as much as they want while they're there.

## People power

The other aspect of the *real* Internet is people. All the information you'll find is put there by real people, often simply because they want to share their knowledge, skills, interests or creations with anyone who's interested. The people themselves may be companies keen to promote their products; organisations such as universities, charities and governments; or individual users like you and me.

Along with people, of course, comes communication, and the Internet is a great communications system. You can exchange messages (**email**) with other users, hold conversations or online meetings by typing messages back and forth or by actually sending your voice over the Internet using a microphone instead of a telephone, and take part in any of 50 000 discussion groups on every subject under the sun.

In addition, the Internet can be immensely useful, or just plain fun. Here are a tiny sample of some of the things you can do on the Net:

▶ Control robots and movie cameras on other continents while the live camera footage is beamed straight to your desktop.

▶ Book a skiing holiday online, and check the snow conditions in your chosen resort with up-to-the-minute pictures.

▶ Explore 3D 'virtual reality' worlds, and play games with people visiting the same world.

▶ Manage your bank account, transfer money, and pay bills at any time of the day or night, or do all your shopping in online supermarkets and stores.

▶ Download the latest versions and updates of your software long before they hit the shops, or be among the first to use brand new 'test editions' of major software titles (known as **beta releases**).

**JARGON BUSTER**

## Download

The act of copying a file from one distant computer across a network of computers and telephone lines to your own hard-disk. The opposite term is 'upload' – copying a file from your own disk to a remote computer.

# The popular Internet services

What you've read is a general taste of what's on offer on the Net, but all the things you want to do (or get, or see) will be scattered around the world on different computers. In other words, these computers offer the services you want to use. The Internet is made up of a bundle of different services, but here's a quick look at the five most popular:

▶ **Email** is the oldest and most used of the Internet services with millions of messages whizzing around it every day. Most email messages are just ordinary text, but you can attach almost any type of computer file you want to send along with it (such as a spreadsheet, a picture, or a small program), and encrypt the message so that no-one except the intended recipient will be able to read it.

▶ **The World Wide Web**, often known simply as the Web, has had so much publicity and acclaim that you might think it *is* the Internet. In fact it's the Net's new baby, born in 1992. It's a very lively, gurgling baby though, packed with pictures, text, video, music, and information about every subject under the sun. All the pages on the Web are linked together, so that a page you're viewing from a computer in Bristol might lead you to a page in Tokyo, Brisbane or Oslo with a single mouse-click. Many individual users have their own pages on the Web, along with multinational companies, political parties, universities and colleges, football teams, local councils, and so on and so on.

▶ **Newsgroups** are discussion groups that focus on particular subjects. The discussions take place through a form of email, but the big difference is that these messages are posted for the whole of each group to read and respond to. You can join any group you like from a choice of over 50 000, with subjects ranging from spina-bifida support to alien landings and James Bond films to Turkish culture.

▶ **Chat** isn't chat as in 'yakety-yak', more 'clickety-click'. You can hold conversations with one or more people by typing messages back and forth which instantly appear on the screens of everyone involved. Some chat programs allow 'whiteboarding' (drawing pictures and diagrams in collaboration), private online conferences, and control of programs running on someone else's computer.

▶ **Voice on the Net** *is* chat as in 'yakety-yak'. As long as you've got a soundcard in your computer, and a microphone plugged into it, you can talk to anyone in the world just as you do with the telephone. Add a Web camera to that setup and you can make video phone calls (albeit with rather jerky video). Best of all, an Internet phone call to Australia will cost you little more than an ordinary phone call to your next-door neighbour.

Although other services exist, these are almost certainly the ones you'll be using most (and you may use nothing but email and the World Wide Web – the services are there if you want them, but you don't *have* to use them).

# Understanding Internet addresses

So the Internet is big, the computers that form the Internet are counted in millions, and yet somehow all that information manages to get wherever it's supposed to go. How does that tiny, helpless file find its way from deepest Africa to your own computer all by itself?

In much the same way that an ordinary letter manages to arrive at your house: it has an address attached to it that identifies one single house in the whole world. Every single computer on the Internet has a unique address, called its **IP address**, which consists of four numbers separated by dots, such as 194.72.6.226.

## Domain names – the easier way

Of course, if you need to connect to one of these computers you'll need to know its address. But don't panic! You don't have to remember streams of meaningless numbers: there's an easy way. As well as this numerical IP address, each computer is given a much friendlier **domain name**. Going back to that IP address I mentioned just now, the domain name of that computer is the much more memorable **btinternet.com.** Best of all, most of the Internet programs you'll be using will store these addresses for you so that you can just recall them with a few mouse-clicks.

## Talking in dots

If you're ever in that awkward situation where you have to say a domain name out loud, use the word 'dot' to replace the dot itself, such as 'bbc dot co dot uk' for **bbc.co.uk**.

# What do you need?

To begin with, of course, you'll need a computer. Contrary to popular belief, it doesn't have to be a stunningly fast or powerful computer: you'll get more from the Net's multimedia aspects with a soundcard and 2 MB of RAM on your graphics card, but these days it's hard to find a computer that doesn't. Your computer will need a modem connected (or a terminal adapter or ISDN card), either as an internal expansion card or as a separate external unit, which we looked at in Chapter 6.

You'll also need a telephone line, with a socket fairly close to your computer so that you can plug your modem into it. For a pound or two you can buy an adapter to let you plug a phone and a modem into the same socket which is a worthwhile investment. If you find yourself spending a lot of time online, you might want to consider installing a second phone line just for Internet access so that people can still telephone you while you're surfing (or upgrade to BT's Home Highway service, mentioned in Chapter 6), but that's a decision for later.

## Turn off Call Waiting!

If you have the Call Waiting service on your phone line, make sure you turn if off every time you go online (by dialling # **43** #) and back on again when you've finished (* **43** #). Otherwise an incoming call at the wrong moment could disconnect you and cancel anything you were doing.

Finally, you need a way to connect to a computer that's a part of the Internet. There are hundreds of companies in the UK who specialise in selling dial-up links to the Internet via their own computers, so the next step is to choose one of these companies and set up an account with them.

This leads to the main decision you have to make: do you want an account with an **Internet access provider** (often just called an IAP) or with an **online service**?

# Online services and Internet access providers – what's the difference?

The most important thing that access providers and the major online services have in common is that they both let you connect to the Internet. It's the way they do it and what else they have to offer that makes them different, along with their methods of deciding how much you should pay. To round off this chapter, and help you decide which path to follow, let's take a look at the two options and the pros and cons of each.

## Online services

You may have heard of the 'big three' online services, **America Online** (AOL), **CompuServe** (CSi), and the **Microsoft Network** (MSN). In fact, if you buy computer magazines, you're probably snowed under with floppy-disks and CD-ROMs inviting you to sign up to one or other of these. One of the main plus-points about these online services is the speed and ease with which you can sign up: just this one disk and a credit or debit card number is all you need.

But it is important not to confuse online services with the Internet itself. An online service is rather like an exclusive club: once you subscribe you'll have access to a range of members-only areas such as discussion forums, chat rooms and file libraries. Although you can 'escape' to the Internet from here, non-members can't get in. You won't find much in the members-only areas that you can't find on the Internet itself, but online services do have the combined benefits of ease of use, online help if you get lost, and a friendly all-in-one program from which you can reach everything you need. Although the Internet certainly isn't the chamber of horrors that some newspapers would have you believe, there's little control over what gets published there; online services carefully filter and control their members-only content, making them the preferred choice for getting the whole family online.

So online services give you the Internet, plus a bit more. In the past, what counted against online services was the monthly charge, but with the arrival of free Internet access providers, the online services have had to run to keep up. America Online, for example, now charges a fixed £9.99 per month and subsidises the cost of your connection phone calls, leaving you with a flat rate of 1p per minute. If you spend more than about 10 hours a week online, an online service could be the cheaper option.

Finally, online services tend to offer Internet access as an 'extra' – when you step out on to the Net itself you might find that the information doesn't travel as quickly as it does on a direct Internet connection.

## Internet access providers

An Internet access provider gives you direct access to the Internet, plain and simple. When you dial in to your access provider's computer, you'll see some sort of message on the screen that tells you you're connected, but you won't feel the earth move. Instead, you'll start your email program or your Web software and start doing whatever you wanted to do.

The IAP account has several valuable points in its favour. The first is that you'll have far greater flexibility in your choice of software. Most access providers will give you a bundle of programs when you sign up, but you don't have to use them – just pick and choose between programs (many of which are free) until you find the ones you're comfortable with.

The second benefit is pricing: the competition among companies to gain subscribers means that you can now access the Internet without paying for anything but your phone bill. Rather than charging you a subscription, free service providers make their money from a combination of advertising and a rake-off from the cost of your phone call. So if you're rarely online your charges will be low; if you go on holiday for a month, you won't pay for an Internet account you haven't used.

## Free Internet access? What's the catch?

**GOOD QUESTION!**

The main catch is that you'll be paying upwards of 50p per minute for phone calls to the company's help line if you get stuck. It's a pretty small catch, though – you're not going to get stuck very often, and you may never need to call the help line at all.

Of course, there are plenty of access providers out there still willing to take your money if you prefer to pay. It may seem silly to suggest you should pay for something you can get for free, and I'd certainly recommend picking a free service to begin with, but there may be reasons for choosing a subscription service later. Free service subscribers are almost all home users, so they all tend to pile on to the Net at the same time – evenings and weekends – which can result in a rush that the service can't cope with. The free access concept is still very new, so it remains to be seen whether this turns into a big issue, but Internet access may soon become a case of 'you get what you pay for'.

# Phone calls and connections

Whether you've chosen to hook up with an IAP or an online service, you shall have to dial in to that company's computer every time you want to go online. This means that if you connect for 20 minutes you pay for a 20-minute phone call (although it's your modem using the line, not your phone). So how much are these phone calls going to cost?

## It may be free!

**BY THE WAY**

Service providers are starting to offer premium-rate services (at around £10 per month) which give you free Internet calls during evenings and weekends. You can also subscribe to a British Telecom package called SurfTime which gives completely free Internet calls all day long for around £30 per month or at evenings and weekends only for about £18. If you have one of these packages, you can probably ignore some or all of this section!

The good news is that you should always be able to connect through a local phone number. At the time of writing, British Telecom's local call rate (per minute) is 4p peak, 1.7p cheap, and 1p at weekends. Add your access number to your 'Friends & Family' list and you'll save a useful 10 per cent or more. If your phone bill is high enough to qualify for the Premier Line scheme you'll be able to knock off another 15 per cent.

**24**

# MAKING THE
# CONNECTION

Now that you've made the all-important decisions, this is where things start to happen – after following the instructions in this chapter you'll be online and ready to start exploring the Internet. Right now you're only two steps away from connecting: you need to choose and subscribe to an access provider or online service, and install the software they give you.

## Choosing an access provider

Okay, it's decision time again! There are countless IAPs in the UK, and new ones are starting up all the time. In particular, more and more *free* services are appearing. Well-known names like Dixons, Tesco, Barclays and the Mirror now offer free Internet access; telecommunications companies are trying to steal us away from BT by providing free access combined with lower call charges; and established IAPs like Virgin Net and BT Internet have introduced free accounts to cling on to their existing users.

You'll find a list of several dozen UK access providers in the Directory at the back of this book, and the first decision to make is whether to plump for a free or a subscription service. The chances are you'll take the free option. If so, it's best to choose a service that you've heard good things about, but it's not vital – if you have problems or you're not happy with the service, it's easy to switch to another and there's nothing to cancel.

## Asking questions – six of the best

It never hurts to ask a few questions, and if you've opted for a subscription service you want to know what you're going to get for your money! When you've picked a promising candidate, give them a ring and ask a few questions.

First, check any details from the back of this book to make sure they're accurate and up-to-date. Then work your way down this list:

1   **What is your monthly subscription fee?** A common price is about £12 including VAT. Although this question doesn't usually apply to free IAPs, a few offer a two-tier service with which you can opt to pay a low monthly fee instead of paying a premium rate for calls to their support line.

2 **Do you charge extra for the time I spend online**? The correct answer to this is 'No we don't'. If they get this one wrong, go no further!

3 **Do you support my modem type**? You probably have a 56-kbps modem, but there are currently three different standards in use known as K56Flex, X2 and V.90 (see page 54). If you look in your modem's manual it should tell you that it supports one or more these. Make sure your chosen IAP supports at least one of the same standards.

4 **Do you have a local access number for my area**? You need to know the location of the computer you're dialling in to (usually called a PoP or Point of Presence) – you *must* be able to dial in using a local phone number. Many providers have PoPs all over the UK, or provide a single local-rate 0345 number. Others might be smaller companies with, perhaps, a single PoP in Blackpool. This could be ideal if you live in the Blackpool area, but if you're in Torquay, forget it.

5 **When is telephone support available and is it free**? These days, getting online is as quick and simple as installing a new software program, and you may never need to call a support line for help. In case you do, though, make sure it will be available when you're most likely to need it (for example, during evenings and weekends) and whether it's a premium-rate call.

6 **Do you provide pre-configured connection software for my computer**? The answer should be 'yes', but if you're not using Windows 95 or 98 you may get a 'no'. (The software will usually be on a CD-ROM – very few companies use floppy-disks these days.) You should be able to pop the CD into the drive, follow some simple instructions, and be online in a few minutes.

When you've found the access provider of your dreams, you're almost ready to subscribe. But first …

# Choosing your username

When you start a subscription with an access provider, you'll be identified by your choice of **username** (some companies refer to it as a user ID, logon name or member name). You'll need to quote this when you call the support line with a question, and when you log on to the provider's computer to surf the Internet. More importantly, it forms the unique part of your email address. If you were to start an account with **mycompany.co.uk**, your email address would be *username*@**mycompany.co.uk** and this is the address you'd give out to friends and colleagues so that they could send you email. As an example, my username is **rob.young** and my IAP is **btinternet.com**, so my email address is **rob.young@btinternet.com**.

## Pick a name, any name...

You don't have to use your own name, you can use just about anything you want. It will be easier for you (and other people) to remember if it doesn't contain numbers, but there's nothing to stop you having a username like **jellyfish** or **zapdoodle**, as long as your IAP doesn't already have a zapdoodle on their subscriber list.

The rules on usernames vary a little between providers. They can't contain spaces (in common with any Internet address), but dots, dashes and underscores are usually okay. Most importantly, it must be a username that hasn't already been scooped by another subscriber to your chosen access provider, so it's worth putting a bit of thought into a second and third choice in case your first is unavailable.

## And now ... subscribe!

It's time to get your hands on the software you need to set up your account. Depending on which IAP you chose, you may already have the software on the cover disk of a computing magazine, or you may have to go to a high-street store such as Dixons (for Freeserve) or Tesco (for Tesco Net) and ask for a CD-ROM. More often than not, you'll have to call your chosen IAP and ask them to send you a disk. What happens next will depend on the individual access provider, but it'll usually be one of the following:

▶ Following the instructions on the CD-ROM will install the software you need and then dial the IAP's central computer to create your subscription. At some point during this process you should be told the **username** and **password** you've been assigned. Make a note of these somewhere safe before continuing. At the end of this short process your computer will be ready to connect to the Internet.

▶ You may receive a disk of software and some documentation that tells you how to install it and how to configure your computer yourself.

You may also receive a wonderfully technical-looking list of IP addresses, domain names and so on. Even if your software is pre-configured for quick and easy installation, make sure you hang on to this list for reference – you might need to enter some of these settings into other software you use in the future.

# Choosing an online service

This should be an easy choice to make – not only is the list of online services fairly short, but most offer a free 30-day trial, so you've got nothing to lose by picking one at random. All the same, it's better to make an informed choice if you can, so let's take a look at the two most popular UK online services, **CompuServe** and **America Online**.

## CompuServe

CompuServe has over 1000 different areas covering just about every conceivable subject including finance, news, TV listings, articles from popular magazines, travel information, movie and music previews, along with interactive chat rooms. Many retail companies have their own forums offering advice and product support, and business users will probably find more to interest them on CompuServe than the other services. The program used to move around this lot is smart and fairly formal, although not quite as easy to get to grips with as America Online. UK-specific content is sparse for a company with so many UK users, but CompuServe are trying to improve things in this area. Parents can download a program called Cyber Patrol to restrict kids' access to areas of CompuServe itself or the Internet, and limit the time they can spend online.

### Parental control

BY THE WAY

Even if you haven't opted for an online service account, there are many good programs available that you can use with an Internet access provider account to restrict access to different areas of the Net, or to particular types of information.

## America Online

In comparison with CompuServe, America Online (AOL) has a very sunny, friendly and informal feel to it, making it a good choice for children and inexperienced computer users. The content provided is very similar to that of CompuServe, with a couple of differences: business content, although growing, is still far from comprehensive, but you will find plenty of UK content. Parental controls are very good, although there's currently no way to restrict how long your kids stay online. One major bonus is that AOL allows an account holder to have up to five different member-names (AOL calls them Screen Names), which means that you can have five email addresses; for families or small businesses, this allows everyone to receive their own personal email. More importantly perhaps for families, it also means that you can bar access to areas of the service by your children without restricting your own use.

# How do you sign up?

The first job is to get your hands on the free connection software. These disks are regularly glued to the covers of computer magazines so you may have dozens of them already. If you have, make sure you pick the most recent. If you haven't, either take a trip to your newsagent or phone the services and ask them to send you the correct software for your computer and operating system. You'll find their contact details in the Directory at the back of this book.

That was the tricky part! Somewhere on the disk you'll be told how to start the program that signs you up, and the whole process will advance in simple steps. The exact routine will vary from one service to another, so I can't tell you exactly what to expect, but here are a few tips to bear in mind:

▶ Somewhere on the disk packaging you'll find a reference number (perhaps on a small label, or perhaps on the disk itself). Don't lose it – you'll have to enter this into the software to start the sign-up procedure.

▶ Make sure you've got your credit card or debit card handy. Although you won't be charged for the first 30 days' access, you'll have to enter the card number and its expiry date when you sign up.

▶ You may be asked to choose a dial-in phone number from a list covering the whole country. If so, make sure you choose a *local* number. (In some cases, the software will work out the best dial-in point for you, based on your own phone number, or it may use a local-rate 0845 number.)

▶ After you've entered all the necessary personal details, the program will dial up the service's computer and set up your subscription automatically. Within a minute or two you'll receive a username and password. These are your entry ticket, so write them down and keep them safe.

## Secure your password!

Keep your password private. Never include it in an email message, don't type it in front of anyone, and make sure you change it at least once a month (you'll find instructions for this online). If possible, use a combination of letters and numbers at least five characters in length. And don't even consider using the word 'password' as your password!

# How do you use an online service?

When you dial in to your online service and log on using your username and password (which should happen automatically), you won't actually be *on the Internet*. At the click of a few buttons you can enter chat rooms or join in with other activities and forums, and you'll find plenty of assistance if you get lost, both in help files and online support areas.

Access to the Internet itself will be marked as one of the areas you can visit, and you'll probably see a big friendly button marked 'Internet' that will take you there. In most cases any extra software needed for Internet access was installed when you signed up, but you might be told that you need to download it yourself. If so, another friendly button will probably appear in front of you and all the spadework will be done for you while you sit back and wait.

I'm not going to dwell on the members-only areas of online services in the following chapters. But once you have clicked that big friendly button, you're surfing the same Internet as everyone else.

# EXPLORING THE WORLD WIDE WEB

## ▶ IN THIS CHAPTER

Discover the amazing World Wide Web

Learn to use your Web browser and start surfing

Keep track of where you've been and where you're going

Start downloading files and saving Web pages

The World Wide Web is the jewel in the Internet's crown, and the whole reason for the 'Internet explosion'. A large part of the Web's popularity lies in its simplicity: you don't have to be a networking genius or a computer whiz to use it, you just point with the mouse and click. In this chapter you'll learn the basics of finding your way around this powerful system.

# Understanding the Web

The 'pages' you find on the Web contain a scattering of words that are underlined and highlighted in a different colour from the text around them. Just move your mouse-pointer on to one of these words or phrases (you'll see it change into a hand with a pointing finger when you do so, as shown in the next screenshot) and click. Hey presto, another page opens. The entire 'web' of pages is being 'spun' by millions of people at the rate of several million new pages per day, and every page includes these point-and-click links to many other pages.

▶ To jump between pages, move the pointer over the coloured hypertext and click to open the related document.

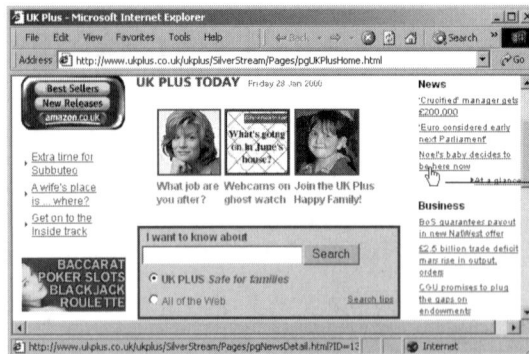

The hand pointer shows that this text is a link

## Web page

A 'page' is a single document that can be any length, like a document in a word-processor. Pages can contain text, graphics, sound and video clips, together with clever effects and controls made possible by new programming languages such as Java and ActiveX.

JARGON BUSTER

This system of clickable text is called **hypertext**, and you've probably seen it used in Windows help files and multimedia encyclopaedias as a neat way to make cross-references. The Web takes the system a few stages further:

▶ These links aren't restricted to opening a document stored on the same computer: you might see a page from the other side of the world.

▶ A hypertext link doesn't have to be a word or phrase: it might be a picture that you click on, or it might be a part of a larger picture, with different parts linking to different pages.

▶ The link doesn't necessarily open a new Web page: it might play a video or a sound, download a compressed archive (.zip file) or an application, display a picture, run a program … the list goes on.

The Web is made up of millions of files placed on computers called Web servers, so no-one actually *owns* the Web itself. The Web servers are owned by many different companies, and they rent space (or give it away for free) to anyone who wants to put their own pages on the Web. The pages are created using an easy-to-use, text-based language called **HTML** (HyperText Markup Language).

Once the newly-created pages are placed on the Web server, anyone who knows their address can look at them. This partly explains why the Web became such an overnight success: a simple page can be written in minutes, so a Web site can be as up-to-date as its creator wants it to be. Many pages are updated daily, and some might even change every few minutes.

**JARGON BUSTER**

## Web site

'Web site' is a loose term that refers to the pages belonging to an individual or company. A site might be just a single page that your Auntie Ethel wrote to share a nice fruitcake recipe, or it might be hundreds of pages belonging to a supermarket chain.

## What do you need?

To view pages from the World Wide Web you'll need a program called a **browser**. In fact, this single program will be the most powerful weapon in your Internet arsenal, and not just because you'll be spending so much time on the Web – you can use this program to handle many of your other Internet-related tasks as well. Although there are many different browsers available, the most popular and capable is Microsoft's **Internet Explorer**.

If you're using Windows 98 Second Edition (which should be installed on any PC bought since Autumn 1999) a recent version of Internet Explorer is already installed and you should see its icon on the desktop (a blue 'e'). A copy of Internet Explorer is also included with the original Windows 98 and with some editions of Windows 95. It may be installed on your system already, or you may have to install it yourself from the **Windows Setup** tab of Control Panel's Add/Remove Programs applet, but you may prefer to install the more recent version included on the CD-ROM accompanying this book.

# Start browsing

When you open Internet Explorer, the first thing you'll see is your **Start Page**. Unlike a word-processor or a paint program, the browser must always display a document, and until you tell it which document you want to look at it'll display the document set as its Start Page. By default, Explorer is set to display the first page of Microsoft's Internet site.

Although Internet Explorer calls this page the Start Page, there's a button on the toolbar with the word 'Home' beneath it. Wherever your Web wanderings lead you, just click the **Home** button to return to your Start Page anytime you want to.

# Anatomy of a Web page

Now it's time to get acquainted with the basic workings of the browser and with the Web itself. If you look at the Start Page you should see several hypertext links (underlined, coloured text). Move your mouse-pointer on to any link that looks interesting and click. When you do that, your browser sends a message to the server storing the page you want. If everything goes according to plan, the server will respond by sending back the requested page so that your browser can display it.

Spend a little time following links to see where they lead. Don't limit yourself to clicking textual links alone, though – many of the pictures and graphics you see on a page will lead somewhere too. Take a look at the page shown in the following screenshot from Time Out Magazine's site **(http://www.timeout.com)** for a few clues to the type of thing you'll find on a Web page.

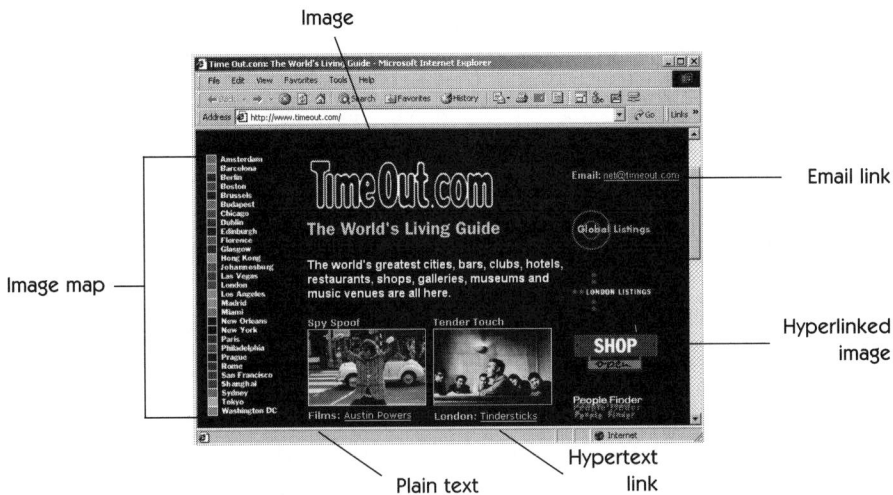

▶ Some of the main elements that make up a Web page.

▶ **Plain text**. Ordinary readable text. Click it all you like – nothing will happen!

▶ **Hypertext link**. A text link to another page. HyperText links will almost always be underlined, but their text colour will vary from site to site.

▶ **Image**. A picture or graphic that enhances a Web site. Like most pictures, it paints a thousand words, but it won't lead anywhere if you click it.

▶ **Hyperlinked image**. Clicking this image will open a new page. In most cases a hyperlinked image will look no different from an ordinary image, but it may have a box around it that's the same colour as any hypertext links on the page.

▶ **Image map**. An image split up into small chunks, with each chunk leading to a different page. In this case, every city name is linked to its own page, listing forthcoming events in that city.

▶ **Email link.** Click on this link and your email program will open so that you can send a message to the Web page's author. The author's address will be automatically inserted into the message for you.

## How can I tell an ordinary image from one that links somewhere?

**GOOD QUESTION!**

The trick is always to watch your mouse pointer: when you move the pointer on to any link (image or text), it will turn into a hand shape with a pointing finger. In a well-constructed image map, the different areas of the picture itself should make it clear what each link will lead you to.

## Charting your course on the Web

By now you should be cheerfully clicking links of all descriptions and skipping from page to page with casual abandon. The problem is, you can only move *forwards*. If you find yourself heading down a blind alley, how can you retrace your steps and head off in a different direction? This is where the browser itself comes to your rescue, so let's spend some time getting acquainted with its toolbars and menus.

▶ Internet Explorer's button bar and address bar.

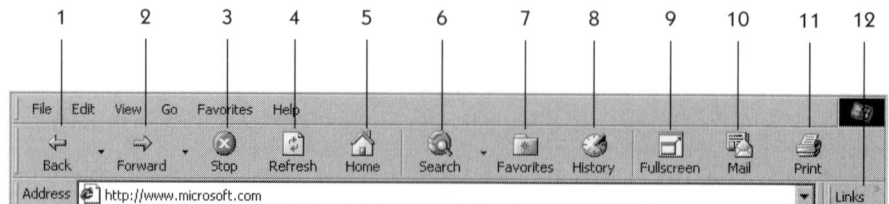

1 File 2 Edit View Go Favorites Help 3 Stop 4 Refresh 5 Home 6 Search 7 Favorites 8 History 9 Fullscreen 10 Mail 11 Print 12
Back Forward

Address http://www.microsoft.com Links

1 **Back.** Clicking this button will take you back to the last page you looked at. If you keep clicking you can step all the way back to the first page you viewed this session.

2 **Forward.** After using the Back button to take a second look at a previously-viewed page, the Forward button lets you return to pages you viewed later. This button will be greyed-out if you haven't used the Back button yet.

3 **Stop**. Stops the download of a page from the server. This can be useful if a page is taking a long time to appear and you're tired of waiting, or if you clicked a link accidentally and want to stay where you are.

4 **Refresh**. Clicking this tells your browser to start downloading the same page again. See *Sometimes things go wrong …* on p. 295 for reasons why you might need to Refresh.

5 **Home**. Opens your Start Page.

6 **Search**. Opens a Web search site from which you can search for pages by typing in several descriptive keywords relating to the subject you want to find out more about.

7 **Favorites**. See *Many happy returns – using Favorites* on the next page.

8 **History**. Opens a list of sites you've visited recently, letting you revisit one with a single click (see *Retracing your steps with history* on p. 293).

9 **Fullscreen**. Expands Internet Explorer's window to fill the screen, covering the Windows taskbar and everything else, and leaving just a tiny toolbar visible for navigation.

10 **Mail**. Opens a menu from which you can run your email or newsreader software, or open a blank form to send an email message.

11 **Print**. Prints the current page. Your can choose the printer to use and change printing options from the File menu.

12 **Links**. If you click on this word a new button bar will slide across revealing links to Microsoft's own site and some useful jumping-off points for your Web travels. To hide the Links bar again, click the word 'Address' to its left.

## More cyber-space

BY THE WAY

You can find all these options on Explorer's menus as well, and most have keyboard shortcuts. If you'd like to see more of the pages themselves in Explorer's window, head off to the **View** menu and click on **Toolbar** to turn it off.

One useful extra tool is a facility to search the page you're viewing for a particular word or phrase. Open the **Edit** menu, choose **Find (on this page)...** (or press **Ctrl+F**), and type the word you're looking for.

## Many happy returns – using Favorites

One of the most powerful Explorer tools is the **Favorites** system (known as Bookmarks or Hotlists in other browsers). Any time you arrive at a page you think might be useful in the future, you can add its address to your list of Favorites and return to it by opening the menu and clicking the relevant shortcut. To add the current page to the list, open the **Favorites** menu and click **Add to Favorites**. A small dialog will appear giving a suggested title (you can replace this with any title you like to help you recognise it in future). To place the shortcut directly on the menu, click **OK**.

You can also organise your shortcuts into submenus to make them easier to find. Click the **Create in...** button and **New Folder**, then type a name for the folder. Click the folder into which you want to save the new shortcut and click the **OK** button to confirm. (If it ends up in the wrong place, don't worry! Select **Organize Favorites** from the Favorites menu and you'll be able to move, rename and delete folders and shortcuts, and create new folders.)

When you want to reopen a page that you added to your Favorites list, either open the **Favorites** menu and click the name of the site, or click the Favorites toolbar button to open a clickable list in a small frame at the left of the browser's window (shown in the two following screenshots).

▶ Add a new shortcut to a Favorites submenu by clicking the submenu's folder followed by the OK button.

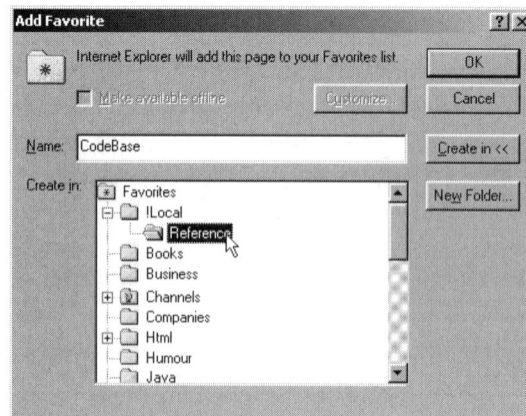

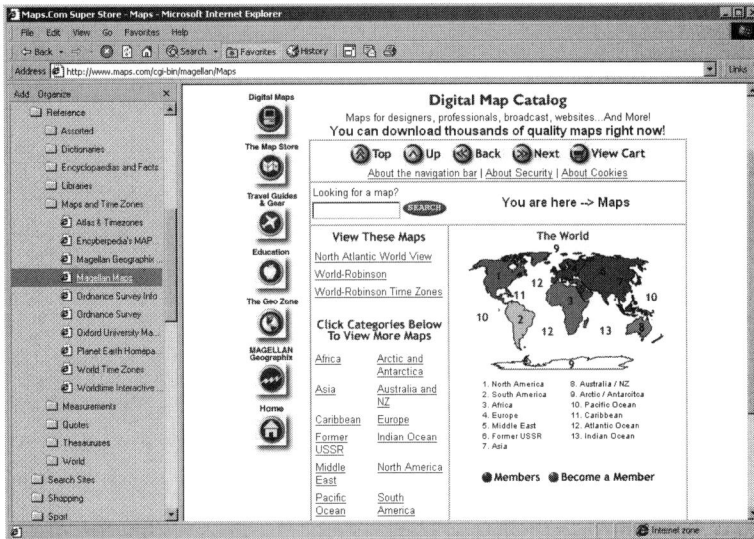

▶ Click the **Favorites** button on the Toolbar, and your Favorites list stays within easy reach while you surf.

## Retracing your steps with History

The History list provides a handy way of finding an elusive site that you visited recently but didn't add to your Favorites list. Internet Explorer maintains this list automatically, and you can open it by clicking the **History** button on the toolbar. The sites are sorted by week and day, with links to the various pages you visited on each site placed into folders. You can revisit a site by finding the week and day you last viewed it, clicking the folder for that site and clicking the page you want to see again. If you're not sure *when* you last visited, click the word **View** at the top of the History panel and choose **By Site** to show an alphabetical list of visited sites instead. You can choose how long Internet Explorer should store details of visited pages by clicking your way to **Tools | Internet Options | General**.

## Offline browsing

You can view some of the pages in History without connecting to the Internet and paying call charges – Internet Explorer keeps copies of some pages on your hard disk. Choose **Work Offline** from the File menu, then move your mouse over sites in the History list. If a site is shown in black text with a usual hand pointer, you can click it to see the stored copy of the page.

# The address bar and URLs

Every page on the World Wide Web has its own unique **URL**. URL stands for uniform resource locator, but it's just a convoluted way of saying 'address'. You'll also notice URLs at work as you move from page to page in Explorer, provided you can see the toolbar (if you can't, go to **View | Toolbars | Standard Buttons** to switch it on). Every time you open a new page, its URL appears in the address bar below the buttons. You can also type a URL into the address bar yourself – just click once on the address bar to highlight the address currently shown, type the URL of the page you want to open, and press **Enter**. For example, if you want to look at today's peak-time TV listings, type: **http://www.sceneone.co.uk** into the address bar. In a similar way, if you find the URL of a site you'd like to visit in an email message or word-processor document, copy it to the clipboard using **Ctrl+C**, click in the address bar, and paste in the URL by pressing **Ctrl+V**.

## Typing URLs

URLs are case-sensitive, so make sure you observe any capital letters. Also, in contrast with the folder paths used in Windows, URLs use backslashes rather than forward-slashes. Actually, these don't matter too much – if you forget and use the wrong type, Explorer will know what you mean.

## Understanding URLs

You'll come into contact with a lot of URLs on your travels around the Internet, so it's worth knowing what they mean. As a specimen to examine, let's take the URL for the Radio 1 Web site at the BBC and break it up into its component pieces. The URL is: **http://www.bbc.co.uk/radio1/index.html.**

    **http://**        This is one of the Internet's many protocols, and it stands for HyperText Transfer Protocol. It's the system used to send Web pages around the Internet, so all Web page URLs have the **http://** prefix.

| | |
|---|---|
| **www.bbc.co.uk/** | This is the name of the computer on which the required file is stored (often referred to as the **host computer**). Computers that store Web pages are called **Web servers** and their names usually begin **www**. |
| **radio1/** | This is the directory path to the page you want to open. Just as on your own computer, the path may consist of several directories separated by backslashes. |
| **index.html** | This is the name of the file you want. The **.html** (or **.htm**) extension indicates that it's a Web page, but your browser can handle any number of different file types. |

# Sometimes things go wrong ...

Things don't always go smoothly when you're trying to open a Web page. To begin with, the server might not be running and you'll eventually see a message telling you that the operation 'timed out' – in other words, your browser waited a minute or so for a response from the server and doesn't think anything is going to happen. If the server *is* running it might be busy. In this case you might get a similar result, or you might get a part of the page and then everything seems to stop dead. You may be able to get things moving by clicking the **Refresh** button on the browser's toolbar, forcing your browser to request the document again, but be prepared to give up, visit a different Web site and try this one again later.

Then there's the mysterious vanishing page syndrome. Although all Web pages contain links, sometimes the pages those links refer to no longer exist and you'll see an error message instead. The reason is simple: on the perpetually-changing landscape of the World Wide Web, pages (and even entire sites) move elsewhere, get renamed, or just disappear. In fact, the average lifespan of a site is a mere 90 days! Anyone putting links to these sites in his own pages has no way of knowing when this happens other than by regularly clicking all the links himself to check them. The endless arrivals and departures are a fact of Web life, but also a part of its magic.

# Saving files from the Web

There are two groups of files you can grab from the World Wide Web – those that are a part of the Web page itself (such as an image), and those that aren't. The second group is huge, covering applications, sound files, videos, spreadsheets, zip files, and a whole lot more. Although the methods of saving *any* file are straightforward enough, that second group is going to lead us into a few complications, so let's begin with the first.

## Saving page elements

**Saving the entire Web page**. If you want to save a copy of the whole Web page (including its images), open the **File** menu and choose **Save As…**. From the **Save as type** box, choose either **Web Archive for Email** or **Web Page, Complete**. The Web Archive is the neater format, but the Complete option may save some multimedia elements from the page that the Archive ignores.

**Saving the Web page's text**. To save just the text from the page, follow the procedure above but select **Text File** from the **Save as type** box. Alternatively, if you only need a portion of the text on the page, you can highlight it using the mouse, copy it to the clipboard by pressing **Ctrl+C** and then paste it into another application.

**Saving the Web page's source**. The **source** of a Web page is the text you see in your browser plus all the weird codes (part of a language called HTML) added by the page's author that make the page display properly. To save the HTML source document, follow the same routine as above, but choose **Web Page, HTML only** from the **Save as type** list. (If you just want to have a peep at the source, right-click the Web page's background and choose **View Source** from the context menu.)

**Saving images from the page**. As you learnt above, it just takes a right-click on any image to save it to disk (or a drag, if you prefer). You can also save the **background**, a small image file that the browser tiles to fill the entire viewing area. In addition to the **Set as Wallpaper** option mentioned above, you can right-click the background and choose **Save Background As…** to save the image file to the directory of your choice. You can also copy images or the background to the clipboard with a right-click, ready to paste into another application.

## Saving other types of file

Although most of the links you find on Web pages will open another page, some will be links to files that you can download (don't worry – it should be obvious, and if it isn't, just hit the Cancel button as soon as you get the chance). As I mentioned earlier, this is where things get a bit more complicated. Come what may, the file *must* be downloaded to your own computer before you can do anything with it all, but how you choose to handle the download will depend upon what you want to do with the file itself. The browser may be multi-talented, but it can't display *every* type of file that exists!

What it can do, however, is to launch an **external viewer** to display the file. An external viewer is just a slightly technical way of saying 'another program on your computer'. Two vital elements are required for your browser to be able to do this:

▶ You must have a program on your disk that can open the type of file you're about to download.

▶ The browser needs to know which program to use for a particular type of file, and where to find it on your disk.

After you click the link, Internet Explorer will start to download the file it refers to and then show the dialog below. It wants to know what to do with the file when it has finished downloading: do you want to save the file and carry on surfing, or open it immediately using an external viewer?

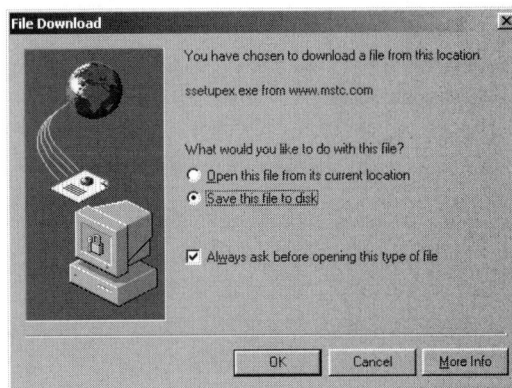

▶ Explorer wants to know whether it should open this file after downloading, or save it to your hard-disk.

**Save this file to disk**. If you choose this option, Explorer will present a **Save As** dialog so that you can choose a directory to save the file into, followed by a smaller dialog that will keep you posted on the progress of the download and how much longer it should take. While the file is downloading you can wait, or continue surfing the Web, and there's a handy **Cancel** button you can use if you change your mind halfway through, or the download seems to be taking too long. The **Save this file to disk** option is the best (and safest) option to use.

**Open this file from its current location**. For a file that you want to view or play straight away, you can select the **Open** option. If Internet Explorer hasn't previously been told how to handle files of this type, it will then prompt you to choose the program you want to use to view the file once it has been downloaded, so click the **Browse** button in the next dialog to locate and double-click a suitable program on your hard-disk, and then click **OK**. Explorer will download the file and then launch that program to display the file. There's also a checkbox labelled **Always ask before opening this type of file**. If you remove the checkmark from this box, and then use the Browse button to select a program to use, Explorer will always use that program whenever you download the same type of file in the future.

You can view and edit the settings for different types of file by opening My Computer and selecting **View | Folder Options | File Types**. Click a file type from the list, and click the **Edit** button. If the box beside **Confirm open after download** isn't checked, this type of file will always be opened – you can check this box if you'd like the chance to save this type of file in future or use a different program to open it. To find out *which* program will open this type of file, click on either **Play** or **Open** in the **Actions** box, then click the **Edit...** button.

## Check for viruses!

Always run a virus-checker before running any program you've downloaded. Although people get a bit too hysterical about it, there's a small risk that a program might contain a virus. It only takes a few seconds to do and might just save a lot of hassle later.

**26**

# EXCHANGING MESSAGES BY EMAIL

Email is the old man of the Internet, one of the reasons the network was constructed in the first place. It's one of the easiest areas of Net life to use, and one of the *most* used – for many people, sending and receiving email is their only reason for going online. By the end of this chapter you'll be able to send email messages to millions of people all over the world (well, perhaps not *all* of them!) quicker than you can stick a stamp on an envelope.

# Why use email?

First, it's incredibly cheap. A single first-class stamp costs 26p and will get a letter to a single, local (in global terms) address. But for a local phone call costing 5p you can deliver dozens of email messages to all corners of the world. Second, it's amazingly fast. In some cases, your email might be received within just seconds of you sending it. (It's not always quite as fast as that, however: on occasions, when the network conspires against you, it might take several hours.) Third, it's easy to keep copies of the email you send and receive, and to sort and locate individual messages quickly.

**JARGON BUSTER**

## Snail mail

A popular term for ordinary mail sent through the land-based postal service, whose speed is closer to that of a certain mollusc than email.

There's a possible fourth reason, but it should be regarded with some caution. If you agonise for hours over ordinary letter writing, email should make life easier for you. An inherent feature of email is its informality: spelling, grammar and punctuation are tossed to the wind in favour of speed and brevity.

# Everybody's first question ...

Whenever the subject of email comes up with Internet beginners, the same question is guaranteed to arise within the first minute. So that you can concentrate on the rest of the chapter, I'll put your mind at ease by answering it straight away. The question is: *What happens if email arrives for me and I'm not online to receive it?*

The answer: email arrives at your access provider's computer (their **mail server**) and waits for you to collect it. In fact it will wait there a long time if it has to: most mail servers will delete messages that remain uncollected for several months, but if you take a week's holiday you can collect the week's email when you return.

JARGON BUSTER

## Newbie

You're a newbie! It's okay, I'm not being abusive. It just means that you're new to the Internet. You wouldn't be proud to describe yourself as a newbie, but you might want to do so when appealing for help in a newsgroup, for example, to keep responses as simple as possible.

# Understanding email addresses

There are two easy ways to spot an Internet 'newbie'. The first is that their email messages begin 'Dear ...' and end 'Yours sincerely'. The second is that they tell you their 'email number'. Don't fall into either trap – email writing isn't as formal as letter writing, and you definitely have an email *address*!

Email addresses consist of three elements: a username, an '@' sign, and a domain name. Your username will usually be the name in which your account was set up, and the name that you log on with when you connect. The domain name is the address of your IAP or online service. For example, if your user name were **joe.bloggs** and you set up an account with Virgin Net, your email address would be **joe.bloggs@virgin.net**. Other companies do things slightly differently: your account name comes after the '@' sign, and you can have unlimited email addresses by putting whatever you like *before the '@'* sign. Joe Bloggs could have the email address **joe@joebloggs.freeserve.co.uk**, and his wife could be **jane@joebloggs.freeserve.co.uk** (though she might be less than thrilled with the prospect!).

## Quoting your email address

If you have to say your email address out loud, replace the dots with the word 'dot' and the @ sign with the word 'at'. So joe.bloggs@virgin.net would be pronounced 'joe dot bloggs at virgin dot net'.

## What do you need?

If you have an account with an online service such as CompuServe or AOL, you don't need anything more – the software you use to connect to and navigate the service has built-in email capability. If you have an IAP account, you'll need an email client (geek-speak for 'a program that works with email'). There are many of these to choose between, but as a Windows 98 user with Internet Explorer installed you also have its sister program, **Outlook Express**, so let's use that.

Outlook Express has greater benefits than just being easily available, though. It allows you to work offline, it can handle multiple **identities** (allowing members of your family to receive their own personal email without receiving or seeing yours), it has a built-in address book, and it lets you organise messages you want to keep by placing them in named folders (just the way you organise files on your hard-disk). You can probably see Outlook Express's icon on the desktop – an envelope with a blue arrow wrapped around it – and you can just double-click that to start the program.

## Offline

Software that lets you work **offline** allows you to read and write your messages without being connected to your IAP or online service and clocking up charges. You only need to go **online** to send your messages and receive any new email. The earliest email had to be written online, which is why speed mattered more than spelling.

# Setting up your email program

Before you can start to send and receive email, Outlook Express needs to know a bit about you and your email account. This simply involves filling in the blanks on a setup page using some of the information given to you by your IAP. The first time you start the program it may prompt you to enter this information, but with luck it won't: most of the setup CDs provided by IAPs will set up Outlook Express automatically.

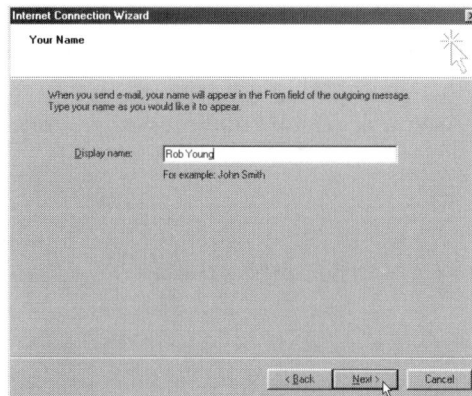

▶ Entering email account details into Outlook Express.

If you are prompted for these details, follow the steps to choose the name that should be displayed as the sender when you write a message (usually your own name), enter your email address, type in your SMTP and POP3 server names, and finally your email account name and password (which are usually the same as those you use for your dial-up connection).

## SMTP server, POP3 server

There are two protocols computers used to move email around, SMTP (used to **send** email messages) and POP3 (used to **deliver** messages to you). Your email program needs to know the name of the computers handling these things (the **servers**). They may both be the same (something like **mail.virgin.net**) or they may be the equally intuitive **smtp.virgin.net** and **pop.virgin.net**. If you need to know, your IAP can tell you, but you may prefer to try these first and perhaps save the cost of a premium call to the support line.

When Outlook Express appears, the main area of the screen will provide a friendly overview of the program. You may prefer not to see that each time you start, and there are one or two others options worth changing, so we'll do those first.

Go to the **Tools** menu and choose **Options**. On the **General** tab, remove the checkmark beside **Send and receive messages at startup**. This prevents your PC dialling up every time you open Outlook Express, which can be annoying when you just wanted to read or reply to a message. You might also want to check **When starting go directly to my 'Inbox' folder**, bypassing that friendly overview screen. On the **Send** tab, remove the checkmark beside **Send messages immediately**. Finally, click **OK**.

## Welcome message

When you first start Outlook Express and go to your Inbox, you'll see one message there. This is actually provided by Outlook Express itself (you haven't just received it) and contains some blurb about the program. If you don't want to keep it, just press the Delete key.

# Sending an email message

You probably feel an overwhelming temptation to email everyone you know and tell them you've 'joined the club', but hold that thought for a moment. Start by sending a message to yourself instead – that way you can check that everything is working, and learn what to do when you *receive* a message as well. To do that, click the **New Message** button on the toolbar.

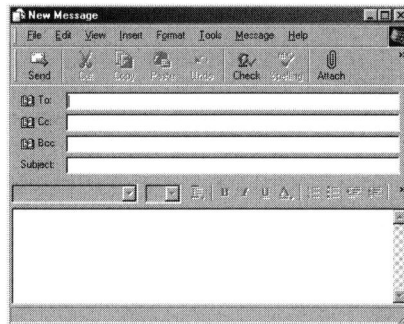

▶ Sending a new message in Outlook Express.

Although all email programs look a little different, the details you need to provide when sending an email message are always the same, so even if you're not using Outlook Express, you'll see similar text fields in the message window. Here's what each field is for:

**To:**        Type the email address of the person to whom you want to send the message .

**CC:**        Carbon copy. If you want to send the message to several people, type one address in the **To** field and the rest in the **CC** field, separated by commas. Using this method, all recipients will know who else received a copy of the message.

**BCC:**        Blind Carbon Copy. If you want to send the same message to several people and you don't want any of them to know who else is getting a copy, place their addresses in this field instead of the CC field. (In Outlook Express, the BCC field won't be shown until you choose **All Headers** from the View menu.)

| **Subject:** | Enter a short description of your message. In some email programs you can send a message with a blank subject line, but avoid doing this. Although most people will open any email they receive (even if the subject is blank), this entry really comes into its own when the recipient is looking for this message again in six months time. |
|---|---|
| **Attached:** | Lists the names of any computer files you want to send to the recipient along with the message. To attach a file, click the paper-clip button on the Toolbar and choose the file from a normal Open File dialog. If you change your mind before sending the message, right-click the file in the Attached list and click **Remove**. |

Below these fields is the area in which you type the message itself. Because you're going to send this message to yourself, type your own email address into the **To** field, and anything you like in the **Subject** field (just to get into the habit), and then write yourself a welcoming message.

Finally, click the **Send** button and the window will close. If you followed my advice earlier and removed the checkmark beside **Send messages immediately** in the Options dialog, this message will be placed in your **Outbox** folder. If you didn't, your PC will connect to the Internet to send the message straight away. The first method is better – if you chose to, you could write more messages with each ending up in the Outbox in the same way, and only connect when you were ready to send them all.

## Return to sender

As Outlook Express sends and receives mail in a single operation, and this message is being passed to your IAP's computer and then back to you, this message you're posting to yourself should come back instantly. Messages you send to other people may take a little longer, and it may be much longer before they connect and check their mail, so don't assume they're ignoring you if you don't get a reply the same day.

When you're ready to send your messages, click the **Send & Receive** (or **Send/Recv**) button in Outlook Express's main window. After your computer has connected, you'll see a dialog indicating that the messages are being sent. As each message is sent, it's automatically moved from your Outbox to your **Sent Items** folder – this is your indication that a message really has been sent. Outlook Express then automatically checks for new mail, and you'll see that arriving in your Inbox. If all goes according to plan, the message you've just sent yourself should appear here. If it doesn't, wait a few minutes, then click Send & Receive again.

## I've got no mail to send, so how can I check for new mail?

GOOD QUESTION!

You can still click the Send & Receive button and Outlook Express will just check for new incoming mail. Alternatively, click the little arrow beside that button and choose **Receive All**; this is a handy option to remember if you don't want to send your mail until you've checked whether there is any new mail waiting.

# You've got new mail!

You really feel you've arrived on the Internet when you receive your first message, and (after the initial excitement wears off) you'll want to read it. In Outlook Express you can simply click on the **message header** (the brief details included on a single line in your Inbox) and see the message in the Preview pane below. If you prefer, you can double-click the message header to read the message in a new window.

At this point you can decide what to do with the message. You can delete it if you want to, and until you do it will remain visible in the Inbox. If you want to keep messages for future reference, it's worth creating some folders to store them in – that way your Inbox can contain just those messages that are still waiting to be dealt with. To create a new folder, right-click on **Local Folders** and choose **New Folder**, type a name for the folder and click **OK**. You can then drag messages from your Inbox and drop them on to the new folder's icon to move them.

## Can I save email messages to my hard-disk?

**GOOD QUESTION!**

Yes, just select the message header, choose Save As from the File menu and select a name and location. Double-clicking the saved file will open it in an Outlook Express message window, but you can read most messages in any word-processor if you prefer.

## Replying and forwarding

One of the things you're most likely to do with an incoming message is send a reply, and this is even easier than sending a brand new message. With the message open (or highlighted in your Inbox) click on the **Reply** button. A new message window will open with the sender's email address already inserted and the entire message copied. Copying the original message this way is known as **quoting**, and it's standard practice in email, helping the recipient to remember what it is you're replying to. You'll see a greater-than sign (>) at the beginning of each line, and you can delete all or any of the original message that you don't need to include in the reply.

The Reply button also inserts the word **Re:** at the beginning of the subject line, indicating to the recipient that it's a response to an earlier message. Although you can change the subject line of a reply, it's often best not to – many email programs have search and sort facilities that can group messages according to subject (among other things) making it easy to track an earlier email 'conversation' you've long since forgotten about.

## Keep it simple

**BY THE WAY**

Remember that email isn't supposed to look like a letter. You don't put the date or the recipient's postal address at the top, or use any letter-writing formalities. On some occasions you might want to include your own postal address and phone number, but for security reasons do this only when the recipient needs to know them.

# Email netiquette

The term 'netiquette' is an abbreviation of 'Internet etiquette', a set of unwritten rules about behaviour on the Internet. In simple terms, they boil down to 'Don't waste Internet resources' and 'Don't be rude', but here are a few specific pointers to keep in mind when dealing with email:

▶ Reply promptly. Because email is quick and easy, it's generally expected that a reply will arrive within a day or two, even if it's just to confirm receipt. Try to keep unanswered messages in your Inbox and move answered messages elsewhere so that you can see at a glance what's waiting to be dealt with.

▶ DON'T SHOUT! LEAVING THE CAPS LOCK KEY SWITCHED ON IS REGARDED AS 'SHOUTING', AND CAN PROMPT SOME ANGRY RESPONSES. IT DOESN'T LOOK AT ALL FRIENDLY, DOES IT?

▶ Don't forward someone's private email without their permission.

▶ Don't put anything in an email message that you wouldn't mind seeing on the nine o'clock news! Anyone can forward your email to a national newspaper, your boss, your parents, and so on, so there may be times when a phone-call is preferable.

# APPENDICES

# THREE FLAVOURS OF PC

▶ **IN THIS APPENDIX**

The differences between desktop, notebook and handheld PCs

# The desktop PC

The desktop PC has long been the established standard, and it's probably what you picture when you think of a computer. As its name suggests, it's designed to sit on your desk and stay there. One big difference between this and the notebook PC is size: the system unit has a mass of free space inside allowing extra components to be fitted that increase the power and flexibility of your machine. Once installed, these new accessories are instantly available every time you switch on your PC. Similarly, it's usually easy to replace existing components with newer, more powerful ones (known as **upgrading**) if the need arises.

Despite its name, the desktop PC's system unit no longer needs to be on the desk. Traditionally, the unit sat behind your keyboard and you plonked the monitor on top of it. In response to demand, a little re-jigging of layout has resulted in a system unit with a **tower** case: in a small room, this has the great advantage that you can stow the unit out of the way under your desk and still be able to pop a disk into its floppy-disk drive without too many physical contortions.

The second major difference between the desktop and the notebook is price. In contrast with many of the products we buy, in the world of PCs *bigger is cheaper*! The technical difficulties involved in building all this power into a smaller box mean that a notebook PC is always more expensive than a desktop with the same specifications.

# The notebook PC

The notebook PC has been known by quite a variety of names over the years: to begin with it was called the **portable**, a term which required a slight stretch of the imagination when trying to carry one any distance. The portable gradually became smaller and lighter and today these early portables tend to be known as **luggables** for obvious reasons. Further downward shifts in scale have given us the **laptop**, and now finally the **notebook**, so-called because of its similarity in size to a sheet of A4 paper (apart from being about two inches thicker of course!).

To actually make a PC portable isn't easy. It has to have similar capabilities to the desktop variety in a much smaller case which obviously involves removing a few components and making a number of others more compact. Nevertheless, the fundamentals are all there: the monitor is housed in the hinged lid which flips up to reveal the keyboard; the mouse is replaced by a stick or a touch-sensitive pad which requires less room to manoeuvre; the hard-disk sits beneath the keyboard together with the slot-in rechargeable battery. Most notebooks now come with a floppy-disk drive and either a CD-ROM or DVD-ROM drive, though these may be external units that you have to carry around, and you may not be able to connect both at the same time.

As with the desktop PC, extra accessories can be added to the notebook but, due to the constraints of size, they can't be fitted permanently – there's no space for them! The solution is the addition of slots in the side of the case into which these extras (in the form of credit-card sized devices called **PC Cards**) can be plugged when needed. Another constraint upon notebook users is that upgrading internal components can be difficult, expensive and, in some cases, impossible, so it becomes all the more important to choose your machine carefully.

# The miniature PC

The third type of PC is the 'everything else' category. If you've decided you need a computer, the odds are that you need either the desktop or the notebook variety and you won't need to consider the remaining options. Miniature PCs vary in their power and capability, but what they have in common is that they make significant compromises to bring you something that looks and acts rather like a PC in a much smaller case.

The first of these types is the **sub-notebook**, a device that looks a lot like a notebook PC but is roughly half the size and weight. This means that the screen and keyboard are half the size as well, which may make the PC uncomfortable to use for long periods, but many sub-notebooks are as powerful and capable as a full-sized notebook computer. One of the most popular sub-notebooks is the Sony Vaio.

Scaling down even further, there's the **handheld PC** (HPC, sometimes called a personal digital assistant or PDA). The HPC is small enough to hold in your hand, at around seven inches across by four inches deep. Despite its diminutive size, it still has a screen and tiny keyboard, along with enough storage capacity to hold a bundle of useful programs and files you create yourself. Until recently, the HPC market has been ruled by the US Robotics PalmPilot and the Psion series, but a new range of handhelds has arrived that uses a cut-down version of the Windows operating system called Windows CE. Windows CE enables the HPC to do some of the things a desktop or notebook PC can do, but its main role is still to act as a pocket organizer and scratch pad for times when you're away from your desktop PC. Popular HPCs are Hewlett Packard's Journada series and the Philips Velo 1.

Finally there's the Palm PC, a still smaller device that also uses Windows CE. The keyboard appears as a picture on its tiny screen and letters are 'typed' by touching the screen. This little unit can record voice messages and recognize your handwriting when you write on its screen with a stylus. Like the sub-notebook and handheld PCs, you can connect this to your main PC to transfer files back and forth between the two.

# THE NOTEBOOK AND PORTABLE ADD-ONS

▶ **IN THIS APPENDIX**

What to look for in a notebook PC

PC Cards: pocket-sized add-ons

Mobile printing in full colour

Do you really need a desktop PC as well?

When it comes to buying a notebook PC and choosing add-on hardware to use with it, there's good news and there's bad news. The good news is that the choices are much easier to make, but this is largely because of the bad news: there are a lot less to choose from. In this appendix we'll look at the issues to consider when buying the notebook itself, and what options are available for connecting extra devices.

# Get it right first time!

When you buy a desktop PC, you have some leeway to make mistakes. Not that you want to do that, of course, but if you're not happy with your keyboard or mouse, for example, you can buy replacements for as little as £20 each. Even the monitor, though expensive, *can* be replaced.

With a notebook PC, things are not quite as simple. The monitor screen and keyboard are built into the machine, making replacement almost impossible. So the single most important thing to do before deciding what to buy is to spend time in a few computer stores trying out as many notebooks as you can get your hands on. Remember that keyboard and screen quality can vary immensely even between models from the same manufacturer.

The monitor is especially important and the two points to check are size and clarity. Sizes currently vary between about 10.4 inches and 15 inches, and the picture quality will tend to be determined by whether the monitor is dual-scan colour or a more expensive TFT screen. TFT screens are essential if you'll be using your notebook for work that relies on accurate colour representation (desktop publishing, graphics, and so on), and you might feel that the better quality is worth the extra expense even for non-graphics use, especially if this is to be your main PC. The TFT screen is recommended, but, as in anything else you buy, remember that there are good dual-scan screens and poor TFT screens.

Along with the comfort, spacing and layout of the keyboard, the device used to replace the mouse is important. Some notebooks use a trackball, a small thumb-operated ball that sits just below the keyboard, or a finger-controlled stick in the centre of the keyboard. Increasingly, however, new notebooks use a touch-sensitive glide-pad instead, generally making control of the on-screen pointer a lot easier. The size of this pad makes a difference (larger is usually better), and you'll want to be sure that the pad is responsive to a finger tap or drag.

Here are a few additional points to check:

▶ The screen must be capable of displaying a resolution of at least 800×600 dpi.

▶ You'll need at least two Type II card slots for PC card devices, giving one Type III slot (see below).

▶ Battery life can vary between one and five hours. Remember that the quoted battery life will always be slightly optimistic, and check the recharge time.

▶ Most notebooks come with a floppy-disk drive and a CD-ROM or DVD-ROM drive, but some allow you to use only one at a time and they may be separate units that plug into the notebook, giving you more gadgets to carry around.

## Balancing act

BY THE WAY

When buying larger PC Card devices such as CD-ROM drives, make sure the cable between the card and the drive itself is long enough: a short cable might mean you have to balance both notebook and drive on your lap at the same time.

# PC cards and slots

PC card is a more recent name for PCMCIA cards (short for Personal Computer Memory card International Association). Notebook computers have PC card slots into which these credit-card sized devices can be fitted when you need to use them. A PC card device might be a hard-drive, CD-ROM drive, modem, extra memory – almost anything you can buy for your desktop computer can be bought in PC card form. The main difference (if you ignore the high cost of these cards) is that only one or two of these cards can be plugged in at any time, but cards are appearing that combine several accessories into one device (such as combined network/modem/ISDN cards).

PC card slots come in two different sizes: the Type II slot which takes smaller cards such as RAM and modems, and the Type III slot for larger accessories like additional hard-disks. The usual notebook specification now includes two Type II slots mounted one above the other allowing two small cards or one large one to be inserted.

## Power drain

When a PC card is connected to your notebook it's still drawing battery power whether you're using it or not. Make sure you remove any cards after use.

The size and weight of these cards makes them easy to carry around in a pocket or briefcase, but the prices are considerably higher than those for comparable full-sized devices. For notebook users on a budget, one option is to buy the smallest full-size device you can get your hands on and connect it to the notebook's serial, parallel or USB port when you need it, but of course you'll need access to a mains supply and you're now carrying a larger piece of kit plus two cables instead of one small card device.

## Cards on the desktop

PC cards aren't limited to notebook PCs – you can buy a PCMCIA interface card for your desktop machine and use PC cards with that too. Clearly this isn't the kind of expansion option that the typical desktop user will regard as a must-have: why pay twice the going rate for a modem that keeps getting lost amongst your other office clutter? For the confirmed notebook user, on the other hand, it might be a worthwhile investment. If most of your work is done on the notebook and you keep a desktop machine for occasional use, a PCMCIA interface will let you use the accessories you've already bought rather than having to equip the desktop with similar full-size devices.

# The better battery

The external device you can't live without if you have a notebook PC is the battery, or perhaps *batteries* if you'll be relying heavily on your machine. Notebook batteries are all removable and rechargeable, and come in two delicious flavours: nickel metal hydride (NiMH), or lithium.

The NiMH battery is the cheaper and more common of the two, but the more expensive lithium battery can power your notebook for longer. Using PC card peripherals will discharge your battery a lot faster, so it's worth looking for a notebook that uses the lithium battery if you expect to be using these cards for much of your computing time.

## Hidden charges

BY THE WAY

When buying a notebook, always find out how long it takes to recharge the battery (some batteries will recharge fully in as little as two hours) and how many hours you can get from a fully-charged battery in normal use.

# Printing on the move

The first thing to say on this subject is that mobile printing should be avoided if possible. Although portable printers are cheaper than their full-size counterparts, they lag behind in quality and speed. In addition, of course, you're giving yourself another couple of kilos to lug around, so you might prefer to print your documents when you get back to your desktop computer (if you have one) or buy a full-size printer and leave it at home.

If a portable printer is a necessity, you should be looking for a colour inkjet printer such as Brother MP21C (which has the benefit of drawing its power from your notebook), or Hewlett Packard's DeskJet 340. There's a catch with some models to watch out for though: to be truly portable, a printer should be able to run on batteries rather than mains, but some manufacturers insist on regarding the battery pack as an optional extra and charging for it separately!

# At home with the notebook

In the past, many notebook users had a desktop PC at home or in the office that they regarded as their 'main' computer, and the notebook acted as a useful accessory that they would use when they had to. The notebook is easy to use like this: it can run the same Windows operating system and all the applications you use on your desktop PC. Windows' Direct Cable Connection accessory makes it easy to connect the two computers together and transfer files back and forth, and the Briefcase accessory can track different versions of the documents you work on to make sure that you have got the most recent version on both machines.

A couple of years ago, the reason for having both notebook *and* desktop PCs was that the notebook simply wasn't much fun to use: small drab screen, poky keys, fiddly mouse control, and the speed and capabilities of a notebook couldn't come close to matching the power of the desktop. However things have come a long way since then. Although notebook technology still lags slightly behind that of the desktop, these machines are much more useable and, at last, make a credible alternative to the desktop.

This leads to two extra add-ons worth considering that add a little extra flexibility to the notebook as desktop replacement:

**Port replicator**. This is a reasonably cheap device into which you can slot your notebook, which gives you an easy way to connect typical desktop peripherals such as a full-sized monitor, keyboard and printer.

**Docking station**. A more advanced (and expensive) device which adds the other useful abilities of the desktop system unit: drive bays for access to extra disk drives and backup drives, and expansion slots to give you access to the cheaper desktop expansion cards.

In effect, either of the above devices will give you the best of both worlds. Without the full expense of buying and maintaining a desktop PC, you have easy access to the desktop features you need.

# C

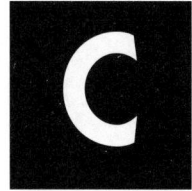

# BUYING A NEW PC

When it comes to choosing a new PC, there's no magic formula that can tell you what to buy: a set of specifications that's ideal for one user may be overkill for another, and hideously under-powered for a third. In theory, you should choose a PC according to the software you want to use – after all, it's the software that makes the PC a useful tool. For example, if you just need to run an integrated package like Microsoft Works or one large application at a time like Lotus WordPro, you don't necessarily need a fast, expensive system. However, while it's obviously sensible to make sure you choose a PC that can cope with your choice of software, it's hard to be sure that that's *all* you'll want to use the PC for in a year's time. So the single most important piece of advice to keep in mind as you decide what to buy is: *think ahead*!

## Power in reserve

BY THE WAY

Many people running high-specification PCs will be using the same two or three applications a lot of the time, but they've got the security of knowing they can get a lot more out of the system whenever they need to.

# Buying a desktop PC

The desktop machine is by far the cheapest route to take both in terms of initial cost and in the price of add-on hardware. All the same, a high-specification PC is still a major purchase so you don't want to get it wrong. The table below shows the specifications of four example computers, ranging from a minimum-specification to a high-spec machine, with a few explanatory notes beneath. These specifications are included for guidance only – to save on initial costs, you can add extra RAM, a CD-ROM drive, soundcard and so on later if you need to. Pay particular attention to processor, monitor and hard-disk capacity, the elements that are expensive or (sometimes) complicated to either upgrade or replace later. The example specifications assume that you want to run Windows 98 and a typical range of the latest home/office software.

| | Minimum | Low | Recommended | High |
|---|---|---|---|---|
| Processor type | Pentium II | Celeron or Pentium III | Athlon or Pentium III | Athlon or Pentium III |
| Processor speed | 400 MHz | 500 MHz | 733 or 750 MHz | 1 GHz |
| RAM | 32 MB | 64 MB | 128 MB SDRAM | 256 MB SDRAM |
| Hard-disk | 4 GB | 6.4 GB | 12 GB | 20 GB+ |
| Floppy-disk drive | 1 | 1 | 1 | SuperDisk drive |
| Backup/archive drive | – | – | – | 1 |
| Monitor size | 14-inch | 15-inch | 17-inch | 19- or 21-inch |
| Graphics card | 4 MB RAM | 8 MB RAM | 16 MB RAM, AGP | 32 MB RAM, AGP |
| 3D graphics accelerator | – | – | Yes | Yes |
| CD/DVD-ROM drive | CD-ROM | CD-ROM | DVD-ROM | DVD-ROM |
| CD-RW drive | – | – | Yes | Yes |
| Modem | – | Yes | Yes | Yes |

**Minimum**. If you hunt around, you might find a new PC with a lower specification, but this is the minimum worth buying. Like each of the four machines listed, this will run Windows 98, but that 32 MB RAM will have Windows trotting rather than sprinting. Although I haven't specified a modem, it's hard to find a new PC package that doesn't include one, and this machine is certainly good enough for full Internet use. It isn't a machine that's intended to be worked hard or used regularly for long periods: that 14-inch monitor is a bit small, there's not enough RAM for a computer that's going to be frequently opening, closing and switching between large applications, and it's not going to be a stunning multimedia or game system. It's a good system for occasional small office/home use with a package such as Microsoft Works, or for someone wishing to 'test the water' before committing to a more expensive system.

**Low**. A far more practical base for running Windows with a reasonable turn of speed. From solid office software such as Microsoft Office to games and multimedia, this machine will deliver. In summary: a good machine for the kids, a more suitable machine for small office/home use than the minimum specification, but lacking in punch for heavy-duty use. This system will quickly start to groan under the demands of next year's software.

**Recommended**. If you're looking for a machine that handles everything well, this is it. The combination of a large monitor and plenty of RAM on its graphics card makes this a pleasant system to work with for long periods, with good support for graphics and image processing. The fast processor and 128 MB RAM make the system responsive, and heavyweight software titles like Microsoft Office and Lotus SmartSuite will perform well. The graphics accelerator pushes this machine into the multimedia zone, making DVD movies and games a pleasure, but it isn't necessary for business use. Similarly, the rewriteable CD drive could be swapped for a cheaper backup drive. The capacity of the hard-disk is enough to hold everything you could throw at it, even if you work with very large files.

## Double version

For frequent use, you may want to consider a double-monitor setup. Windows 98 and 2000 both allow you to add a second graphics card, connect a second monitor to it, and stretch your desktop across two screens. This provides an excellent way to view multiple windows while working, refer to one document while working with another, and so on.

**High**. You want the best, and you don't care what it costs! This machine has everything, and has it in spades. A 21-inch monitor may be overkill unless you work extensively with desktop publishing and large spreadsheets, and might feel uncomfortably similar to sitting a foot away from your TV. This machine probably comes with a 19-inch monitor as standard, and that should be ideal. Here you've got the best 'future-proofing' possible, with the recommended specification unlikely to reach this point for over a year. In summary: if this is *your* system, *we're* envious!

## Buying a notebook PC

Although the purchase of *any* PC should never be taken lightly, buying a notebook takes even more care than buying a desktop since its components are either much more expensive or totally impossible to replace. PC cards give you the ability to add extra RAM or a second hard-disk, but they fill a slot you could be using for something else if the PC itself were better equipped.

The four specifications in the following table assume that you need to use your notebook for exactly the same tasks that you would use a desktop PC for – in other words, as your sole computer. It's worth noting that notebook specifications are always following several steps behind the desktop.

| | Minimum | Low | Recommended | High |
|---|---|---|---|---|
| Processor type | Celeron | Pentium II | Pentium III | Pentium III |
| Processor speed | 366 MHz | 400 MHz | 450 MHz | 600 MHz |
| RAM | 32 MB | 32 MB | 64 MB | 128 MB |
| Hard-disk | 2.5 MB | 4 GB | 6.4 GB | 10 GB |
| Floppy-disk drive | 1 | 1 | 1 | 1 |
| Screen | 11.3-inch Dual-Scan | 11.3-inch TFT | 13- or 14-inch TFT | 15-inch TFT |
| Max. screen resolution | 640×480 | 800×600 | 1024×768 | 1024×768 |
| Slots | 2×Type II | 2×Type II, 1×Type III | 2×Type II, 1×Type III | 3×Type II or 1×Type II + 1×Type III |
| CD-ROM drive | Swappable with floppy drive | Swappable with floppy drive | Yes | DVD-ROM |
| Modem | – | – | Yes | Yes |

# Have I wasted my money?

Regardless of what you buy now, in six months' time you'll see systems with the same specifications advertised at prices perhaps 20 per cent lower. The instinctive feeling is that you should have waited, or that you've somehow been conned, but don't torture yourself! In the computer world technology moves very fast, and there's an endless array of bigger and better products arriving on the market that push down the prices of existing products. If you'd waited six months before buying, you would see exactly the same effect six months after that.

The fact that there's no escaping this cycle serves to underline an important point in computer buying: *buy what you need*. You can interpret that in two ways:

▶ If you know exactly what tasks this computer will have to perform and what software you'll use, a computer that can handle these now will still handle them in ten years' time. Provided you don't hanker after the latest software versions and hardware add-ons every year, you are future-proof.

▶ If you *do* want to keep up with the latest software, multimedia add-ons and PC capabilities, buy with an eye to expansion. A large hard-disk and fast processor, along with vacant drive bays and expansion slots, will take everything you can throw at it for two or three years, and perhaps longer. Eventually you'll reach a point at which some element of your PC can't cope with the device or application you want to use, but a good base machine can be kept alive longer with a few economic upgrades.

# Warranties

All new computers should come with at least a one-year warranty as standard. Many packages (as well as one-off peripheral purchases) give you the chance to extend the warranty to three or more years in return for cash. Don't be tempted! There are two reasons why the standard one-year warranty is enough: first and foremost, if a component is going to curl up and die, it's usually going to do it long before the first year is up; second, if it fails after the first year, prices will have fallen still further and you'll probably be able to replace the part yourself for a lot less than the price of the extra cover.

BY THE WAY

## A little help from your friends

Support is often more useful than a warranty. Ask if there is a telephone support-line you can call – it's more likely that you'll need help installing new hardware, for example, than it is that you'll need the PC to be taken away to be fixed.

Bear in mind that your basic one-year warranty will usually be of the 'back-to-base' type: if something goes wrong, you will have to pack up your machine and send it away for repair. You might want to consider paying extra for an on-site warranty if you rely on your PC for daily use.

# You get free software!

Most computer packages include a range of software, which has usually already been installed when you take delivery (with the exception of games and multimedia titles intended to be run from CD-ROM). This bundle of software will include an operating system (see below), together with a range of productivity software such as an office suite, perhaps a few games, and so on. The software bundle will look very tempting (it's supposed to) and, being free, amazingly good value.

The first point to remember is: *nothing is free*! This software is included in the price you pay and the best you could say is that it's cheap. Being cheap isn't a crime of course, and one of the most popular integrated office applications, Microsoft Works, costs very little even if you buy it at full price. If this is included in the bundle, it's probably worth considering – you're sure to need these types of application at least occasionally, whatever the primary use of your PC. A full office suite like Microsoft Office or Lotus SmartSuite can seem a very attractive proposition, but they are large and powerful applications with many more features than the average user is ever likely to need and you might just find them unwieldy for day-to-day working.

This highlights the second point: do you really need this software? Hopefully you'll have a pretty good idea of what you'll be using your PC for; if this software isn't what you had in mind, you may be able to find a similar computer with no bundled software at a cheaper price, and use the saving to buy the software you want.

Finally, make sure you'll be provided with the manuals for all this software, and the installation disk(s) in case you ever need to re-install the software yourself.

# The all-important operating system

Whether your new PC comes with a bundle of software titles or not, it should definitely include an operating system. The operating system should be installed on the hard-disk already so that you can just switch on and start using the computer. Although installing an operating system is rarely more troublesome than installing any other type of software, you definitely don't want that to be your first computing experience. As with the software bundle, make sure you're provided with the original installation CD-ROM.

Almost without exception, the operating system installed on a new PC will be Microsoft's Windows 98 Second Edition. Almost 90 per cent of the world's computers run a Windows system, and this is the most recent version for which vast numbers of software titles are available.

There are other PC operating systems, of course, but to explain the use of each would be well beyond the scope of this book. Here is a quick description of some that you might see mentioned:

**Windows 3.1**. This version of Windows was available in several forms (such as Windows 3.11), and they are sometimes collectively referred to as Windows 3.x. This was the forerunner to Windows 95 and 98, and was almost as easy to use although it looked very different. A huge amount of software was (and still is) available. Windows 3.x was less power-hungry than 95 or 98, running happily on slow pre-Pentium systems with 4 MB RAM, but it required MS-DOS to be installed on the PC too. Rather than an operating system in its own right, this version of Windows was a 'friendly face' for MS-DOS.

**MS-DOS**. The original PC operating system, which few people use by choice nowadays. Instead of Windows' colourful attractive features, clickable icons, and simple menus, DOS offered a plain screen on which cryptic text commands had to be typed to make anything happen. (If you choose to, you can get a flavour of DOS by clicking the MS-DOS Prompt icon on the Windows Start Menu.)

**Windows NT**. Microsoft's full-strength operating system, aimed at the demanding corporate network environment. The various versions of Windows NT look very much like Windows 3.1 or Windows 95/98, but they are very different under the bonnet and demand a more powerful computer. Certain software designed for the Windows 3/95/98 series won't run on NT, and versions of NT up to 4.0 have very poor support for some of the fancy devices you may want to add, such as scanners or rewritable CD-ROM drives.

**Windows 2000**. This is actually version 5.0 of the Windows NT series, given a more friendly name. It looks just like Windows 98, with a few added features aimed at corporate users and networking. It is a much tougher and sturdier system that Windows 98, and once again demands a more powerful computer.

**Windows Millennium**. The successor to Windows 98, still being developed. This is just a codename that invites the obvious abbreviation to 'WindMill', but there are whispers that it will be released during 2000 as Windows 2000 Personal Edition.

**OS/2 Warp**. This IBM operating system is a sometime challenger to Windows that takes a similar approach to Windows 95/98. Unfortunately, it failed to capture the PC-user's imagination in the same way that Windows did, with the result that there is a comparatively tiny amount of software available and some areas of computing have no OS/2 software at all. Add-ons to the basic OS/2 system do enable it to run some Windows 3.x-compatible software.

**Windows CE**. It's tempting to refer to this as a cut-down version of Windows 98 (although Microsoft wish we wouldn't), and it's the operating system used in many handheld and sub-notebook PCs. It offers a subset of the accessories included with Windows 98, and extra features to help you convert and copy files between the handheld and your main PC.

**Linux**. A free and increasingly popular operating system for PCs. There are various flavours of Linux available, the most popular being Red Hat or SuSE, and you have to pay a moderate price to cover packaging and distribution costs. Although the operating system is the same in each case, these various flavours differ in what extra software is included with them and (to some degree) how easy they are to install. The main point against Linux is that it can't run Windows software. In its favour, though, there's a lot of compatible software available for it (much of which is actually included with the package), it runs happily on a far less powerful system than Windows, and it's probably the most reliable operating system available today.

# Quickfire buying tips

Apart from choosing the PC itself and any other peripherals and software you want, a few other points need attention when buying. Here is a list of the more important ones that apply equally to whole computer systems and to single add-on devices:

▶ For extra security, try to pay by credit card.

- ▶ Always check what the final price will be, including extra peripherals or software you asked to be added, tax and delivery, and get it in writing.

- ▶ When you place an order, tell the vendor what you want to use the computer for. This will give you extra leverage if the PC doesn't prove fit for the task.

- ▶ Find out what your options are for refund or replacement if you're unhappy with your purchase. Make sure you get written confirmation of these terms.

- ▶ If you order by telephone, keep records of who you spoke to and when, and make notes on what was offered and at what price. Follow up with a fax or letter detailing the order, agreed terms and price. If a delivery date was given and is vital, include the words 'Time is of the essence'. This is a legal term that gives you the right to cancel the order if delivery isn't made by the quoted date.

- ▶ When you sign for the delivery, add the words 'Goods not inspected' before your signature.

- ▶ When you receive the goods, set everything up and check it carefully. Make sure you inform the vendor immediately if something is missing or not working – if you leave it too long, you may find it more difficult to justify a refund or replacement.

- ▶ Keep all the cartons and packaging in case you need to return the system or send it for repair sometime in the future.

- ▶ Keep *all* the paperwork that came with the computer in one place.

- ▶ Don't fill in any warranty or registration cards for hardware or software until you know it's complete and it works.

# D

# DEALING WITH
# HARDWARE PROBLEMS

Windows provides a friendly help-based Hardware Conflict Troubleshooter which aims to solve hardware problems in question-and-answer style. Choose **Help** from the Start Menu, click the **Contents** tab, then click **Troubleshooting**, followed by **Windows 98 Troubleshooters** and **Hardware Conflict**. With luck, you will be able to solve the problem without getting tangled up with the technical aspects of the PC. If you're not so lucky, the following pages coupled with your hardware manuals should give you a few clues.

# Understanding resources

With many types of hardware you add to your system, the question of **resource settings** will raise its ugly head, particularly with expansion cards. Resources are one of the most complicated areas of PCs you're likely to come up against, but you shouldn't have to deal with them too often unless you plan on buying new hardware every few weeks. (If you do, they'll soon seem pretty easy anyway!) Let's try looking at this in simpler terms first.

A car has resources; it has petrol, oil, and water. Some of its components need petrol, some need oil, others need water. So car makers *assign* these resources where they're needed: if a particular component needs petrol, for example, they make sure there is a hose connecting it to the petrol tank.

In a PC, there are also three typical resources that different components might need, which should be clearly listed in the device's manual: **I/O Port Address** (also known as Input/Output address or I/O range), **IRQ** (interrupt request line) and **DMA** (direct memory access). Here is a quick description of each:

**I/O Port address**. Identifies a particular area in memory that a single specific device can use.

**IRQ**. Whenever a device is called upon to do something (for example, your soundcard needs to play a sound), it has to interrupt whatever the processor is doing at that time. So it sends a request for processor time (an **interrupt request**) down a line to the processor, and these lines are numbered. The lower the number assigned to a particular device, the higher its priority in the queue when the processor is busy.

**DMA**. These are numbered channels rather like IRQs. A DMA channel is a direct line to the computer's memory, bypassing the processor. This gives an improvement in response times from the device, coupled with the fact that the processor is left alone to get on with other things in the meantime.

The most important aspect of these resources (which, sadly, doesn't remotely fit our car metaphor) is that these settings must be *unique* to each device. For example, if two devices are assigned IRQ2, one or both of them will be unable to work, giving a situation known as a **hardware conflict**.

In a similar way to device drivers, mentioned above, there are two methods of allocating resources to a newly-installed device. If you're lucky (or you bought carefully), the device will come with a program on a disk to help you out. This program will examine your entire system to see which resources are available (that is, haven't been assigned to another device) and tell you which ones you should choose. Most of the time this will be as simple as agreeing to the program's suggestions and letting it update the system for you, but once in a while you might need to change settings on the hardware itself, and the device's manual will explain how to do that.

If you're unlucky, you might have to configure these resource settings yourself. This will involve looking at the resources already allocated to all the other devices attached to your computer and making notes of any available ones. You will then need to check the manual for the new device to see which settings are suitable. For example, despite the fact that there are 15 IRQ lines, some devices (typically the cheaper ones) might be able to work with only two or three of them. If these two or three lines are already being used, you've got the added thrill of checking the manuals of *other* devices to see if you can swap the IRQs around and free-up one of the lines you need.

# Finding system settings in Device Manager

Almost all the nitty-gritty of your system that affects (or is controlled by) Windows can be found in Control Panel's **System** applet. You can either double-click this icon or, for quicker access, right-click on My Computer, and choose **Properties**.

Following the basic information on the **General** page, the first tab you come to is **Device Manager**. This follows the familiar 'tree-structure' used in Explorer's left pane. From this page, you can:

▶ View all the devices connected to your computer.

▶ Add/remove or disable/enable devices.

▶ See which drivers are used for particular devices and change them.

▶ Check and change settings, addresses and IRQs.

▶ Check and alter port settings (mouse, modem, printer etc.).

▶ Make sure that each device is working properly.

It is well worth taking a browse through Device Manager even as an inexperienced user: expand trees, select devices and choose the **Properties** button for each. Provided you don't actually change anything, this is risk-free. For the nervous, the simple way to change nothing is: never click **OK** – always use **Cancel** to close a dialog.

By selecting the **Computer** entry at the top of the Device Manager list and clicking **Properties**, you can view devices by resource: for example, click the **Interrupt Request** radio-button to see which IRQs are in use, and by which devices – useful information to have if you need to find a free IRQ to allocate to a newly-installed device.

## Making resource settings

Assuming your computer has a Plug & Play BIOS, when you install a Plug & Play device Windows allocates the resources for it automatically. On the **Resources** tab of a device's Properties page in Device Manager you should see that the **Use automatic settings** box is checked. This gives Windows the freedom to juggle resources around between different devices if you install more Plug & Play hardware, so this box is always best left checked.

With a Plug & Play BIOS, Windows will still try to allocate correct resources for a *non*-Plug & Play device, but these may not always suit the hardware itself. If they don't, you'll need to clear the **Use automatic settings** checkbox and specify your own settings instead according to the details given in the device's manual.

If neither hardware nor BIOS are Plug & Play compatible, the **Use automatic settings** box will be greyed out and you'll have to identify and set the resources manually.

## Setting resources manually

Different hardware will require different resources, such as **IRQ** (interrupt request), **DMA** (direct memory access) channel, **I/O** (Input/Output) range, and **Memory address**. The following steps explain how to carry out the common operation of changing the IRQ setting. The procedure is the same to change the setting for one of the other resources – just select the resource you want to change in the **Resource Settings** window.

1 Highlight the offending device in Device Manager and click **Properties**.

2 Click the **Resources** tab, and highlight the **Interrupt Request** entry in the **Resource Settings** window.

3 Make sure the **Use automatic settings** box isn't checked; if it is, clear the checkbox.

4 Click the **Change Setting**… button.

5 Change the interrupt setting in the **Value** box, keeping an eye on the lower box for an indication that you've picked a non-conflicting setting, as shown in the next screenshot.

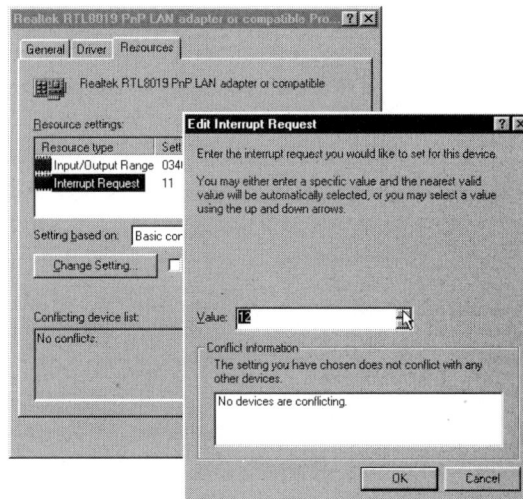

▶ Assigning a different interrupt request to a device.

337

Of course, not only do you have to choose an IRQ that doesn't conflict with other installed devices, it must be one that your device can respond to, and some devices respond to a very limited number. You might be able to juggle IRQs for other devices to free-up a compatible one, but it's possible you'll have to replace the device itself with one with greater IRQ support.

If you can find an available IRQ that *is* compatible with your device, you may have to alter jumper or DIP switch settings on the hardware accordingly – check the device's manuals for details.

## Preset configurations

Some devices offer different preset configurations: before modifying any resource settings, take a look in the drop-down list titled **Setting based on**. A different configuration may give you the settings you need, or may let you change settings that were fixed in a different configuration.

# JARGON BUSTER
# SUPER REFERENCE

▶ **IN THIS APPENDIX**

People who use computers always end up talking in an alien language, one that seems to feature an awful lot of capital letters ('*I opened the DTP file on the CD-R, then converted it to HTML and FTP-ed it to the WWW using my ISDN TA.*') and a fair sprinkling of made-up words like 'modem', 'gigabyte' and 'shareware'. It may not be a language you want to speak yourself, but it helps to have a translating dictionary at the ready.

In this section, you'll find simple explanations of the most popular abbreviations, acronyms and technical gobbledegook in use. Keep a look out for words and phrases in *italic text* – they indicate a related entry.

**application** One of many words for a computer program, a file containing instructions which tell the computer what to do. Some applications play CDs, others let you create pictures and graphics, more let you send faxes, write letters, and so on.

**ASCII** Text that contains characters readable on any type of computer using any word processor or *text editor*. An ASCII file can't contain fancy formatting (bold text, colours, different text sizes, etc.). ASCII is often referred to as 'plain text', and it's the kind of file that the Notepad accessory can open and create.

**backup** A file you copy somewhere (usually on to a different disk) as a safety copy, in case something happens to the original.

**bit** The tiniest possible amount of computer data. A computer only understands the difference between yes/no, on/off, 0/1, etc. and a bit is the amount of data that can store one of these settings. Not being much use by themselves, bits are combined into groups of eight called *bytes*.

**boot** The technical term for starting an operating system, which is what you do when you switch your computer on. When you press the reset key on the system unit (or choose an option that says Restart while you are using Windows) you're 'rebooting'.

**bps** An abbreviation of *bits* per second, used to measure and compare the speeds of computing devices (particularly modems).

**bug** A mistake in a piece of software such as an *application* or an operating system. Software is written by real people, and real people make mistakes. Although software is tested before being released for sale, some bugs only show up when you do some weird combination of things while using the program which no-one had foreseen. Some bugs are just the result of lazy programming and poor testing, of course.

**byte** A group of eight *bits*, and the smallest useful unit of computer data. A byte is enough to store one single character (such as the letter 'a'). See also *gigabyte, kilobyte, megabyte*.

**CD-ROM** An acronym for compact disk read-only memory. A CD-ROM looks just like an audio CD, but it contains computer data that can't be read by an ordinary CD player. The 'ROM' part means that the disk can be read, but no new data can be stored on it. A CD-ROM can hold about 650 MB (*megabytes*) of data.

**clipboard** A temporary storage space built into Windows that any program can access. The Cut and Copy options in a program let you place text, graphics, files and other items on the clipboard (replacing what was there previously), and the Paste option copies the contents of the clipboard to the window you're working in.

**COM port** An abbreviation of communications port (also known as serial ports). Most PCs have two identical COM ports named COM1 and COM2 on the back of the system unit, and traditionally this is where the mouse and modem are connected to the computer. The PS/2 port has largely replaced the use of COM1 for the mouse, and more recently still, the arrival of the *USB* port has replaced pretty much every kind of port.

**context menu** A menu that appears when you right-click on almost anything in Windows. Which options appear on the menu depend on what it was you clicked (in other words, they change according to the 'context').

**CPU** Short for central processing unit, and also referred to as the microprocessor or processor. This is the computer's 'brain', the tiny device in the system unit that handles everything the computer has to do.

**crash** If a program unexpectedly stops taking any notice of mouse clicks or key-presses, or shuts down suddenly, or otherwise becomes unusable, it has 'crashed'. You usually get some warning, such as a *dialog box* stating that the program has 'performed an illegal action and will be closed'. Restarting the program may solve the problem, but program crashes sometimes make the entire system unstable, so it's usually best to shut down Windows and restart your PC.

**cursor** Usually the name of the flashing vertical or horizontal line that indicates where the next piece of text you type will appear. The word is also used for the various shapes and designs of the mouse-pointer.

**desktop publishing (DTP)** A program that can help you create documents containing text and graphics, such as brochures and newsletters. Although some good word-processors have similar abilities, a DTP program offers much finer control over the layout of the pages, along with better features for organising and printing your work.

**dialog/dialog box** A small window that pops open to ask you a question or prompt you for information. The windows that appear when you choose Run or Shut Down from the Start menu are both examples of dialog boxes.

**directory** The *MS-DOS* word for a *folder*, also used in early versions of Windows.

**document** Although it's usually used to describe a file containing text, created in a word processor, Windows uses the word 'document' for any file that you created yourself.

**DOS** See *MS-DOS*.

**download** The act of copying a file from one distant computer to your own computer. See also *upload*.

**DVD** An abbreviation of digital versatile disk. DVD disks look just like compact-disks, but they're able to hold over ten times as much data. DVDs are starting to replace video cassettes in movie distribution, and they'll soon replace *CD-ROMs* for computer use.

**email** Short for electronic mail, a method of sending messages from your computer to someone else's computer over a *network* (usually the *Internet*). Email messages are usually plain text, but it's possible to include fancy formatting and send copies of computer files with the message.

**executable** To do anything with your computer, you have to run (or 'execute') the program you want to use; the difference between a program file and a *document* file is that a program is executable. Executables have the *extension* .exe, .bat or .com. As an example, when you use Notepad, you're running an executable file called 'notepad.exe'.

**expansion card**  A circuit board that plugs into an *expansion slot* inside your PC's system unit giving your computer extra capabilities. An expansion card might contain a *modem* or a graphics adapter, for example.

**expansion slot**  One of around eight slots in your PC's system unit into which *expansion cards* can be installed. Modern PCs have one AGP slot for a graphics adapter, several PCI slots for other types of device, and (usually) two ISA slots for older types of device. These slots are all different sizes, so comparing the connectors on a new card with the sizes of the slots will tell you where the card should go.

**extension**  The names of files end with a dot followed by several (usually three) characters, and this is the extension. Windows hides the file extension from you, but uses it to determine which program should be used when you double-click on a file's icon to open it.

**floppy-disk**  A removable $3\frac{1}{2}$-inch storage disk encased in plastic used for storing files. Floppy-disks can't hold much data (roughly 1.44 *megabytes*), but they are useful for carrying small files between one computer and another, or for taking *backup* copies of important (but still smallish) files. Floppy-disks are inserted into the floppy-disk drive, a slot in the front of your PC's system unit, when you want to use them.

**folder**  A storage place for files on a disk. Folders can contain any number of files, and can also contain more folders (known as *subfolders*) each containing yet more files. Folders are generally used to organise the files you create yourself into logical groups so that you can easily find the file you're looking for.

**font**  A set of characters that all have the same design. Windows includes a variety of fonts, including Arial and Times New Roman.

**format**  1 To format a disk means to prepare it so that your computer can store files on to it and read them again later. Most floppy-disks are already formatted when you buy them, but you can re-format them to erase all data and use them again. 2 To change the layout or styling of a text document (or part of it), by applying bold or italic effects, for example, increasing the width of the margins, or using different *fonts*.

**freeware**  Software that you do not have to pay for. Freeware often turns up on magazine cover CDs, and it's available in abundance on the *Internet*.

**FTP (File Transfer Protocol)**  A *protocol* used by computers to handle the transfer of files between one computer and another on the *Internet*. Good FTP programs make this as easy as copying files from one *folder* to another on your own computer.

**gigabyte (GB)**  The largest unit in common use for measuring the storage capacity of disks such as *hard-disks* and *DVDs*. A gigabyte equals 1024 *megabytes*, or 1 048 576 *kilobytes*.

**hard-disk**  The fixed disk inside your computer's system unit that holds your Windows operating system, all the programs you have installed, and all the files you create yourself. The hard disk is usually named C:, and can often hold 10 GB (*gigabytes*) or more of data (equivalent to thousands of *floppy-disks*).

**HTML (HyperText Markup Language)**  The language in which pages on the *World Wide Web* are written. The language consists of 'tags', small pieces of text between < and > signs, which determine how items on the page should be displayed. For example, <B> is a tag that turns on bold text, so <B>Hello!</B> would be displayed as **Hello**!

**icon**  A small picture you see on the screen that represents a file or device on your computer – a file, a folder, a printer and so on.

**insertion point**  A flashing horizontal or vertical bar in a word-processor that tells you where you are in the document. Text you type will appear immediately to the left of this bar. (The insertion point is also known as the *cursor*.)

**Internet**  A giant worldwide *network* of computers. Unlike smaller networks, in which all the computers might be physically connected together using cables, the Internet's computers use telephone lines to talk to one another, requiring the use of a *modem* to translate the sound into computer data and vice versa.

**intranet**  A sort of mini-*Internet*, owned and used by one company or organization as a method of sharing documents and information between employees without making it accessible to the world at large.

**IRC (Internet relay chat)**  A method by which you can connect to chat rooms on the *Internet* and hold live 'conversations' with others in the same room by typing messages. Messages you type are visible to everyone else in the room, and you'll see what everyone else is saying.

**ISDN**  An abbreviation of integrated services digital network. Using a *terminal adapter* or an ISDN *expansion card* instead of an ordinary *modem*, your PC can make digital connections to other computers at speeds of up to 128 kbps.

**kilobyte (K, kB)**  A unit for measuring the sizes of files, or the storage capacity of disks and memory. A kilobyte is equals to 1024 *bytes*.

**megabyte (MB)**  Like the *byte*, *kilobyte*, and *gigabyte*, this is one of the computing units for measuring size and capacity. A megabyte equals 1024 kilobytes, or 1 048 576 bytes.

**menu, menu bar**  The menu bar is a strip along the top of most windows containing words such as File, Edit and Help. Clicking one of these words opens a menu, a list of available options from which you can select an option by clicking it. See also: *context menu*.

**microprocessor**  See *CPU*.

**modem**  A device used by your computer to convert computer data into sound so that it can be sent down a phone line to another computer, and to convert the sound it receives back into data. The fastest modems can receive data at 56 kbps (56 000 *bits* per second), but this speed is hugely dependant upon the quality of the phone line, as well as how fast the data is being sent from the other computer.

**MS-DOS**  The operating system for PCs that was the fore-runner to Windows. DOS gave you a plain black screen with a flashing *cursor*, and making the computer do anything required you to type (sometimes quite involved) commands. Modern PCs still use a chopped-down version of DOS, and you can select the MS-DOS Prompt item from the Start Menu to get a taste of DOS running in a window.

**multitasking**  Windows computers let you have several programs running, a file being printed, and an active connection to the *Internet*, all at the same time. This ability to do lots of things at once is known as multitasking.

**network**  Two or more computers connected to each other and able to access some or all of each others files and, sometimes, devices such as printers or *modems*. The *Internet* is the best known example of a network, but many companies and organisations have computer networks, and as computer prices fall, some home users buy a second PC and link the two together.

**notebook**  A small and (supposedly) portable computer with a screen in its hinged lid, a built-in keyboard, and a small stick or touch-sensitive pad to replace the mouse. Notebook computers are more expensive than desktop computers with similar features. Add-on devices such as modems can be bought in PC-card format (credit-card sized devices which slot into the computer). The term 'sub-notebook' is also used, meaning a scaled down notebook that is truly portable. While a notebook could easily replace a desktop system, a sub-notebook really is intended for use on the move and could be tiresome to use for long periods.

**online**  In the *Internet* world, being online means your computer has dialled up and connected to the Internet. More generally, anything that is attached to your computer, switched on and ready for use is said to be online, such as a printer.

**parallel port**  A single socket at the back of your PC's system unit into which your printer and/or scanner may be plugged. Your PC will usually refer to this as LPT1.

**path**  The full name of a file or folder on a computer disk. The path starts with the name of the drive (C:, for example), followed by the names of all the folders that must be opened before the item is reached, each preceded by a \ sign, and finally the name of the item itself. An example is C:\Program Files\Accessories\Mspaint.exe, which is the usual path to the Windows Paint program.

**peripheral**  Any device that is (or could be) attached to one of the ports and sockets at the back of your computer's system unit. Peripherals are optional devices, not essential to the use of the computer (although the keyboard and mouse tend to be thought of as peripherals, and it's essential to have at least one of those).

**pixel** The picture you see on your computer's monitor is made up of hundreds of thousands of individual dots, and these dots are known as pixels (stemming from 'picture cells'). See also *resolution*.

**plug & play** When you attach a new device to your computer that has plug & play features, your PC should be able to communicate with it, find out what it is, and handle the software configuration required to make it work without any help from you. You may be asked a few simple questions, but if all goes according to plan, you'll just click a button that says the equivalent of 'Yes, that's it, sort it out'.

**processor** See *CPU*.

**protocol** A set of rules that determines how two computers communicate with each other to carry out a certain task. The result is similar to a Czech and a Norwegian who don't speak each other's language, but may agree to talk to each other in French.

**RAM (random access memory)** The most important type of memory fitted in your PC. Any program or file you work with is loaded into RAM first, giving the computer extremely fast access to it. When the available RAM is filled, the computer starts using slower alternatives, so there's no such thing as too much RAM! More RAM can be installed in the form of DIMM chips (or SIMM chips in older computers). RAM is only a temporary store – when you close a file or program, the memory it was using is freed up for other uses, and the RAM is emptied when you shut down your computer.

**read-only** Something that can be read, viewed or opened, but can't be modified or deleted. Files and folders can be set as 'read-only', allowing you to view their contents. If you edit a read-only file and try to save it, you'll be prompted to choose a different name or location to protect the original file.

**resolution** The number of *pixels* your monitor is displaying. Resolution is noted by the number of horizontal pixels multiplied by the number of vertical pixels (e.g. 800 × 600, or 1024 × 768). Higher numbers mean a higher resolution with more dots used to create the displayed image, items on the screen will appear smaller but you will see more information on screen at any one time.

**ROM (read-only memory)** Any type of memory or storage that is *read-only*, i.e. you can read its contents but you can't change them. A good example is CD-ROM: the contents of the disk can be read, but you can't erase the disk or store anything new on it.

**root folder** The primary folder on every computer disk, which ultimately contains every folder and file on that disk. The root folder of your hard-disk, for example, contains your Windows folder, Program Files folder, and probably several files with unusual names. The root folder has the same name as the drive, plus a '\' sign, so your hard-disk's root folder is C:\ and your floppy-disk's root folder is A:\.

**serial port** See *COM port*.

**shareware** A popular method of distributing and selling software, particularly via the *Internet*. The software can be used for a specified period while you decide whether you like it. If you do, you pay for it; if not, you stop using it. The software will usually stop working when the trial period expires, unless you've paid for your copy.

**status bar** A strip at the very bottom of some windows that provides information about the contents of the window, or about an item you've selected in that window. The status bar often has a triangular 'size grip' at its right which you can click and drag to resize the window.

**subfolder** Any folder that's inside another folder is said to be a subfolder. The folder it's inside is said to be its parent folder. You can create subfolders inside any folder, but it's best to avoid adding or altering anything inside folders you didn't create yourself (the exception being the My Documents folder).

**Taskbar** The horizontal strip along the bottom of your screen. This remains visible all the time you are using Windows. Each program or window you open will add a button to the Taskbar, and you can click these buttons to view a window hidden behind others. The Taskbar can be moved to any edge of the screen by clicking on a blank area and dragging it to the desired location.

**terminal adapter (TA)** This is the *ISDN* equivalent of a *modem*. If you have an ISDN phone line and want to make high-speed digital connections from your computer to others, you need a terminal adapter (or its internal version, an ISDN card) rather than a modem.

**text editor**  A program used to create and edit plain-text (*ASCII*) files. Windows includes its own text editor accessory, Notepad.

**toolbar**  A horizontal strip found in most program windows that contains buttons you can click to select options. Most of these options can usually be found on the same program's *menu bar* too, but the toolbar generally provides easier access to the most-used options.

**tooltip**  A tiny box that appears when you hold the mouse over a button on a toolbar or (in some cases) an icon on the desktop, giving a brief explanation of what that item is for.

**tray**  Sometimes boringly referred to as the 'notification area', this is the recessed area at the right of the *Taskbar* which contains the clock and one or two (or perhaps many more) small icons for programs that are running. Right-click any of these icons to see the options available, or double-click the clock to change the time or date.

**upload**  The act of copying a file from your computer to some remote computer, and the opposite of *downloading*.

**UPS  (uninterruptible power supply)** Something you can plug your PC into which, in the event of a power cut, will keep your computer going long enough for you to save your work and shut down properly.

**USB (universal serial bus)**  A relatively new type of socket found on recent PCs that aims to replace *parallel ports* and *COM ports*. Devices are connected to these sockets, and to each other, by cables, with multiple devices connected to a single USB port. USB ports are faster than the ports they replace, and new devices can be connected without the need to turn off your PC first, and (with a bit of luck) without getting bogged down in complicated installation procedures, due to the wonders of *plug & play*.

**virus**  A program written and sneakily distributed by someone with a warped mind, usually by hiding it inside another program. Some types of virus can replicate themselves to invade other programs, fill your hard-disk with gobbledegook, or otherwise make your PC unusable. Other types can be relatively harmless, perhaps just making your computer go 'beep' once a year.

**World Wide Web (WWW, the Web)** An area of the *Internet* that consists of documents (Web pages) viewed using a program called a Web browser. These documents can contain text, images, sounds, animations, movies, and much more. The pages are written in a simple text-based language called *HTML*, and a page can contain clickable links to any of the billion-or-so other pages stored on computers anywhere in the world.

**write-protect** Floppy-disks have a little tab in one corner which, when shut, prevents any new data being written on to the disk and protects the existing data on it from being deleted. To write-protect a disk, just snap this little tab upwards so that you can see through the hole it was covering. Some other types of removable disk also have write-protect options, though these are usually accessed using a software program rather than by changing something on the disk's case.

# DIRECTORY

# 1: UK Internet access providers

Use the list below to find an IAP with the services you're looking for and a local POP, then give them a ring and check some of the details mentioned. All IAPs noted here offer the basic services of email, World Wide Web, FTP, Telnet, Gopher, IRC and newsgroup access. Extra details are included under *Notes*.

Bear in mind that this is not an exhaustive list, and these details change regularly – for example, over the last year many Web-space allocations have risen from 5 MB to 25 MB or more – so it doesn't hurt to ask if the details don't exactly match what you are looking for. Most IAPs have special packages for business users and a choice of home-user accounts. If you already have Internet access, an increasing number of free and subscription IAPs will let you sign up online.

| | |
|---|---|
| Company: | Abel Internet |
| Telephone: | 0131 445 5555 |
| Email: | info@abel.net.uk |
| WWW site: | www.abel.net.uk |
| POPs: | UK coverage |
| Notes: | ISDN, 10 MB Web space, unlimited email addresses |

| | |
|---|---|
| Company: | BT Internet |
| Telephone: | 0800 800001 |
| Email: | support@btinternet.com |
| WWW site: | www.btinternet.com |
| Notes: | ISDN, unlimited Web space and email addresses Free weekend calls |

| | |
|---|---|
| Company: | City NetGates |
| Telephone: | 0117 907 4000 |
| Email: | sales@netgates.co.uk |
| WWW site: | www.netgates.co.uk |
| Notes: | ISDN, 3 MB Web space, five email addresses |

| | |
|---|---|
| Company: | CityScape |
| Telephone: | 01223 566950 |
| Email: | sales@cityscape.co.uk |
| WWW site: | www.cityscape.co.uk |
| Notes: | ISDN, 6.5 MB Web space, 24-hour support |

| | |
|---|---|
| Company: | ClaraNET Ltd |
| Telephone: | 0800 072 0723 |
| Email: | sales@clara.net |
| WWW site: | www.clara.net |
| Notes: | ISDN, various account offers, reduced call charges |

| | |
|---|---|
| Company: | Demon Internet |
| Telephone: | 020 8371 1234 |
| Email: | sales@demon.net |
| WWW site: | www.demon.net |
| Notes: | ISDN, 20 MB Web space, unlimited email addresses, 24-hour support |

| | |
|---|---|
| Company: | Direct Connection |
| Telephone: | 0800 072 0000 |
| Email: | sales@dircon.net |
| WWW site: | www.dircon.net |
| Notes: | ISDN, 20 MB Web space, unlimited email addresses |

| | |
|---|---|
| Company: | Dorset Internet |
| Telephone: | 01202 659991 |
| Email: | sales@lds.co.uk |
| WWW site: | www.lds.co.uk |
| Notes: | ISDN, 25 MB Web space, two email addresses, 24-hour support |

| | |
|---|---|
| Company: | Enterprise |
| Telephone: | 01624 677666 |
| Email: | sales@enterprise.net |
| WWW site: | www.enterprise.net |
| Notes: | ISDN, 25 MB Web space, unlimited email addresses |

| | |
|---|---|
| Company: | Force 9 |
| Telephone: | 0800 073 7800 |
| Email: | sales@force9.net |
| WWW site: | www.force9.net |
| Notes: | ISDN, unlimited Web space and email addresses |

| | |
|---|---|
| Company: | Frontier Internet Services |
| Telephone: | 020 7536 9090 |
| Email: | info@ftech.net |
| WWW site: | www.ftech.net |
| Notes: | ISDN, 25 MB Web space, unlimited email addresses |

| | |
|---|---|
| Company: | Global Internet |
| Telephone: | 0870 909 8043 |
| Email: | info@globalnet.co.uk |
| WWW site: | www.globalnet.co.uk |
| Notes: | ISDN, 50 MB Web space, unlimited email addresses |

| | |
|---|---|
| Company: | Internet Central |
| Telephone: | 01270 611000 |
| Email: | sales@netcentral.co.uk |
| WWW site: | www.netcentral.co.uk |
| Notes: | ISDN, 2 MB Web space, five email addresses |

| | |
|---|---|
| Company: | NetDirect Internet |
| Telephone: | 020 7731 3311 |
| Email: | info@netdirect.net.uk |
| WWW site: | www.home.netdirect.net.uk |
| Notes: | ISDN, 25 MB Web space, unlimited email addresses |

| | |
|---|---|
| Company: | Nildram |
| Telephone: | 0800 072 0400 |
| Email: | sales@nildram.co.uk |
| WWW site: | www.nildram.co.uk |
| Notes: | ISDN, 25 MB Web space, unlimited email addresses |

Company:            Primex Information Services
Telephone:          01908 643597
Email:              info@alpha.primex.co.uk
WWW site:           www.primex.co.uk
Notes:              ISDN, 25 MB Web space, unlimited email addresses

Company:            Wave Rider Internet
Telephone:          0121 603 3888
Email:              info@waverider.co.uk
WWW site:           www.waverider.co.uk
Notes:              ISDN, 50 MB Web space, six email addresses

Company:            Zetnet Services
Telephone:          01595 696667
Email:              info@zetnet.co.uk
WWW site:           www.zetnet.co.uk
Notes:              ISDN, 25 MB Web space, unlimited email addresses

Company:            Zoo Internet
Telephone:          020 8961 7000
Email:              support@zoo.co.uk
WWW site:           www.zoo.co.uk
Notes:              ISDN, 5 MB Web space, two email addresses

# 2: UK Free access providers

Company:            BT ClickFree
Telephone:          0845 7576333
Email:              btclickplus-support@btinternet.com
WWW site:           www.btclickplus.com
Notes:              Phone for software or download

Company:            Cable and Wireless Internet
Telephone:          0800 0923001
Email:              –
WWW site:           www.cwcom.net
Notes:              Phone for software or download
                    20 MB Web space, five email addresses

Company:           Connect Free
Telephone:         0870 742 1111
Email:             info@connectfree.net
WWW site:          www.connectfree.co.uk
Notes:             Sign up online
                   Unlimited Web space and email addresses

Company:           Free-Online
Telephone:         0870 7060504
Email:             sales@free-online.net
WWW site:          www.free-online.net
Notes:             Unlimited Web space and email addresses, free
                   support

Company:           Freeserve
Telephone:         –
Email:             –
WWW site:          www.freeserve.net
Notes:             Free disk from Dixons or PC World, or sign up online
                   15 MB Web space, unlimited email addresses

Company:           ic24
Telephone:         0870 9090262
Email:             ic24@mgn.co.uk
WWW site:          www.ic24.net
Notes:             Phone for software or download
                   10 MB Web space, five email addresses

Company:           SoftNET
Telephone:         0870 727 4444
Email:             –
WWW site:          www.softnetfree.co.uk
Notes:             Phone for software
                   10 MB Web space, unlimited email addresses

Company:           Virgin Net
Telephone:         0500 558800
Email:             advice@virgin.net
WWW site:          www.virgin.net
Notes:             Sign up online
                   10 MB Web space, five email addresses

# 3: UK software companies

| Company | Telephone | World Wide Web |
| --- | --- | --- |
| Adaptec | – | www.adaptec.com |
| Adobe Systems | 020 8606 4008 | www.adobe.co.uk |
| Apple | 020 8308 8614 | www.apple.com |
| Asymetrix/Click2Learn | – | www.asymetrix.com |
| Attica Cybernetics | 01865 791346 | www.attica.com |
| Autodesk | 01483 303322 | www.autodesk.co.uk |
| Berkeley Systems | – | www.berksys.com |
| Borland | 01734 320022 | www.borland.com |
| Broderbund | 01753 620909 | www.broderbund.com |
| Brooklyn North Software Works | 0500 284177 | www.brooknorth.com |
| Claris/Filemaker | 0800 422322 | www.claris.com |
| Corel | 0800 581028 | www.corel.com |
| Delrina | 020 8207 7033 | www.delrina.com |
| Digital Workshop | 01295 254590 | www.digitalworkshop.co.uk |
| Dorling Kindersley | 020 7753 3488 | www.dk.com |
| Dr Solomons | 01296 318733 | www.drsolomon.co.uk |
| Electronic Arts | 01753 549442 | www.ea.com |
| Gold Disk | 01753 832383 | www.golddisk.com |
| Health Perfect | 020 8200 8897 | www.healthperfect.co.uk |
| IBM | 023 9249 2249 | www.software.ibm.com |
| Interplay | 01235 821666 | www.interplay.com |
| Intuit | 01932 578500 | www.intuit.co.uk |
| JASC, Inc | – | www.jasc.com |
| Lotus Development | 01784 445808 | www.lotus.com |
| Macromedia | 020 8358 5858 | www.macromedia.com |
| McAfee | 01753 827500 | www.mcafee.com |
| MetaCreations | 020 8358 5858 | www.metacreations.com |
| Micrografx | 0191 510 0203 | www.micrografx.com |
| Microsoft | 0345 002000 | www.microsoft.com |
| Mindscape | 01444 246333 | www.mindscape.com |
| Nico Mac Computing, Inc | – | www.winzip.com |
| Ocean | 0161 839 0999 | www.infogrames.co.uk |
| Oki | 01753 819819 | www.oki.co.uk |
| Pegasus Software | 01536 495000 | www.pegasus.co.uk |
| Psygnosis | 0151 282 3000 | www.psygnosis.co.uk |
| Quark Systems | 01483 451818 | www.quark.com |

| Company | Telephone | World Wide Web |
|---|---|---|
| Quarterdeck UK | 01245 494940 | www.symantec.com |
| Sage | 0191 255 3000 | www.sage.com |
| Serif | 0800 376070 | www.serif.com |
| SoftKey | 020 8789 2000 | www.softkey.com |
| SoftQuad | 020 8387 4110 | www.sq.com |
| Starfish Software | 020 8875 4455 | www.starfish.com |
| Steinberg | 020 8970 1924 | www.steinberg-us.com |
| Symantec | 020 7616 5600 | www.symantec.com |
| Visio | 0800 132047 | www.visio.com |
| Wang UK | 020 8568 9200 | www.wang.com |

# 4: UK hardware companies

| Company | Telephone | World Wide Web |
|---|---|---|
| AMD | 01256 603121 | www.amd.com |
| Award | – | www.award.com |
| Aztech | 01189 810118 | www.aztech.co.uk |
| Brother UK | 0161 931 2354 | www.brother.com |
| Canon | 0990 143723 | www.europe.canon.com |
| Casio | 020 8450 9131 | www.casio.com |
| Cirrus Logic | – | www.cirrus.com |
| Compaq | 0845 270 4065 | www.compaq.com |
| Creative Labs | 01245 265265 | www.creaf.com |
| Data Becker | 01420 22707 | www.data-becker.co.uk |
| Dell | 0870 152 4699 | www.dell.co.uk |
| Diamond Multimedia | 01189 444400 | www.diamondmm.com |
| Epson UK | 01442 261144 | www.epson.co.uk |
| Fujitsu | 0870 128 2829 | www.fujitsu.co.uk |
| Gravis | 01296 397444 | www.gravis.com |
| Hauppauge | 020 7378 0202 | www.hauppauge.com |
| Hayes | 01276 704400 | www.hayes.com |
| Hercules | 01635 294300 | www.hercules.com |
| Hewlett Packard | 0990 474747 | www.hp.com |
| Hitachi | 020 8848 8787 | www.hitachi.com |
| IBM | 0870 601 1036 | www.ibm.com |
| Iiyama | 01438 314417 | www.iiyama.com |

| Company | Telephone | World Wide Web |
| --- | --- | --- |
| Imation | 01344 402200 | www.imation.com |
| Iomega | 0800 973194 | www.iomega-europe.com |
| JVC | 020 8208 7654 | www.jvc.com |
| Kodak | 01442 261122 | www.kodak.co.uk |
| IMC (Umax) | 01344 872800 | www.imcnet.com |
| Intel | 01793 404900 | www.intel.com |
| Lexmark | 01628 480640 | www.lexmark.com |
| Logitech | 020 8308 6581 | www.logitech.com |
| Matrox | 01753 665500 | www.matrox.com |
| Maxtor | 01483 747356 | www.maxtor.com |
| Microsoft | 0870 601 0100 | www.microsoft.com |
| Mitsumi | 01276 29029 | www.mitsumi.com |
| NEC Computer Products | 020 8993 8111 | www.nec.com |
| Nikon | 0800 230220 | www.nikon.com |
| Oki | 01753 819819 | www.oki.co.uk |
| Olivetti | 0990 111145 | www.olivetti.com |
| Pace | 0990 561001 | www.pacecom.co.uk |
| Packard Bell | 01628 508 200 | www.packardbell-europe.com |
| Panasonic | 0990 357357 | – |
| Phoenix Technologies | – | www.phoenix.com |
| Pioneer | 01753 789789 | www.pioneer-eur.com |
| Plextor | 01782 54777 | www.plextor.com |
| Primax | 01235 535524 | www.primax.net |
| Psion | 01908 261686 | www.psiondacom.com |
| Samsung | 020 8391 0168 | www.samsung.com |
| Seagate | 0800 783 5177 | www.seagate.com |
| Sharp | 0990 274277 | www.sharp-uk.co.uk |
| Sony UK | 0990 42424 | www.sony.com |
| Syquest | 0118 538 5857 | www.syquest.com |
| Taxan | 01344 484646 | www.taxan.co.uk |
| Toshiba | 01932 828828 | www.toshiba.co.uk |
| Trust Peripherals | 01376 502050 | www.trust.com |
| Umax | 01344 871344 | www.imcnet.com |
| US Robotics | 0800 225252 | www.usr.com |
| Viewsonic | 01293 643900 | www.viewsonic.com |
| Visioneer | 01908 260422 | www.visioneer.com |
| Western Digital UK | 01372 360055 | www.wdc.com |
| Xerox | 01429 855060 | www.xerox.com |

# 5: UK retailers

| Company | Telephone | Products/World Wide Web |
|---|---|---|
| AJP | 020 8208 9744 | Notebook PCs<br>www.ajp.co.uk |
| Byte Direct | 0500 888910 | PCs/Peripherals/Software |
| Carrera | 020 8307 2800 | PCs/Notebook PCs<br>www.carrera.co.uk |
| Choice Systems | 020 8993 9003 | PCs/Notebook PCs<br>www.choicesystems.co.uk |
| Compaq | 0845 270 4065 | PCs/Notebook PCs/Peripherals<br>www.compaq.com |
| Currys | 01442 888000 | PCs/Peripherals |
| Dabs Direct | 0800 138 5120 | PCs/Peripherals/Software/Consumables<br>www.dabs.com |
| Dan Technology | 020 8830 1100 | PCs<br>www.dan.co.uk |
| Dell | 0870 152 4674 | PCs<br>www.dell.co.uk |
| Dixons | 01442 888000 | PCs/Peripherals/Software/Consumables |
| Elonex | 0800 542 2935 | PCs/Notebook PCs<br>www.elonex.co.uk |
| Evesham | 0800 496 0800 | PCs/Notebook PCs<br>www.evesham.com |
| Gateway 2000 | 0800 142000 | PCs/Notebook PCs<br>www.gateway.com/uk |
| Grey Matter | 01364 654200 | Software<br>www.greymatter.co.uk |
| Insight | 0800 073 0730 | PCs/Peripherals/Software/Components<br>www.insight.com/uk |
| Javelin Computers | 01254 505505 | PCs/Peripherals/Components<br>www.javelincomputers.co.uk |
| Mesh Computers | 020 8208 4701 | PCs<br>www.meshplc.co.uk |
| MX2 | 01481 253526 | Consumables<br>www.mx2.com |

| Company | Telephone | Products/World Wide Web |
|---|---|---|
| NEC Direct | 0870 010 6321 | PCs/Notebook PCs<br>www.necdirect-europe.com |
| PC World | 0990 464464 | PCs/Peripherals/Software/Consumables<br>www.pcworld.co.uk |
| Pico Direct | 0870 729 6111 | Notebook PCs/Notebook peripherals<br>www.picodirect.co.uk |
| Palmtops Direct | 01491 822604 | Handheld PCs<br>www.palmtops.co.uk |
| Panrix | 0113 244 4958 | PCs<br>www.panrix.co.uk |
| Qual Technology | 01737 855800 | PCs/Notebook PCs/Peripherals<br>www.qual.co.uk |
| Simply | 020 8498 2100 | PCs/Peripherals/Software<br>www.simply.co.uk |
| Software Warehouse | 0800 035 5355 | PCs/Software/Peripherals/Consumables<br>www.software-warehouse.co.uk |
| Tech Direct | 020 8286 2222 | PCs/Printers/Peripherals/Consumables<br>www.techdirect.co.uk |
| The Link | 01442 888000 | PCs/Peripherals |
| Technomatic | 0800 248000 | PCs/Peripherals/Software/Components |
| Time Computer Systems | 0800 316 2317 | PCs<br>www.timecomputers.co.uk |
| Tiny Direct | 0800 731 7283 | PCs<br>www.tiny.com |
| Viglen | 0990 486 486 | PCs/Notebook PCs<br>www.viglen.co.uk |
| Virgin Megastore | 020 7631 1234 | Software<br>www.virgin.co.uk |
| Watford Electronics | 0800 035 5555 | PCs/Software/Peripherals/Components<br>www.watford.co.uk |

# 6: UK general services

* **Data transfer, conversion, duplication**

| | | |
|---|---|---|
| AL Downloading Services | 020 8994 5471 | www.aldownloading.co.uk |
| Media Direct | 0800 000441 | |

* **Data recovery (disk failure, corruption, viruses)**

| | | |
|---|---|---|
| DataQuest International | 023 9258 1263 | |
| OnTrack Data Recovery | 0800 1012 1314 | www.ontrack.co.uk |
| Vogon International | 0800 581263 | www.vogon-international.com |

* **PC rental**

| | | |
|---|---|---|
| MC Rentals | 01952 603534 | |
| Hire-Ring | 020 8838 5495 | |
| Skylake Rentals | 0800 373118 | |
| Team Management PC Hire | 020 7702 9242 | www.pchire.com |

* **PC security/anti-theft**

| | |
|---|---|
| Microcosm | 0117 983 0084 |
| Secure PC | 020 7610 6611 |

* **PC memory**

| | | |
|---|---|---|
| AW Memory | 01382 807000 | |
| Crucial Technology | 0800 013 0330 | www.crucial.com/uk |
| Memory Express | 0870 900 9500 | |
| Offtek | 0800 698 4100 | www.offtek.co.uk |
| UKMemory.com | 01948 663666 | www.ukmemory.com |

* **Printer consumables**

| | | |
|---|---|---|
| Big Rom | 0800 074 4283 | |
| Cartridge Club | 0800 328 5072 | |
| Cartridge Express | 0800 026 7023 | www.consumables.net |
| CompuJet | 0800 026 7435 | |
| InkSpot | 020 8953 9192 | www.inkspot.co.uk |
| Inky Fingers | 0870 241 0229 | www.inkjetuk.com |
| Jetica | 01603 748002 | |

| Manx Print Care | 0800 056 6610 | www.mcb.net/jettmanx |
| Squire International | 0800 698 7474 | www.squire.co.uk |
| Themis | 0800 376 8980 | |

**\* Blank disks/storage**

| Owl Associates | 01543 250377 | |
| Product Trade and Services | 0800 136502 | |
| Squire International | 0800 698 7474 | www.squire.co.uk |

# 7: Useful Internet sites

**Search pages**

| AltaVista | www.altavista.com |
| Excite | www.excite.co.uk |
| Filez Search | www.filez.com |
| Hotbot | www.hotbot.com |
| Infoseek Search | www.infoseek.com |
| Lycos Search Page | www.lycos.co.uk |
| Mirago | www.mirago.co.uk |
| Starting Point | www.stpt.com |
| WebCrawler | www.Webcrawler.com |
| UK Plus | www.ukplus.co.uk |
| Yahoo! | www.yahoo.com |
| Yahoo! UK and Ireland | www.yahoo.co.uk |

**Internet software and general sites**

| 32Bit.com | www.32bit.com/software |
| Jumbo Software Archive | www.jumbo.com |
| No-Nags Internet Software | ded.com/nonags/main.html |
| Shareware.com | www.shareware.com |
| Jungle.com | www.jungle.com |
| Thingamabobs | www.thingamabobs.com |
| Tucows Internet Software | tucows.cableinet.net |
| Virtual Software Library | abyss.idirect.com/cgi-bin/vsl-front |

# INDEX

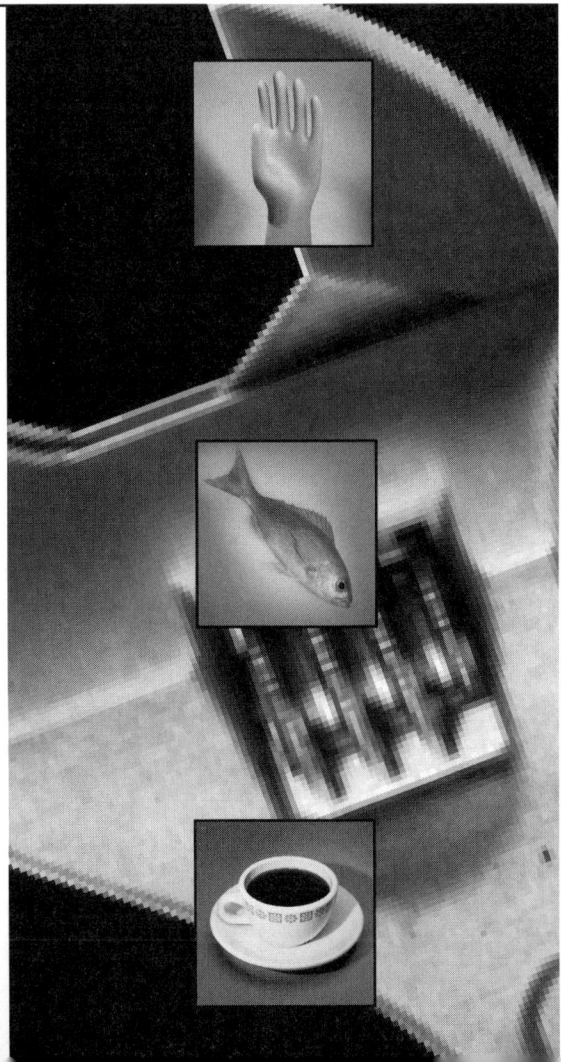

## Welcome to Virgin Net

We're here to give you the best Internet service there is. That's it. Once you've tried it we hope you will stay with us for a long time. Exploring the **Internet** [1] can be a confusing experience at first. Virgin Net is here to provide a helping hand – we will guide you through the pitfalls and help you get the best from the Internet. Once you get online you'll find that we've provided you with a guide to some of the best things on the Internet, and a number of features of our own. Please feel free to contact us if you have any comments on how we might improve our service or if there are any new things you would like to see included.

### If you feel yourself getting into trouble when registering, please call our local call rate helpline.

**24-hour registration helpline: 0845 650 0000**

Your calls may be monitored for training purposes.

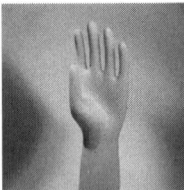

## 1. Internet
**Millions of computers storing billions of files accessed by tens of millions of people. But don't panic: we'll show you around the basics before turning you loose.**

### AND WE'LL ALWAYS BE CLOSE AT HAND TO HELP.

## Virgin Net is simple to use. You don't need to know anything about the Internet

This section contains simple step-by-step instructions for getting on to the Internet, and will guide you through to a successful connection within a few minutes.

All you need is a PC or a Mac, a **modem**[1], an **ordinary telephone line**[2] and the installation pack on the CD.

Within minutes, you'll have access to the world's biggest reference library, CD collection, department store and news-stand. You'll be able to search for information, communicate with people all over the world, discuss your interests and share ideas.

## 1. Modem

**A box of electronics that allows your computer to communicate through a telephone line. It's like a TV aerial tuned to Virgin Net, receiving all the things that you see on your screen. But unlike an aerial, your modem also sends your commands back.**

## 2. Ordinary telephone line

**Your computer is connected to Virgin Net by telephone. No matter where your computer is getting information from, you only pay for a local rate call. Remember: while you're connected, you can't use that line to make or receive calls.**

## What you will need

1. A **personal computer** [1]. You will need a PC running Windows 3.1 or **Windows 95** [2] or an Apple Mac running MacOS 7.1 or better.

2. A modem. Plug its phone lead into a working telephone socket, and, unless your computer has an internal modem built inside it, plug the other lead into the appropriate socket in the side or back of your computer.

3. The CD included with this book.

4. The following information:

• Your name, address and postcode.

• The make and model of your modem.

### 1. Personal computer
**Detailed hardware requirements are provided at the back of this section.**

### 2. Windows 95
**If you are running Windows 95, you may also need your original Windows 95 CD or floppy disks.**

## Software pack

The Virgin Net software pack contains all the programs you need to connect to and use the Internet. Most of the information and entertainment you'll find on the Internet is linked by the **World Wide Web**[1]. You navigate through the World Wide Web using a browser. A browser is a program which knows how to play and display the many different types of pictures, sounds, movies or text files that you will find on the 'Web'. The browser is also your tool for moving around the Web, just using clicks of your mouse. It will also let you send and receive **e-mail**[2] and read and send messages to **newsgroups**[3]. The Virgin Net software pack includes both Microsoft Internet Explorer and Netscape Navigator. During this installation we will recommend which browser is appropriate for your computer.

### 1. World Wide Web
An easy way of finding most of the information on the Internet. The Web is made up of millions of linked pages of text and pictures, which you can display on your computer.

### 2. e-mail
Keep in touch with your friends and colleagues by sending electronic messages. It's cheaper than a phone call.

### 3. newsgroups
Whatever your interest or hobby, you'll find people talking (in writing) about it in a newsgroup. Anyone can post messages to a newsgroup, and anyone can read them.

## In addition to the browser

We will also install the following Virgin Net programs.

These are:

**Global Chat**
Lets you talk live to other people on the Net by typing messages.

**Real Audio**
Allows your browser to play sound files without downloading them first.

We also provide two optional extras, Cybersitter and Shockwave.

Full instructions can be found on the Help service once you are online.

**Cybersitter**
This program allows you to control your children's access to the Internet.

**Shockwave**
This program allows your browser to place animated graphics and movies.

## How to install Virgin Net

First, make sure that you have shut down any other programs and applications that are running on your computer, except **Windows 95** [1] or Windows 3.1 or MacOS. Next, put the CD into your CD drive. The Installation program will do some tests on your computer, to see if you have disk space for the Virgin Net programs and test whether your machine can run them. If there's a problem, the Installation program will tell you exactly what it is. Some problems you can solve easily by following the on-screen instructions. If the problem is more serious, call our 24-hour helpline on 0845 650 0000. Before you call, take a note of the problem message from the Installation program it will help our team guide you through the solution.

**24-hour registration helpline: 0845 650 0000**

## 1. Windows 95

During installation, you may be asked to insert your Windows 95 CD or floppy disks, so keep them handy. Virgin Net uses certain Windows 95 programs to connect your computer and modem to the Internet. These files may not have already been installed.
Remember: if you have any problems, simply call the 24-hour Virgin Net registration helpline on 0845 650 0000 for advice.

## Window 95 and 98 users only

(If the installation starts automatically, you can skip straight to step 4.)

1. Select start on the Taskbar.

2. Select run in the Start menu.

3. If you are using a CD, type D:/virgin.net/setup.

4. Click OK and follow the on-screen instructions.

## Window 3.1 users only

1. Open program manager.

2. Select file from the Menubar.

3. Select run.

4. Type D:/virgin.net/setup.

5. Click OK and follow the on-screen instructions.

## Mac users only

1. Double click on the 'Virgin Net' icon in the desktop.

2. In the 'Virgin Net' folder, click the 'Installer' icon.

3. Follow the on-screen instructions.

# Registration

Once installation is complete you are ready to register with Virgin Net. Before you start, be sure to check that your modem, telephone line and computer are all properly linked up and that the modem is switched on. Then just follow the simple on-screen registration instructions. The Registration program will make a local rate telephone call to Virgin Net using your modem, and then will ask you for your **name and address**[1]. The information you provide is used to set up your account. As soon as you have done this, Virgin Net will send you a unique Username and Password. Your Username will tell us who you are when you go online with Virgin Net. Your Password allows us to confirm that you are who you say you are. Please make a note of both your Username and your Password as you will need them every time you want to connect to Virgin Net. In addition, your Username will be used to set up your e-mail address on Virgin Net.

## 1. Name and Address
This information is confidential and secure. Your details are sent by a direct link to our private computer, which is not connected to the Internet. The information you send cannot be intercepted or read by any other Internet user.

## Problems with registration

If the Installation procedure has been successful, it should have taken you directly to our online registration screen. But if it hasn't, don't worry. First try this:

1. Check that your modem is turned on and plugged in correctly.

2. Check that your **telephone line**[1] is working properly. Do this by plugging in an ordinary telephone and dialling the special Virgin Net Registration number, **0645 50 54 40**. You should first hear the line ringing and then something that sounds a bit like a fax machine or static on the radio.

If after these checks you still cannot register, call:

**24-hour registration helpline on: 0845 650 0000.**

## 1. Telephone line
Make sure that no one is on the phone before you try to connect to Virgin Net. It won't work and they're likely to hear a horrible screeching.

## Whenever you want to connect to Virgin Net

All you need to do is:

1. First, make sure that your modem, telephone line and computer are properly connected.

2. Then turn your modem and computer on and **double-click**[1] the Virgin Net icon on your Windows 95/MacOS desktop or in the Virgin Net Program Group if you are using Windows 3.1.

3. If you are using Windows 95, you will need to confirm your Username and Password.

4. Finally, click the connect button. Your modem will connect you to Virgin Net by making a **local rate phone call**[2].

## 1. Double click
Tap the left-hand mouse button twice, quickly. Usually used to start a program. Remember: once you're using your browser, you only need to click ONCE to jump to a new link.

## 2. Local rate phone call
Wherever you are in the country, your telephone connection to Virgin Net's computers is always charged as if you were making a local call.

## Once the connection has successfully been made

The browser will **download**[1] on to your screen the Virgin Net **homepage**[2]. Your homepage is always the first thing you see each time you connect to the Internet, and the Virgin Net homepage is designed clearly and simply to:

1. Help you to search for useful, entertaining or important information.

2. Give you direct links to the places we recommend.

3. Bring you up-to-the-minute news, sport and entertainment.

4. Let you download and play games or use your computer to connect to **websites**[3] containing recorded and even live sounds, such as **Virgin Radio**[4].

 That's it. The rest is up to you. Remember, you're in charge. From now on, we're just here to help.

### 1. Download
Get information or files from a computer on the Internet and copy it on to your own computer.

### 2. Homepage
The place you'll begin your exploration of the Internet from. And don't worry if you ever get lost because one click of the HOME button on your browser will take you straight back there.

### 3. Websites
What a programme is to TV and a book is to a library, a website is to the Internet.

### 4. Virgin Radio
1215AM & 105.8FM. The world's greatest radio station, of course.

# Help - and where to find it

We have made Virgin Net as simple and easy to use as possible.

Even so, we know that for newcomers the Internet can be a strange

and confusing place. That's why we've created a Help service that

will answer the **questions**[1] you're most likely to ask.

## 1. Questions

There are some questions that come up again and again. They're referred to as "Frequently Asked Questions" or FAQs. Before asking a question – either in Virgin Net or a newsgroup it's a good idea to check to see if the answer is already in the relevant FAQ.

## Electronic mail

Electronic mail, better known as e-mail, is so useful that many people get on to the Net just to use it. It's that good. Unlike old-fashioned 'snail mail', you don't need a stamp and it travels at the speed of light. Once you start using e-mail, you will be able to send messages and documents quickly, cheaply and at any time of the day or night to anyone in the world with an e-mail address.

To start using e-mail, press on the mail button on **the browser**[1]. This will open Outlook Express the e-mail program. To receive e-mail, click on the send & receive button. Outlook Express will go to the **Virgin Net computers**[2], check to see if you have new mail waiting for you there and download any new messages on to your computer.

## 1. The browser
If you are using Netscape click GET MAIL to receive an e-mail, TO MAIL to send one and RE: MAIL to reply.

## 2. Virgin Net computers
Giant, mysterious black cabinets covered in thousands of flashing lights and quietly leaking white coolant fumes. No? Actually they look pretty much like your machine, except a bit faster. Probably.

## Electronic mail

New messages will appear in bold and you can read them by double-clicking on them. To send e-mail, click on the compose message button and an empty message window will appear. Type in the e-mail address of the person you want to write to, and then type your message. Send it by clicking on the send button. To reply directly to an e-mail that you have received, the simplest way is by clicking on the reply to author button. A window will open showing the original message with the sender's return e-mail address already filled in. Just type your reply and press the send button. To learn more about using e-mail, use the Virgin Net **Help service** [1], where we have prepared a full guide to using and getting the best out of e-mail.

## 1. Help service

We want to make using the Internet as easy as possible. And that means having the best help service you'll find anywhere. As well as our 24-hour helpline, we've prepared an online tutorial to take you through the basics, step by step. We've written reference pages that answer the most commonly asked questions. You can find the Help service on our homepage.

# Detailed hardware requirements

## PC requirements:

• Windows 95, Windows 98 or Windows 3.1

• 486dx processor or better (100MHz for IE4)

• 6Mb free hard disk space (75Mb for Internet Explorer)

• 14.4Kbps or faster modem

• 256 colour display monitor

## Apple Mac requirements:

• MacOS System 7.1 or above

• 68040 processor or better

• 16Mb free hard disk space (24Mb recommended)

• 14.4Kbps or faster modem

• 256 colour display monitor